Ancient Objects and Sacred Realms

THE LINDA SCHELE SERIES IN MAYA AND PRE-COLUMBIAN STUDIES

This series was made possible through the generosity of William C. Nowlin, Jr., and Bettye H. Nowlin, the National Endowment for the Humanities, and various individual donors.

Requests for permission to reproduce material from
this work should be sent to:
    Permissions
    University of Texas Press
    P.O. Box 7819
    Austin, TX 78713-7819
    www.utexas.edu/utpress/about/bpermission.html

⊛ The paper used in this book meets the minimum
requirements of ANSI/NISO Z39.481-992 (R1997)
(Permanence of Paper).

Library of Congress Cataloging-in-Publication Data

Ancient objects and sacred realms : interpretations of Mississippian
iconography / edited by F. Kent Reilly, III and James F. Garber ;
foreword by Vincas P. Steponaitis. — 1st ed.
    p.   cm. — (The Linda Schele series in Maya and pre-Columbian studies)
Includes bibliographical references and index.
 ISBN: 0292721382

1. Mississippian culture.   2. Mississippian art.   3. Symbolism in art —
Mississippi River Valley.   4. Symbolism in art — Southern States.
5. Supernatural in art — Mississippi River Valley.   6. Supernatural in art —
Southern States.   7. Indians of North America — Southern States — Antiquities.
8. Indians of North America — Mississippi River Valley — Antiquities.
9. Mississippi River Valley — Antiquities.   10. Southern States — Antiquities.
I. Reilly, F. Kent.   II. Garber, James.
E99.M6815A52 2007
976'.01 — dc22
                                                    2006022618

Ancient Objects and Sacred Realms

Interpretations of Mississippian Iconography

Edited by *F. Kent Reilly III and James F. Garber*
Foreword by *Vincas P. Steponaitis*

University of Texas Press, Austin

To Phil Phillips, who started the process.
For Linda Schele, who showed us the way,
and for the Lannan Foundation,
whose continuous financial support made both
the Texas State University conferences and this volume possible.

Contents

Foreword

From time to time, a book appears that completely changes the landscape in a field of study. This is such a book. For more than sixty years, scholars have tried to make sense of the corpus of pre-Columbian art known as the Southeastern Ceremonial Complex (SECC) or "Southern Cult." The studies presented in these pages sketch out a new paradigm for understanding this imagery, a paradigm that is based on rigorous methods and is deeply grounded in American Indian ethnography. The new interpretation that emerges sees these images not as depictions of "real-world" actors and rituals, but rather as representations of a larger, multilayered cosmos populated by heroes and supernatural beings whose exploits and powers were widely known by Indian peoples throughout eastern North America.

This book took shape through a series of workshops that were organized by Kent Reilly in the 1990s. Having been trained as a Mesoamerican archaeologist by the late Linda Schele, Reilly had experienced firsthand the breakthroughs in deciphering Maya iconography and script that happened during the 1970s and 1980s. He reasoned that the same methods might lead to similar breakthroughs in North American archaeology, so he decided to give them a try.

A key factor in the Mesoamerican advances had been the annual Maya Meetings hosted by Schele at the University of Texas in Austin. These advanced workshops would bring together a relatively small group of scholars with diverse perspectives, who would spend the better part of a week working intensively on a set of specific problems. Reilly adopted this model for attacking the problems of the SECC. The first of his workshops was held in March of 1993, in conjunction with the Maya meetings in Austin. Two years later, in 1995, the SECC workshop moved to Texas State University–San Marcos and took on its own identity as the Texas State Mississippian Iconography Conference. One hallmark of these workshops has been the diversity of participants: archaeologists, folklorists, art historians, anthropologists, and Native religious practitioners all have come to these gatherings. Besides Reilly himself, those who attended the first meeting were Alex Barker, James Brown, C. Randall Daniels-Sakim, Judith Franke, James Garber, Robert Hall, Mary Helms, Alice Kehoe, Vernon J. Knight, George Lankford, Patricia O'Brien, Mallory M. O'Connor, and Amy Trevelyan; later meetings included Garrick Bailey, M. Kathryn Brown, Christopher Carr, Carol Díaz-Granados, David Dye, Mary Johns, William Johnston, Adam King, Shirley Mock, Dan Penton, George Sabo, Clay Schultz, Robert Sharp, Dee Ann Story, Richard Townsend, Chet Walker, Sam Wilson, Kenneth York, and me. Many of these individuals have contributed chapters to this book.

Although their subject matter differs, all the chapters share elements of a common approach that was fostered by these workshops. The first is a rigorous formal analysis that searches out all occurrences of a given theme or motif and critically examines the range of variation and substitution. The second is a heavy reliance on ethnographic texts from throughout eastern North America as a way of interpreting these images and giving them meaning. Indeed, a key insight is that ethnographic texts from the eastern Great Plains and western Great Lakes are a valuable resource in understanding the imagery of the pre-Columbian Southeast—in a sense, these texts proved to be the Rosetta Stone that led to many of the interpretations presented herein.

Whether one agrees with these interpretations or not, this book has clearly laid the groundwork for a new approach to iconographic problems in eastern North America. The interdisciplinary approach and creativity fostered by these workshops has set a tone and direction that is likely to continue generating insights for many years to come.

Vincas P. Steponaitis
Chapel Hill, N.C.
March 7, 2006

Acknowledgments

The editors would like to gratefully acknowledge the Lannan Foundation and the Department of Anthropology, Texas State University–San Marcos, for their financial support of the Texas State Mississippian Iconography conferences, the results of which led to the publication of this volume.

1. Introduction

F. Kent Reilly III and James F. Garber

Between A.D. 900 and 1600, the native peoples of the Mississippi River Valley and other areas of the Eastern and Southeastern United States conceived and executed one of the greatest artistic traditions of pre-Columbian America. Many of the artistic and iconographic elements that make up this complex had originally been defined as the *Southeastern Ceremonial Complex* (Waring and Holder 1945). Objects of this complex were produced in the media of copper, shell, stone, clay, and almost certainly wood, although little of this material has survived in the soils of the eastern woodlands. Many of these ritual objects were incised or carved with a complex system of symbols and motifs. In many ways it has been this symbolic system of communication along with the extraordinary objects that carry it that has sparked the most intense scholarly interest.

Simply stated, this Mississippian Period artistic tradition consists of the artifacts, symbols, motifs, and architectural groupings that provide the physical evidence for the ritual activities practiced by the numerous ethnic groups comprising the demographic and cultural landscape of the Mississippian Period. It is also the discernible cosmology, ideology, and political structures of those various Mississippian Period groups. This physical evidence is examined primarily through structural analysis of Mississippian iconography and the identification of style regions, combined with the ethnohistorical approach.

With its beginnings around A.D. 900, the Mississippian Period and its numerous cultural and ethnic traditions came to an end with the French destruction of the Natchez polity in 1731. The Mississippian Tradition emerged from an earlier tradition that flowered in the Woodland Period (500 B.C.–A.D. 500). Just as the Mississippian Period witnesses an artistic florescence in its latter half, so too does the Woodland Period, with its analogous florescence commonly referred to as Hopewell.

The Hopewell artistic tradition is partially identified by its naturalistic depictions of birds and animals, while the Mississippian artistic tradition features often-bizarre configurations of dragon-like creatures whose images invoke mystery and hidden knowledge (Chapter 5). Previously, any explanation of these images primarily rested on the pioneering work of Antonio Waring. In 1945 Waring and Preston Holder organized ritual objects and symbols into a series of four lists of traits, which they categorized as a Southeastern (centered) Ceremonial Complex (SECC). Within the SECC, the organizational categories consisted of motifs, god-animal representations, ceremonial objects, and costume details, and were perceived as an internally consistent system of symbolic communication with a brief temporal duration. They also conceived of the complex as a specific cult manifestation that originated with the Muskhogean speakers of the lower Southern United States. Since the classic Waring and Holder identification of the SECC, scholarly opinion has expanded the definition while using the trait list as the foundation for a critical analysis of the entire system concept. Most significant for the recent and expanding efforts at interpretation have been the recognition of specific styles and themes within the SECC definition, the realization that symbols and themes can change over time, and the linkage of these changes to specific geographic areas.

In contrast to the Waring and Holder trait list approach, Jon Muller (1989:11–25) has proposed a more archaeologically centered procedure for defining the Mississippian artistic tradition, placing it within the social evolution of the chiefdom-level societies of the Mississippi Valley and the lower Southeastern United States. Muller accurately suggests that a temporal organization that views such objects and symbols as a series of interrelated traditions that change over a definable period of time would be a more productive model for identifying and interpreting this material. Within this model, Muller temporally classifies the complex into five horizons. He defines each of these horizons as a discrete tradition that saw not only the origin of a specific number of motifs, symbols, and ritual objects, but also specific developments in political structure and long-distance exchange.

The first of these periods Muller labels as "Developmental Cult." Developmental Cult (A.D. 900–1150) is marked by the appearance of such distinctive objects as the "long-nosed god" shell and copper masks and the "square cross" symbol. Muller identifies a "Southern Cult Period" (A.D. 1250–1350) as the apogee of the tradition. During this brief century, perhaps a century and a half, there was a rapid expansion of exchange networks, particularly in terms of such prestige materials as copper and shell. The Southern Cult Period is also the temporal point at which a number of the traits defined by Waring and Holder (bi-lobed arrows, striped pole, baton/mace, fringed apron, ogee, and the chunkey player) make their appearance. In the "Attenuated Cult Period" (A.D. 1350–1450) the long-distance exchange networks that so typify the preceding Southern Cult Period appear to diminish if not disappear altogether. Interestingly, the motifs and symbols that were, in the previous period, carried on stone, copper, and shell migrate to the medium of clay. Muller also sees an emphasis on styliza-tion in the art of the Attenuated Cult Period. He implies that this stylization is linked in some way to the collapse of such important Mississippian centers as Cahokia. Muller associates his "Post–Southern Cult Period" (A.D. 1450–1550) to the rise of a large number of regional artistic traditions that manifest distinct stylistic differences in their art, specifically in the production and ornamenta-tion of carved shell gorgets. Muller also associates the production of large shell masks with this increased regionalization and hypothesizes that these masks and gorgets reflect a period of dramatic social and ideological change throughout much of the lower southern United States. Muller's final period, "Historic Times Period" (after A.D. 1550), is the termination of the ideological and artistic formats of the complex, as well as the transformation of the chiefdom-level societies of the pre-Columbian Eastern Woodlands into the tribal social orders that were described by the French and English explorers and colonists in the seventeenth and eighteenth centuries. While we generally agree with Muller's chronologi-cally focused model, it does not incorporate the importance of regional variation in the meaning of the SECC art and symbols in its various contexts.

However, Muller's categories that are based on a temporal organization force a reexamination of the SECC concept in its entirety. As previously stated, when first proposed some sixty years ago, the interpretation of Mississippian iconog-raphy, as well as the objects that carried the motifs and elements of this symbolic system, was organized under the label of the Southeastern Ceremonial Complex or SECC. However, in the past decade many students of ancient Native American archaeology in general and the Mississippian Period in particular have become convinced that this SECC label is woefully inadequate as a cultural, religious, and artistic identifier.

The results of the decade-long study of SECC material that has emerged from meetings held at Texas State University only emphasize the inadequacy of this SECC label. After much thought and discussion we believe the term *Mississip-pian Ideological Interaction Sphere* or MIIS appears better suited as an organiza-tional phenomenon for this large corpus of art and symbols currently classified as the SECC. Certainly the interaction sphere model more accurately describes a Mississippian Period ideologically derived symbolic system and its accompany-ing artistic output. Unquestionably, a close examination of MIIS objects within their archaeological and temporal context reveals a large number of regional and stylistically distinct systems that appear to have their origin in the Greater or Classic Braden Style. However, within the corpus of MIIS symbols there are several symbols that appear to cross recognizable regional and stylistic boundaries that exist in the eastern United States through both time and space. The number of these shared symbols varies as to the time and the proximity of these specific style regions.

At the beginning of the MIIS (Muller's Developmental and Southern Cult Horizons), MIIS symbols and motifs in all of the style regions are primarily carried by objects created from exotic materials, the majority of which are mica, marine shell, imported stone, and copper. Over time the exchange system that was the mechanism for the procurement of these exotics disappears, and by Muller's Post–Southern Cult Complexes Horizon, much of the MIIS symbolism has migrated from exotics to clay vessels or gorgets created from easily obtainable riverine shell, though marine shell remains an important resource throughout the Mississippian Period.

That several of these symbols consistently cross stylistic and regional boundaries over time is undoubtedly due to the fact that these symbols and motifs carry the fundamental tenets of an overarching religious system that covered the enormous geographical area that included the diverse ethnic and cultural boundaries of the then Native American Eastern United States (Lankford: personal communication). The studies that are recorded in this volume clearly demonstrate that the MIIS was affected by the multiethnic complexity of its origin and its broad geographical distribution. The action, or indeed the interaction, of these cultural and stylistic areas underlines the importance of the interaction sphere model, particularly in the light of the recognition of the importance of specific style regions outside of what was previously thought to be the point of origin of this great body of art in the Southeastern United States.

Most of the authors who have contributed to this volume readily recognize that style distinctions are clearly apparent within the corpus of MIIS objects and symbols. Also, even though the themes are conservative and relatively limited, we believe that the MIIS label is an adequate organizing principle that covers such diverse factors as ideological emphasis, temporal change, style distinctions, and multiethnic adoption and adaptations, as well as shared thematic and aesthetic qualifiers within the seven-hundred-year life span of this truly remarkable ancient Native American ideological and artistic phenomenon.

One of the successes of the Texas State University Mississippian Iconography conference series has been the general acceptance of Cahokia as the point of origin for the "Greater Braden Style." Furthermore, there is a general consensus that the Greater Braden Style (Chapter 9) was the primary "mother style" from which many of the regional styles of the MIIS were derived.

Thematically, there has also been a general acceptance that much of the Mississippian imagery and symbolism has a linkage to ethnographic material that describes the location of the "realm of the dead" and the journey of dead souls to that otherworld location (Chapter 8). Additionally, much of the imagery presented on Spiro shell engravings executed in the Braden and Craig styles consists of vignettes occurring in the celestial realm of the Mississippian cosmological model (Chapters 2 and 3). This hypothesis interprets this celestial imagery as depictions of the "Path of Souls" and the otherworld actors that ethnographic sources describe as occupants of that starry path (Chapter 8).

There is a general consensus that another set of images, figures, and regalia details is associated with sets of deities and/or mythological heroes. In particular, among these otherworldly entities is the celestial deity Morning Star, who, within the ethnographic literature, carries the epithets "Red Horn" and "He Who Wears Human Heads in His Ears." This Above World/Otherworld hero was strongly associated with elite rule in at least Muller's Developmental Cult Period, and perhaps in other periods as well.

Iconographic studies conducted at the Texas State meetings generally concluded that there is a link between the ethnographic figure of Morning Star and the image of the widely recognized Hawk Dancer or Falcon Impersonator. These figures most often appear on the media of copper or shell. Mississippian elites who validated their elite status in rituals in which they impersonated this Above World deity would wear an elaborate headdress centered on a copper plate that depicted a falcon, hawk-wing cape, raptorial bird beak, and forked eye markings (Chapter 4). The elite Morning Star impersonator usually carried a mace or club in one hand, and often a severed head in the other. Many examples of these maces and clubs have been recovered by collectors, and more recently by archaeologists. They are magnificently crafted from single pieces of stone or slate, but they would have been useless as weapons, since they would have shattered at the first blow. Nevertheless, the carrying of these weapons and their associations with severed heads in the iconography have caused most scholars of the subject to link the Falcon Impersonator with warfare (Chapters 4 and 7).

The function of art as a material expression of cultural (and therefore mental) constructs is a well-documented phenomenon among ancient civilizations as well as contemporary small-scale societies. A common characteristic of such societies is the construction of analogies between the social order and the natural world, expressed in religious beliefs and practices (i.e., ritual) and given tangible form in art. Many of the authors in this volume note that the function of the

Mississippian objects was twofold: (1) serving as ritual regalia, and (2) providing a visual validation for the elite authority of the rulers of the various chiefdoms that populated the Mississippian Period geographical landscape. In order
to understand the interrelatedness of these two essentially ideological functions,
it is necessary to understand both the role of art in the ritual activity of pre-
Columbian Native Americans and the meanings carried by the MIIS motifs and
symbols (Chapter 3).

Traditionally, theories of the evolution of political society have been framed
in terms of "Western" economic models, which stress the importance of the
control of limited resources and military force. Ongoing research in Mesoamerica, Central and South America, as well as the pre-Columbian United
States, has shown that in the Americas the evolution of political power was
based equally on ideological factors. This demonstrates that forms of political validation among the ancient chiefdoms of the Midwest and Southeastern
United States were functionally identical to those of many other chiefdoms of
the Americas. Various chapters illustrate that within Mississippian art, cosmological imagery was used to publicly validate the power of a stratified elite social
order. An analysis of symbols that carry this cosmological imagery illustrates
that the cosmic model described by these symbols deals primarily with the celestial realm of gods and heroes and the realm of souls (Chapters 2 and 8). Furthermore, the repeated use of zoomorphic supernatural imagery on the costumes
and ritual objects of Mississippian elites demonstrates that these individuals
were incorporating major concepts of ideology and their ritual expressions into
these striking visual forms of political validation (Chapter 7).

During the workshops and meetings held at Texas State University, a methodology was developed to recover these ancient Native American "cultural constructs." This methodology consists of a fourfold approach, including recognition of style regions, visual structural analysis, archaeological content, and
ethnographic analogy. The plethora of ethnographic data comes primarily from
past and more recent studies of the Native American cultures of the Midwest
and Southern United States. Some of the most important ethnographic data
have been collected by Native Americans themselves. Archaeological data from
the ongoing excavations at Mississippian and Woodland Period sites have also
proved critical for our ongoing study. The authors of this volume contend that
the Mississippian artistic output can only be properly understood within this
archaeological context.

The authors represented in this volume have produced chapters that in many
ways are pioneering efforts in the structural analysis, style recognition, and interpretation of Mississippian artistic material. Structural analysis alone has been

extremely fruitful in our endeavors and has led to the recognition of a cosmic model as well as specific categories of supernaturals (Chapters 5 and 6).

These same authors have either considered an iconographic problem or have dealt with questions of meaning, chronology, interpretation, or ideological foundations within the art of the Mississippian Period. It is our hope that the discussions and conclusions contained within this volume, along with the workshop interdisciplinary methodology that has led to those conclusions, will provide specialist and interested readers with new definitions, along with fresh and critical interpretations of a superb body of Native American art that has been too long neglected by professional scholars as well as the general public.

2. Some Cosmological Motifs in the Southeastern Ceremonial Complex

George E. Lankford

Similar prehistoric iconographic images on shell, copper, and ceramics have been found across a wide geographic area in the Eastern Woodlands and the Plains. Even if the area is reduced to its presumed major centers for diffusion, such as Spiro, Moundville, and Etowah/Tennessee Valley, it still seems certain that the Southeastern Ceremonial Complex was international in nature, encompassing groups speaking different languages and manifesting somewhat different cultural traditions. The sharing of a visual symbol system such as the SECC suggests the sharing of some sort of belief system which lies behind and is manifest in the iconography. Such a belief system, like the iconography, must be beyond the boundaries of culture and the particulars of environmental adaptation.

Ethnographic evidence from various groups across several centuries provides many clues to such similarities in beliefs, and the clearest focus for such commonalities is the structure of the cosmos. The belief that the world is layered appears to be universal across the Woodlands and Plains. That layered cosmos is inhabited by a fairly small number of Powers, most of whom are recognizable as they shift their forms and meanings from one group to another. Both the structural elements of the cosmos and the Powers which inhabit it, furthermore, have qualitative meanings, as is to be expected in a religious belief system. None of these insights is new, of course, but it is important to recall that the basic beliefs of an ancient North American international religion are already known, at least in the forms in which they yet survive. Thus an attempt to match some of them to an international iconographic system is not so great a conceptual leap, and, in fact, has been done before.

This chapter is a consideration of the elements comprising a generalized cosmological model from the Woodlands and Plains, into which is incorporated an explication of iconographic elements that appear to be visual expressions of the beliefs. The crucial cosmological information is contained in mythology,

FIGURE 2.1. Two shell gorgets from the Tennessee Valley region. *Left:* the Cox Mound style. *Right:* the Hixon style.

in statements of belief, and in descriptions of ritual, all gathered through the last few centuries by ethnographers of varying trustworthiness. It is the argument of this chapter that in light of the knowledge of the cosmological beliefs of Native America, which is greater than is generally thought, these iconographic images are not as obscure as the visual presentation alone makes them seem. While the interpretations cannot be proved—what would constitute "proof" in iconographic study?—it is possible to present a strong case for them.

This study seeks to identify some of the basic structural motifs of cosmology in the SECC images, as well as some of the nonhuman characters who inhabit that cosmos. Such a project could very quickly get out of hand, given the large number of images and visual motifs that are contained in the SECC, and it thus seems wise to limit the present demonstration to the interpretation of a few basic images. Therefore, two shell gorget designs will be the focus of this investigation, each of them found in a long series in the Tennessee River Valley and Etowah. They are known by type names assigned in this century on the basis of similarity of design. One, which has twenty-three known examples, is called the Cox Mound style (Fig. 2.1 [left]). The other, found in thirty examples, is called the Hixon style (Fig. 2.1 [right]) (Brain and Phillips 1996:9–15).

Interpreting these gorgets should take place on at least two levels. The focus in this chapter is on ideological content—to what empirical or conceptual realities do the elements of the designs refer? The second level, which is beyond the limits of the present chapter, is that of functional meaning—to what social uses are these iconographic images put? Who wears these gorgets, and what do they say about the wearer? The difference between the two realms of interpretation is important, because it is difficult to claim that a symbol has been exegeted properly until both realms have been explored. An analogous situation from Western history is the case of the Christian cross—an explanation of it in terms of the New Testament story of the crucifixion and its ramifications is an interpretation of the first type. There is, however, the meaning of the different forms of the cross (Maltese, St. Andrews, and so on) as signifiers of religious orders or national traditions, as well as the meaning of crosses as parts of personal insignia (rank in an order or priesthood, participation in a Crusade, and so on)—a set of interpretations which go far beyond the conceptual meaning of a religious philosophy. It seems fair to consider that engraved shell designs such as the Cox Mound style and the Hixon style, because they are represented in multiple forms and found in situ in graves as costume elements, should be examined from this twofold perspective of conceptual and functional meaning. Unfortunately, the brevity of this article limits the interpretation to the first realm only.

The theses of this chapter can be listed briefly: (1) the two gorget styles are cosmological models, one a view from above, the other a side view; (2) both of the symbols and the field they occupy have meanings related to the believed structure of the cosmos and the cultural practices of the societies which created the images; and (3) those meanings, at least in the limited denotative sense described above, can be understood from beliefs, myths, and practices known from many different societies across the Eastern Woodlands and Plains, and they can be plausibly linked to the iconographic symbols. In order to present the support for these arguments, this chapter analyzes each of the two gorget styles in turn, with excursi into the ethnographic material at several points to bring into the discussion relevant religious understandings.

The Cox Mound Style Gorgets

In order to facilitate analysis, the gorget art needs to be broken down into fields or elements. The first image, the Cox Mound style, has five basic fields (Fig. 2.2).

The first field, on the left, is the center of the design; in this example of the Cox Mound style it is occupied by a square cross. The second field is a circular pointed surround, in this case with eight rays. The third is a square with loops at the corners; the composition of the square usually appears as bands, although the number of lines varies. The fourth is a set of four bird heads in quadripartite arrangement. The fifth field is the circular piece of shell itself; while it can be seen simply as the raw material from which the gorget is carved, it will be argued further on that both the material (shell) and the shape (circular) are part of the message embodied in the gorget. Since each of the symbols appears in

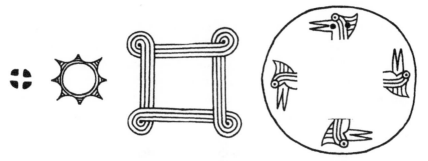

FIGURE 2.2. The five fields of the Cox Mound style gorget.

other SECC images and thus seems to have an independent life of its own, the fields have distinct meanings, and each can be explored separately.

Within this particular cluster of images—the twenty-three known examples of the Cox Mound style gorgets—there is actually very little variation (Brain and Phillips 1996:9–12). A brief survey of the gorgets by field makes this fact clear. While a few of the gorgets are fragmentary and only six are pictured in the Brain and Phillips catalog, the accompanying text points out the variations. In Field 1 there is one line cross (+) and one swastika, while there are eight which are unspecified, which probably means no observable variation from the norm, which is a solid cross. Since it is not difficult to see a line cross as a simplified version of the solid cross, only the single swastika is left as a possibly significant variation in meaning.

In Field 2 almost all of the gorgets agree on a circle with triangular rays surrounding it. Field 2 is omitted in one gorget, and it consists of a double circle in one. In twenty-one it seems that there is agreement on the rayed circle (if the silence in Brain and Phillips indicates similarity for those not pictured). Other than the two deviant ones, there is variation only on the number of rays; eight seems to be the norm, but two have only six rays, and nine- and twelve-ray forms are represented by one gorget each. It may be that the number of rays is an aesthetic judgment by the artist and is not significant iconographically.

Field 3 consists of a looped square composed of parallel lines. In most of the examples there are four lines (making three bands), but there are at least two which have only three lines (two bands). Most of the loops have pits engraved in their centers, but the presence or absence of a loop-pit seems insignificant. Two of the squares reverse the loop (in regard to which band overlaps the other at the corners), but Brain and Phillips (1996:10) concluded that this is "probably a non-significant variation."

Field 4 consists of four bird heads. While the artistic execution of the birds seems to vary significantly, a feature that has caught the attention of students from Holmes to the present, the structure is the same across the board. There are two gorgets in which the birds face clockwise rather than the standard counter-clockwise, but there seems to be little reason to suspect iconographic significance in that aberration. Despite the artistic range, the viewer is immediately aware that the birds of Field 3 are the same bird. This conviction is given by two major features—the straight, sharp beak and the crest on top of the head. These two features, and especially the crest, appear to be so characteristic that it seems a safe operational procedure to label them as identifiers of this bird, whatever its meaning and artistic context. For clarity, this creature will henceforth be re-ferred to as the "Crested Bird." As will be seen, the crest as an identifying motif is important in recognizing this particular creature when it is encountered in other SECC contexts.

Field 5 is the circular form of the shell of which the gorget is constructed. In every case the gorget is of shell and is roughly circular. No known examples of this total design—the combined five fields—have appeared in any other me-dium, such as copper or ceramics. Furthermore, the Cox Mound gorget is "char-acteristically decorated on the convex side" (Brain and Phillips 1996:9). Only two of the twenty-three gorgets break this rule and engrave the design on the concave side, and, again, there seems little reason to suspect iconographic mean-ing in those deviations.

By way of summary, it may be said that there appear to be no significant variations in any of the five fields identified for this image. The content is clear and standard for each field:

Field 1: cross
Field 2: rayed circle
Field 3: looped square
Field 4: Crested Birds
Field 5: circular shell

With minimal variation of motifs and a limited range of artistic idiosyncra-sies, the Cox Mound style appears to be remarkably pure. The geographical dis-tribution is also limited, for these gorgets, with a single exception, have been found only in the Cumberland and Tennessee river valleys (Fig. 2.3).

The single exception is a gorget found in Pickens County, Alabama, in the Tombigbee drainage. It is probably significant that the upper Tennessee has not produced examples of this gorget style; the distribution starts in the Chatta-nooga area and moves downstream. The same is true for the Cumberland. This

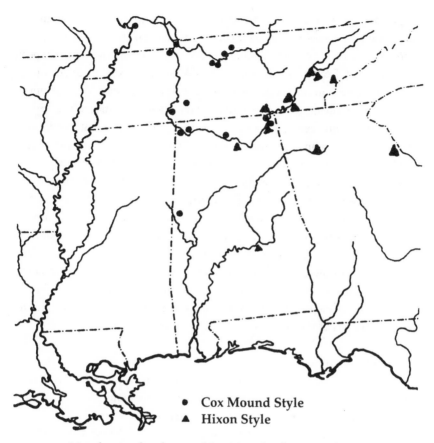

FIGURE 2.3. Map showing distribution of Cox Mound and Hixon style gorgets.
Adapted from Brain and Phillips 1996:9, 16.

restricted distribution, when coupled with the general lack of variation in the
design and the close similarity of some of the gorget executions, has led Brain
and Phillips to hypothesize a "Master" of this style, and possibly a "workshop"
of that Master as a primary source of these gorgets. This situation suggests that
these gorgets were produced in a fairly limited geographical area within a restricted time frame, a fact that may prove to be significant when the function of
these gorgets is considered. For the purposes of the present chapter, it is enough
to conclude that this design was rigidly replicated, which in turn suggests that
each of the fields had a clear meaning and was perhaps widely understood. The
strong similarities may also indicate that there was no reason (or time?) to develop significant variations.

How can the denotation of the iconographic motifs be determined? The only empirical possibility is to argue that the content of the field has a naturalistic referent which is self-evident. This course has been taken by many researchers through the years. The consequence has been frustrating disputes over species and varieties ("Exactly which bird is intended in the Crested Bird?"), but even a general agreement on a naturalistic referent would still leave the problem unsolved, for the "meaning" of the motif must inevitably be in the realm of culture, not nature. It thus seems clear that any further pursuit of the interpretation of the field designs cannot be empirical, for any attribution of meaning to them will have to originate in the mind of the interpreter, whether by dealing directly with the artistic symbol or by interpreting the natural phenomenon which the symbol is suspected to represent. The alternative is to go directly to the ethnographic information, even though there are many well-known difficulties in identifying trustworthy analogies (Wylie 1985). Nonetheless, the ethnographic approach seems the only one likely to shed light on the iconographic motifs. Since it is the thesis of this chapter that this particular image is a cosmological model, it seems best to become familiar with a generalized cosmological model derived from ethnographic and mythological materials before proceeding to a detailed analysis of the possible significance of the five fields.

A COSMOLOGICAL MODEL

In looking for relevant ethnological information to interpret prehistoric iconography, researchers would prefer to examine the ethnographic and mythic collections from the descendants of the people responsible for the images, for that procedure would limit the major ambiguities to the diachronic dimension. Unfortunately, the ethnic identity of the people responsible for the Cox Mound style gorgets is not known. The geographic locations of the gorgets suggest, for reasons no more profound than later habitation in those areas, either (or both) Shawnee or Muskhogean (Creek, Chickasaw, Choctaw, Koasati, and Chakchiuma) peoples. As it happens, the diachronic ambiguity with both of these groups is great enough to be a serious problem. In the case of the Shawnee, there is reason to believe that their mythology underwent significant alteration in the eighteenth and nineteenth centuries, largely due to a series of nativistic revitalization movements (Schutz 1975; see Chapter 5 in particular). In the case of the western Muskhogean speakers, their mythological materials were collected only sparsely and late. Even their kinsmen to the east, the various Creek towns, produced only what has to be described as a fragmentary mythological corpus at the beginning of the twentieth century, and there are reasons to believe that they, too, experienced important religious and philosophical changes in the two preceding centuries (Swanton 1928a, 1929; Lankford 1987; Martin 1991).

It is an awkward problem. The probable descendants of the makers of the gorgets have not provided the information that might interpret the iconography, and researchers are thus forced to broaden the scope of the inquiry to include other peoples whose mythology, although it might well be relevant, is not directly in the historical line. For the concerns of this chapter, this is not as great a problem as it might be with other SECC designs, for the argument here is that these are cosmological motifs, and it is not difficult to discern a great agreement on the basic structure of the cosmos among most of the peoples of the Eastern Woodlands. In many respects the mythology of the Southeast is closely parallel to the mythology of the northern Algonkian peoples and the Siouan speakers, who were formerly part of the Woodlands world. It thus may not be too great a leap to examine their beliefs and myths concerning the structure and creation of the cosmos in the hope of shedding light on the meaning of the Cox Mound style.

The paramount agreement in cosmology is that the cosmos is organized in layers. The Above World is the world of the air, but it is comprised of one or more solid vaults on which beings live. The Above World is thus a celestial realm which is layered in itself. The Beneath World is composed primarily of water, although the logic of the Earth Diver myth indicates that the water resides in something solid, for at the bottom lies some soil. (See references in Lankford 1987:Chap. 5.) The Beneath World, like the Above World, may also consist of several layers, as elaborated by the particular society. In the middle of the two worlds is the Middle World, the earth-disk on which live humans, plants, and other creatures. On this basic structural vision there is massive agreement. How this is elaborated, though, is a matter of local and regional tradition. It might be argued that the very fact of the existence of variation in the details of the cosmic scheme is an indicator of antiquity, particularly when coupled with the wide geographic spread of the common cosmological vision.

With so widespread a phenomenon, it is difficult to know where to focus to get clarity, but one key to the problem is to find a coherent and well-collected body of beliefs, ritual, and mythology. The Central Algonkian peoples appear to be excellent candidates for such a focus. They are a useful group for the examination of Eastern Woodlands cosmology, because their corpus is large and their presence in the territory north of the Ohio River appears to be of long duration. Then, too, the Shawnees are part of that cultural tradition, and some of the Muskogee mythology shows close affiliation with some of the Central Algonkian narratives (Sauk and Fox, for example). (See Lankford 1987 for a discussion of some of these affiliations.) Their worldview is characterized by a particular creation myth—focused on the culture hero Nanabush—and a multilayered universe. Complicating the understanding of their cosmology is the historical existence of an association of religious practitioners in most of the tribal groups, and their rule of secrecy has left question marks over some of the interpretation of Algonkian religious beliefs. Their basic understanding of the structure of the world is that there are two divisions, earth and sky, and that each of those is divided into four strata. As Barnouw (1977:41) summarized the Ojibwa belief:

> The Indians say that this earth has four layers. The bottom layer does not look like the one we are on now. It is night there all the time. That is where the manitou is who is the boss that rules the bottom of the earth. He rules all four layers . . .
>
> The sky has four layers too. In the top layer of the sky there is a manitou who is equal in power to the manitou at the bottom of the earth. It is always day there. It is never night. This manitou has no name, but you can call him Gicimanitou (Great Spirit). There is no name for the top layer. We're right in the middle in between the four earth layers and the four sky layers.

The Ojibwa cosmology is thus a fairly clear one, featuring layers of the world stacked on top of each other, half comprising the Underworld and Underwater, half comprising the sky. The Middle World consists of a flat earth-disk floating on the water between the Above World and the Beneath World. The layers are united by a cosmic tree, and the central plane, the earth-disk interface between earth and sky, is characterized as a sacred geography marked especially by the Directions and the Winds. The master of the sky is the Gitchi-manitou, and the master of the Underworld is the Matchi-manitou. The two realms are represented in the human Middle realm by the Thunders (sometimes quadripartite) and the Underwater Panther, who are forever at odds (Barnouw 1977; Smith 1995).

This is virtually the same cosmology that is believed by the other Central Algonkian peoples—Menomini, Sauk, Fox, Miami, Illinois—all of whom had pretty much the same mythological corpus and at least some form of the Medicine Society. The myths make it clear that the layered cosmos is further structured by various powers which inhabit specific locales. These powers (manitouk—singular: manitou) vary slightly from tribe to tribe, even among the Central Algonkian. Again, however, there is basic agreement, and the lists of powers and functions are similar. Sauk informants provided a roster of power points in the cosmology, printed here in a brief list form for clarity:

- *Getci Mu'nito* is thought to be an old white-headed man of majestic appearance who sits everlastingly in the Heavens, smoking . . .
- *Wi'saka,* the culture hero, founder of the Medicine Dance, dwells on earth in the north . . .
- *The Thunderers* . . . giant eagles inhabiting the western Empyrean, but some maintain that they resemble human beings . . .
- *The Water Spirits* consist of monstrous snakes and enormous panthers . . .
- Four of the *great serpents* support "this island," the earth, on their backs . . .
- *Underworld Panthers* have spotted bodies like wildcats, and tails of enormous length . . .
- *Tepe'kininiwa,* the "night man," . . . Master of Fire . . .
- *"Chief Snakes* or Powers" . . .
- *Ketcikumi Manitu* is the God of the Sea, while the
- *Paia'shiwuk* are two brothers, dwarfs, who dwell under the water . . .
- *"Our Grandmother, the Earth,"* is the earth personified as an old woman. She figures prominently in Sauk mythology as the old grandmother who raised the hero Wi'saka. She is frequently invoked and to her are offered tobacco sacrifices which are buried in the ground. She owns the roots and herbs which are the hairs of her head . . .
- *Shawa'natasiu* is the manitu of the south . . . He is personified as a great serpent, and was desired as a dream guardian . . .
- *Ya'pata* is the brother of Wi'saka, the Culture Hero, and has charge of the realm of the Dead . . .
- *Po'kitapawa,* known as "Knocks-a-hole-in-the-head" or "Brain-Taker," guards the bridge on the trail to the afterworld. (Skinner 1923a:34–36)

Missing, but probably implicit, in this listing are two of the most important powers, the Sun and the Great Serpent, Mishebeshu (to use the Ojibwa name). The former is a primary religious image, and it may be a focus for the Great Spirit or the culture hero; the latter, the master of the Beneath World, may be present in this Sauk listing as Ketcikumi Manitu, Water Spirits, Chief Snakes, or all of them. Whether or not this Sauk pantheon is to be taken as the one best expressing the general cosmology, it makes it clear that the powers were well known and assigned to structural positions in the cosmos. They create a complex structural form by their relationships—their alliances and conflicts—and it is in this world of powers that the creation of humanity occurs. For the

Central Algonkian, the basic story is the well-known and widespread myth of the culture hero Nanabush, which has many texts. Smith and Vecsey have each summarized the elements which are common to all the variants:

> The Underwater manitouk always kill Nanabush's companion, the wolf . . . Nanabush . . . always seeks vengeance against the killers. Further, Nanabush never fails to kill the ogimaa [master, "boss"] Mishebeshu, and the surviving Underwater manitouk invariably flood the earth in retribution. And, finally, it is Nanabush who escapes the water by building a raft or climbing a tree and sends the earth divers to the bottom for mud. Nanabush takes the tiny bit of mud and forms the earth. Additionally, he is usually aided in his actions by birds and along the way almost always kills a toad medicine woman so that he can gain entrance, in her stead, to Mishebeshu's lodge. (Smith 1995:158; see Vecsey 1988)

As a result of the presence in the human layer of connectors to the other layers, each manitou and its set of powers may also be understood in terms of its social meaning within human life—who controls a particular power, how did he/she get it, and what does it mean? The cosmology has cultural referents in the structure of human society. The cosmological structure of the two halves of the world thus consists of both geographical locations and qualitative signifiers. Any reference to the creatures or to their locations in the cosmology may therefore be a metaphor on several levels at the same time. This becomes quite clear in an examination of the major manitouk in the Central Algonkian cosmos.

Just as the structure of the world appears to be an oppositional dualism, so too does the relationship between the manitouk of the different halves seem to be an active dualism. The principal players are Gicimanitou, probably symbolized by the sun, and the Matchi-manitou, the "boss" at the bottom of the earth. Some believe that this latter figure is a post-contact creation linked to the Christian devil communicated in missionary mythology (Vecsey 1983:82; Smith 1995:104). A strict structural approach, however, suggests that such an "ultimate" figure is needed, for the major oppositional manitouk who appear in popular imagery and mythology are below the level of the Great Spirit; in fact, they are the representatives of the two realms which meet in the small layer within which live the human people. Those two are the Thunders of the upper realm and Mishebeshu, the master of the lower realm. Each is elaborated by subordinates, allies, and alter egos, each located somewhere within the various layers of the Above World and the Beneath World. All together, they form the larger complex of the oppositional dualism.

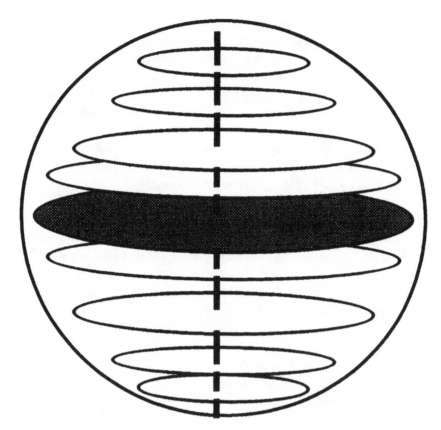

FIGURE 2.4. A generalized model of the cosmic structure, based on the Central Algonkian understanding.

Connecting all the layers in the world is the cedar tree, which was driven through the planes by Bear at the beginning of ceremonialism (or specifically the Midewiwin). Ritually, the equivalent of the cedar is the sacred drum, which creates a sound column which binds together all layers and opens portals, making possible communication between them (Grim 1983:84). There are other axes mundi, as will be shown below, but the tree is a classic image for the northern people, almost certainly stemming from the ancient circumpolar shamanistic tradition (Fig. 2.4).

The two worlds of earth and sky, divided into at least eight categories, are thus united into a single structure by vertical axes. The creatures of the Middle World stand at the center of this cosmos. Within the various species of the Middle World, including humans, there are individuals who can travel with impunity to other levels of earth and sky and visit the manitouk who dwell there, bringing their power back for use on earth. As Smith points out, "[H]umans are meant to live on the island of the earth, and just as it is risky to travel to the nests of the Thunderbirds, so too venturing beneath the ground or water signals a challenge to the accepted boundaries of the world. Only the most experienced and powerful shamans travel routinely through these layers" (Smith 1995:144).

While the details, such as the number of the layers, may differ from tribe to tribe, this layered cosmos is common to most of the peoples of the Eastern Woodlands, regardless of language affiliation. Hudson confirms this same picture for the Southeastern people in his survey of the religious beliefs of that region (Hudson 1976:Chap. 3; see also Swanton 1928b).

Some Cosmological Motifs

The Cox Mound style gorget is a plan figure—a map—of the cosmos just described. There are some slight variations present, but they are easily accommodated within the larger array of cosmological details in the Eastern Woodlands. The easiest way to clarify the nature of the cosmogram is to examine each of the motifs, identified above as Fields 1 through 5.

FIELDS 1 AND 2. The rayed circle of Field 2 has been interpreted by every writer on the subject as the sun, largely because it is difficult to envision an alternate meaning for a rayed circle. The cross of Field 1 is a little more troubling, because there are alternate forms which can fit into the sun circle. Waring solved the problem by considering the two fields as a single motif, and he included all variants as equivalents:

> [Cross and Sun Circle] are the motifs most easily identified with a conceptual complex on the historic level, namely the fire-sun-deity complex. Holmes [1906:105] and Willoughby [1932:59] both regarded these motifs as "sun," "cosmic," or "world" symbols . . . The concept of a holy fire identified with the sun and fed by four symbolic logs oriented to the four cardinal points is the most widespread and basic ceremonial concept in the Southeast . . .
>
> In view of the distribution of this complex, of the similarity of its position in the various individual conceptual systems of the Southeast, and of its association with the symbolic cruciform arrangement of logs, it seems obvious that the Cross and Sun Circle are essential symbols of the fire-sun-deity conceptual complex. (Waring 1968:33–35)

In a lengthy exposition Howard agreed with Waring's interpretation, especially the focus on the ritual significance of the four-log structure of the sacred fire which is found at the center of the Creek square grounds (Howard 1968). That fire is not a minor element in Southeastern religion, for it is the very center of the ceremonial and political life of the *talwa* ("town") (Hudson 1976:126; Lankford 1987:54–57). It is directly related to the sun, in that it is a reflection of the light/heat/rays of the sun itself on the earthly plane—the Middle World's major representative of the Above World. In that philosophical sense, the fire and the sun are not equivalents. They are related, but not to be equated. The difference between the two becomes apparent when a widespread Muskogee practice is recalled: the fire becomes polluted through time and must annually be extinguished so as to make way for a "new fire" to be created, one that will more purely embody the presence of the Sun in the Middle World (Swanton 1928b). Thus, although the interpretations of Waring and Howard seem sound, there is a good reason for distinguishing between the two fields. Since the fire and the sun are not the same thing, as Waring's characterization of the "fire-sun-deity conceptual *complex*" suggests, the iconographic cross and sun circle should not be understood to be the same.

One of the consequences of making the distinction is that it is easier to see an important conceptual difference in the symbols—Field 1 is a reference to the Middle World, while Field 2 points to the Above World. Spatially, then, it is easy to see the two as together forming a vertical axis, demonstrating an important uniting principle of the cosmos (Fig. 2.5).

FIELD 3. The looped square is a sign for the Middle World. That identification is a reasonable surmise based upon the symbol's context in the cosmogram. If this full design is a map of the cosmos, then the Middle World must be indicated in some fashion, and this symbol is the logical candidate. There are, however, ethnographic clues which lend support to the identification.

What is the Middle World? In mythology, it is a disk of rock and earth floating on the water of the Beneath World. It came into existence by magical expansion of a particle of dirt brought from beneath the water by one of the water creatures. The Earth Diver myth has been studied by many scholars from perspectives ranging from historic-geographic diffusion to psychoanalysis (see Lankford 1987:106–110). It has attracted this sort of attention both because it is presumed to be one of the most ancient creation myths of humanity and because it is the creation myth common to the Eastern Woodlands. The problem for the "creator," whoever that figure is in each particular version of the myth, is to determine what will support the floating disk and/or make it stable. The two functions are not quite the same, and solutions vary. Some solve the problem by ignoring it—the disk is there. For others, the support of the earth-disk may be sufficient, or the earth may float unsupported but needs some stabiliz-

FIGURE 2.5. The Sun circle in the Above World makes a columnar connection with the Sacred Fire of the Middle World.

ing force. Or both support and braces may be called for. One major theory in the Eastern Woodlands was that the earth was deposited on the shell of a turtle, who thus became the support (and symbol) of the earth-island. "This belief was not only held by the Iroquois but by the Delaware and other Algonquian tribes in the Eastern Woodlands" (Speck 1931:44–47; Fenton 1962). According to the Shawnee Prophet, the Shawnees were among them (Schutz 1975:100).

Yet others focused more on the technique of stabilizing the earth as it floated in the water. Some, perhaps more influenced by quadripartite thinking, saw the earth's stability as the result of the teamwork of four creatures. The Mandans believed that the earth rests upon the backs of *four* tortoises, who were presumably able to counteract the rocking motion of the water (Catlin 1967:75). The Cherokees believed that there are four ropes which hang down from the celestial vault and support the earth at the four corners (Mooney 1900:239). Hudson implies that this was the general Southeastern view, but the Muskogee understanding was not articulated by any informants, and it seems safer to conclude that the four-rope solution was unique to the Cherokees (Hudson 1976:122).

As was noted above, the Sauk saw the placement of four of the Beneath World's serpents as the key to stabilizing the earth-disk: "Four of the *great serpents* support 'this island,' the earth, on their backs . . ." (Skinner 1923a:35). That same theoretical approach was taken by the Winnebagos, even though in the evolution of their religious views the Earth Diver dropped out, probably as part of the same process by which "Earthmaker" eclipsed the Sun.

> Earthmaker looked on the earth and he liked it, but it was not quiet. It moved about as do the waves of the sea. Then he made the trees and he saw that they were good, but they did not make the earth quiet. Then he made the grass to grow, but still the earth was not quiet. However, it was nearly quiet. Then he made the four directions (cardinal points) and the four winds. On the four corners of the earth he placed them as great and powerful people, to act as island weights. Yet the earth was not quiet. Then he made four large beings and threw them down toward the earth, and they pierced through the earth with their heads eastward. They were snakes. Then the earth became very still and quiet. (Radin 1923:164; see also 302)

Even though the Shawnees stood with the Delawares in their vision of the turtle as the support of the earth, they also maintained a belief in the four stabilizing forces. The ethnographic information from the Shawnee informants makes clear a general ambiguity about those four figures—they are referred to as snakes, as Powers, as people (whether human in form or not), as Directions, as "weights," and possibly as Winds. Part of the problem is that there are other foursomes present in some of the mythological material, including the Thunders, the Winds, and the Directions, and these appear in some cases to be combined in different ways. It is instructive to read Schutz's summary of the various Shawnee informants as they articulated this group of Powers:

> Among the more important deities are the "grandfathers" of the winds, assigned to their stations at the four corners of the earth. These are specifically mentioned by Trowbridge in both the accounts of the Shawnee Prophet and Black Hoof (Kinietz and W. E. Voegelin, 1939:42 and 60–61). The Shawnee Prophet's comment is in reference to religious practices, saying that the Shawnee "pray also to the four serpents who occupy the four cardinal points—to these their supplications are secretly made, accompanied by an offering of tobacco, thrown into the fire." The term translated "snakes" almost certainly being manetooki which is used for various deities

in the sense of "supernatural beings" or powers. The term is specifically used in regard to these beings of the quarters of the earth in C. F. Voegelin and John Yegerlehnder (1952 (Ms):7, line 217).

Black Hoof's account relates specifically to the creation (pp. 60–61): "When he had accomplished the formation of this island he made some very large animals and placed them upon it, at the four cardinal points of the compass, to keep it steady." These surely refer to the grandfathers of the four quarters of the earth . . .

. . . the four personages are characterized in different ways: Winter Man . . . rules half of the year and causes the leaves to fall from which medicines are made to cleanse and purify. Summer Man . . . rules the other half of the year and brings useful things, such as the Spring, the time for planting, and the promise of food. The grandfather who sits in the West brings a feeling of well-being gotten during sleep, and the grandfather of the East is a reservoir of wisdom obtained from the Creator. All of these deities have great power and superior knowledge to man, and it is their duty to guide and care for mankind under the control of the creator. It is likely that in any reconstruction of proto Algonquian mythology the four grandfathers of the earth's quadrants will figure prominently. (Schutz 1975:102–103)

This brief survey makes it clear that there was a variety of understandings as to how the Middle World was given stability as it floats upon the waters, but it also affords some reassurance that the basic cosmological principle was wide-spread—some Powers are located at the "four corners" of the earth-disk. It is proposed here that those four powers are symbolized in the four sides of the looped square of the Cox Mound style. It does not seem possible to say precisely how they are to be glossed—ropes, serpents, or other—but the principle seems clear. The Middle World has four Directions, and they are benign Powers. They also define the boundaries of the earth-disk, and they are the source of support and stability. In the artistic form of the Cox Mound style, they interlock at the corner loops, providing a visual unity of the four. The looped square is thus a twofold image—it points toward the Four, reminding the knowledgeable of the various qualities, powers, and functions of each direction, and it points to the single unified reality which the Four embody—the stable Middle World, which resides inside the figure.

FIELD 4. The Crested Birds are, like the Middle World itself, in quadripartite form, which indicates another characteristic connected to the cardinal directions. Moreover, they are placed with heads (only) located at the edges of the earth-disk, as if to specify location. As already observed, the heads provide two major identifying visual characteristics, the straight sharp beak and the feather crest. Their location further suggests that the Crested Birds are surely part of the complex of directional powers already introduced, and their identification is most likely in the realm of the Winds or Thunders. One of the Shawnee characterizations of the "Grandfathers" of the cardinal directions is as "grandfathers of the winds."

Are these wind or storm powers? It is helpful to look at the lore concerning those powers. Winds are the focus of some Siouan myths. The Kansas believe that the winds are deities, and they are represented in a song chart by a swastika symbol (Dorsey 1885: 676). According to a Santee informant, the winds are subordinate to the Direction powers:

> The Four Winds are sent by "the Something that moves" at each of the "Four Directions or Quarters." The Winds are, therefore, the messengers or exponents of the powers which remain at the Four Quarters. These Four Quarters are spoken of as upholding the earth, and are connected with thunder or lightning as well as the wind. (Fletcher 1884:289)

In an Omaha origin myth of the Washa'she group, the winds played an important role in the creation of the Middle World. The ancestors in the sky were sent by their sun father and moon mother to live below, which was only water. They called upon elk, who summoned the winds.

> Then he called to the winds and the winds came from all quarters and blew until the waters went upward in a mist. Before that time the winds traveled only in two directions, from north to south and then back from south to north; but when the elk called they came from the east, the north, the west, and the south, and met at a central point, and carried the water upward.
>
> The water then receded from the land, and the hairs of the elk became plants. The Hon'ga group have a similar creation myth, but it continues with the Earth Diver myth, with muskrat, loon, beaver, and the successful crawfish as the players. (Fletcher and La Flesche 1911:63)

The Winds can be easily confused with the weather powers. Generally speaking, the storm powers of the northern area are the Thunderbirds, while the equivalent powers of the Southeast appear to be boys, at least for the Caddos and Cherokees. (See Lankford 1987:70–81 for a look at some Southeastern materials.) Even that distinction, however, is a firmer characterization than is war-

ranted by the ethnographic information. Among the Central Algonkian, for example, the Thunderbird has many variations on the name and several different
forms. For the Sauk, the Thunderers were "giant eagles inhabiting the western
Empyrean, but some maintain that they resemble human beings . . ." (Skinner
1923a:35). As one modern Ojibwa described a Thunder, "It looked something
like a bird and it looked something like a man in places, like his legs, you know,
and part of his body, but the face is something like a bird's face with a beak
and wings on the sides (William Trudeau 1988)" (Smith 1995:77). In perhaps its
most mystical perception, the Thunderbird can be seen sometimes in the storm
cloud itself. It can appear in the mythology as a human or as a bird. The shape-
shifting ability of people of power is a given in the religious practices of the
Native American peoples generally, and it is reflected in the Algonkian variety
of descriptions of the most powerful of players on their stage.

There is even a vagueness in the precise identity of the Thunderbirds. Smith
wrestled with the problem:

> Vecsey understands the four winds and the Thunderbirds to be entirely dif-
> ferent entities (1983, 73, 75); other sources record that they were one and
> the same (Coleman 1947, 37–38; Coleman, Frogner, and Eich 1962, 102;
> Howard, 1965, 92). I would tend to agree with Vecsey, for while Winds
> or Directions and thunders are related, they each have their own discrete
> mythologies. The Winds or Directions are said to be the guardians of the
> four corners. (Smith 1995:80)

A text of the creation myth supports Smith's conclusion that the Winds
and the Directions are not the same as the Thunderbirds. Nanabush told the
Thunders:

> "So come, keep watch over these people! . . . and so now do you depart, to
> all the directions from whence blow the winds do you go." Truly then did
> the birds depart. And so in time they found resting-places where to live at
> all the directions from whence blow the winds. (Jones 1919:551, in Smith
> 1995:182–183)

The organization of the earth-disk by cardinal directions and winds was thus
prior, in the Ojibwa view, to the creation of the Storm powers. The Thunderbirds can readily appear in the singular rather than as a group, and the single
Thunderbird is said to live in the West. Nonetheless, the Thunders are usually
seen as closely allied with the Directions and Winds. To humans who can gain

power from them, the Thunderbirds will grant both thunderstones, for bringing rain and for protection from storms, and feathers, useful in healing (Smith 1995:87–88).

Schutz attempted to characterize the Shawnee concept of the Thunderers, and he concluded that they seem to occupy an intermediate position between the tribes of the Southeast and those further north. He quoted with approval E. W. Voegelin's observation:

The Algonquian-speaking tribes of the East refer to them as Our Grandfathers, and they are included in the beings addressed in prayers, as well as being fairly frequently referred to in myths. Among the Shawnee, a borderline tribe between the Southeast and the Eastern Woodlands, the Thunderbirds are mentioned in myths, but the Thunders are also said to be small boys who use backward speech and can move mountains, but are nonplused over moving a handful of dirt or getting across a very small stream; this latter belief in the Thunders as boys is Southeastern. (Voegelin 1972:1112, in Schutz 1975:104)

It is provocative to note that the Cherokees identify the Twins of the "Kanati and Selu" myth as the Thunders. This image appears to be fairly closely related to the Shawnee belief, particularly as it was articulated by one Shawnee informant who described them as small boys with wings (Schutz 1975:104). As already noted, the Muskhogean myths provide a great deal of ambiguity on the nature of the Thunder powers and the Winds, leaving the question open.

It thus appears that without being able to identify precisely the peoples who created the Cox Mound style gorgets, it is impossible to choose between the Winds and the Thunderers as the correct interpretation of the Crested Birds. It may be the safest path to conclude simply that they are Weather powers of some type, located in and associated with the Cardinal Directions.

FIELD 5. The last field consists only of the circular shell of which the gorget is formed. It is, however, more than merely the raw material, for the shell embodies its own intrinsic meaning. It is by nature a water-related substance, since it comes from river-dwelling or marine creatures, but that is only the naturalistic basis for a complex cultural elaboration. In the general cosmological model, the Below World is understood to consist primarily of water, whether or not there are layers. Water and everything associated with it are therefore symbolically related to the Below World, which includes those powers who dwell there. The major power, widely known and respected throughout the Eastern Woodlands, is the Great Serpent, a complicated figure which will be referred to here by its

Ojibwa name, Mishebeshu. In order to explicate the meaning of the shell disk, it is necessary to understand some of the lore about this power. Since a detailed exploration of Mishebeshu, who is so well known through Native America, is presented in Chapter 5, only a brief sketch is needed here.

In a standard set of myths in the Eastern Woodlands, the Thunderbirds are aggressive in seeking out their prey, the manitouk of the waters (see references in Lankford 1987:74–81). The most powerful dualism in the Algonkian worldview is the fight between the two, which are frequently in ritual and myth reduced to a single Thunderbird and the "master" of the Underwater realm, Mishebeshu. The nature of the enmity between the Thunderbirds and Mishebeshu is cast as that of predator and prey and thus as an extension of the natural order and its ecological rules. "[T]he battles between these manitouk are not experienced as contests between good and evil, light and dark, right and wrong, but between the forces of balance and imbalance, as embodied in powerful persons" (Smith 1995:129). The two manitouk are not opposing principles, but simply persons of power related in the food chain—the earth/Beneath World perpetually feeds the sky. There are some differences in the nature of the Thunders and Mishebeshu, however, as Smith points out in regard to the Ojibwa understanding. The Thunders, while aggressive toward the Underwater manitouk, are friendly to humans and willing to enter alliances with them. Mishebeshu is much more reserved toward human relationships, and the underwater manitouk frequently seize people and drag them beneath the water.

There are indications that the outcome from a human attempt to gain power from the sky layers was more likely to be successful than a similar attempt to join in partnership with Mishebeshu. "Mishebeshu could be courted by shamans eager to share in his great power, but such alliances with the monster carried great risks for human beings" (Smith 1995:109). Mishebeshu will grant power to humans, but not willingly. Nonetheless, within Ojibwa society Mishebeshu is understood to have been the primary source of the power of the Midé Society, which was founded by the culture hero, Nanabush. Possibly precisely because it was considered such a mark of achievement for human spirit travelers to be able to use the power of the Underwater Panther, the Midé Society claimed to be able to harness that power to all other powers to produce a major focus of cosmic power. Among the gifts of Mishebeshu to human people of power were copper and megis shells. The shells, which were the primary symbol of the Midé Society, were thought to be scales of Mishebeshu (Howard 1965:125; Smith 1995:185, 187).

Although it is irrelevant for the present examination of two sets of gorgets found only on shell, it is instructive to note that copper, like shell (and therefore probably functionally equivalent to it), also "belongs" to Mishebeshu, who is sometimes described as covered with copper, and especially his horns. Copper and shell are thus substances which participate in the Underwater world and have connotative meanings related to that world.

As part of the body of Mishebeshu, a shell disk like the gorget was not just a display area for an engraving, but was itself an object of power. In the Cox Mound style, the shell disk, as part of a cosmogram, had two meanings: while it intrinsically represented the Beneath World and its power (which was probably true for all shell gorgets, regardless of design), it also represented the lowest part of this particular design. In an artistic sense, the Winds/Thunders, the Directions, the earth-disk, and the fire are all resting on the surface of the shell, the waters of the Beneath World. The sun, as the representative of the Above World, can be understood to float well above the shell/water disk. The Cox Mound style cosmogram thus contains the symbols for an important group of cosmic powers—Sun, Fire, Directions, Earth-supports, Winds/Thunders. Having no engraved symbol, Mishebeshu, Lord of the Beneath World, is nonetheless present in the circular shell disk which underlies all the other symbols (Fig. 2.6).

The Hixon Style Gorgets

There are thirty known examples of the Hixon style gorgets (Brain and Phillips 1996:12–16). They have been known informally for decades as the "turkey-cocks" design, because the birds have long since been identified naturalistically as turkeys. The identification is based largely on the fact that many of the examples have flared tails, reminiscent of turkey tails, and some of them have an additional vertical line down the neck which has been referred to as "wattles." This chapter disagrees with the turkey identification and argues, instead, that this is but another artistic form of the Crested Bird already encountered on the Cox Mound style gorgets (Fig. 2.7).

The basic thesis is that the Hixon style gorgets have as content the same cosmic elements as the Cox Mound style, but that the vantage point is different—the Hixon style presents a side view of the cosmos, whereas the Cox Mound style provides a plan view. The analysis is best organized along the same lines as the approach to the Cox Mound style, by fields. The same fields will be used in order to facilitate comparison, even though it creates a little less clarity in looking at the Hixon style in isolation (Fig. 2.8).

FIELDS 1 AND 2. In side view, the Fire-cross and Sun circle become a pole. That the relationship between the two realms—Middle World/fire and Above World/Sun—spatially would create a column was presented above. In this gorget style it is made manifest. The column, a world axis, takes the form of a

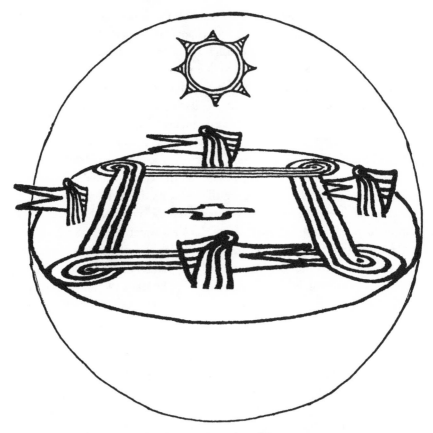

FIGURE 2.6. The Cox Mound style cosmological model.

striped pole. Of the thirty examples of the Hixon style, at least twenty-two have
the central pole. The others are eroded, but it seems probable that they follow
the pattern. There are variations in the decoration of the pole—the direction
of the stripes changes, and in one series (the "conventionalized" form) the stripes
become an "x" pattern, which creates diamonds.

None of the surviving Hixon gorgets shows signs of having been painted,
so it is impossible to tell whether the gorgets were once colored. That would
be of particular interest in regard to the pole, because colors usually possess
symbolic qualities, and it could be important to know how the stripes were envisioned by the native beholders. If these striped poles were red and white, for
example, it would permit speculation concerning the Southeastern use of the
Above World's white in conjunction with the Beneath World's red, with a possible reference to the union of the two worlds (see Lankford 1993 for an ex-

ploration of the meaning of these two colors in Southeastern thought). With only the lines, however, the striped pole stands as a world axis with no further elaboration.

As has been mentioned, in the Central Algonkian belief system there is reference to a cedar tree as a world axis, and the beating of the drum also creates a mystical sonic axis. It is not difficult to find mythical trees in the literature of Native America, for they range from the Iroquois tree of light which stands in the center of the Above World to the Yuchi cedar tree which was surmounted by the decapitated head of a "monster" in primeval times (see Lankford 1975 for a survey of some of the mythological tree presentations). The examination of the Cox Mound style produced the image of another mystical axis mundi, one created by the invisible relationship between Sun and fire. It is an easy leap from that concept to the microcosmic nature of the earthlodge, from the Plains to the Southeast, in which the central fire pit is directly below the circular smoke hole in the center of the vault, thus creating that same invisible conceptual column.

Such cognate forms of world axes are not difficult to see once the basic cosmological model is understood, for poles in ritual life may very well carry symbolic burdens along with their pragmatic functional roles. Thus the four poles supporting the dome of some of the earthlodges become recognizable as the Direc-

FIGURE 2.7. The Hixon style gorget. These examples are from Etowah and Hixon.

FIGURE 2.8. The analytical fields of the Hixon style.

tional powers, surrounding the central axis of fire pit and smoke hole. Then, too, there is the rich symbolism of the pole used in the Plains Sun Dance ceremonies. In the recognition of these potential forms of the world axis it is also possible to understand the use of different forms of the axis—tree, pole, light column, sound column—as motifs which can be substituted for each other within the same structure, and thus related to the same basic concept. Moreover, it is possible to see them blended in an easy metaphoric complex in which one can be called by the name of another, without doing violence to religious reasoning. From this perspective, it is provocative to read a mythological account of the Sacred Pole of the Omaha people:

> The son of one of the ruling men was off on a hunt. On his way home he came to a great forest and in the night lost his way. He walked and walked until he was exhausted with pushing his way through the underbrush. He stopped to rest and to find the "motionless star" for his guide when he was suddenly attracted by a light . . . it was a tree that sent forth the light. He went up to it and found that the whole tree, its trunk, branches, and leaves, were alight, yet remained unconsumed. He touched the tree but no heat came from it . . . At last day approached, the brightness of the tree began to fade, until with the rising of the sun the tree with its foliage resumed its natural appearance . . . As twilight came on it began to be luminous and continued so until the sun again arose . . . four animal paths led to it . . . it was clear to them that the animals came to the tree and had rubbed against it and polished its bark by so doing." (Fletcher and La Flesche 1911:217–218)

A passage from an Omaha text describing this wondrous tree becomes almost a description of the cosmogram under discussion:

> The Thunder birds come and go upon this tree, making a trail of fire that leaves four paths on the burnt grass that stretch toward the Four Winds. When the Thunder birds alight upon the tree it bursts into flame and the fire mounts to the top. The tree stands burning, but no one can see the fire except at night. (Fletcher and La Flesche 1911:217)

The richness of the symbolism becomes apparent when the myth is placed in its ritual context, for this tree is the very one which is cut down and trimmed to a relatively small size for use in the ceremonials. Moreover, it is this tree which is understood to be the connecting force which binds together into a single reality the two realms of the Above World and the Middle World.

> The Omahas have always thought of themselves as a tribe composed of complementary halves, the Sky People (Insta'shunda) and the Earth People (Hon'gashenu). Umon'hon'ti [the Sacred Pole] is a single person in whom these halves have joined. (Riddington 1993)

Although this line of symbolic thought cannot be pursued here, two suggestions should be noted for future examination, one mythological and one iconographic. The Omaha description of the tree which is always burning, but can be seen only at night, sounds like an axis of light. The day and night references sound remarkably like a description of the solar-fire axis already discussed, but the nocturnal equivalent may be the Milky Way, a column of light which nonetheless does not give off heat. If this reading is correct, then the Omaha description of the tree of light refers to a provocative set of symbolic connections: world axis = tree = sun-fire = star column. The iconographic image which may be illustrative of this dual tree concept appears on a Spiro shell. While it appears to be a naturalistic tree (albeit strangely drawn), in the light of this symbolic set of equivalents, it could be interpreted as a visual depiction of the tree of light (Fig. 2.9).

The mysterious tree of the Omaha became a pole in their ritual life, and it is helpful to note a similar usage far removed from the Omaha-Spiro sphere of the southern Plains. The Ais are half a continent removed from the Omaha, and there is little reason to suspect that they have much in common with the Omaha, at least in environment, subsistence strategies, and other material factors. Among these non-agricultural people on the east coast of Florida in late August of 1699, the shipwrecked Dickenson was witness to a lengthy ceremonial in which this occurred:

> It now being the time of the moon's entering the first quarter the Indians had a ceremonious dance, which they began about 8 o'clock in the morning. In the first place came in an old man, and took a *staff about 8 feet long, having a broad arrow on the head thereof, and thence halfway painted red and white, like a barber's pole.* In the middle of this staff was fixed a piece of wood, shaped like unto a thigh, leg, and foot of a man, and the lower part of it was painted black. This staff, being carried out of the cassekey's house, was set fast in the ground standing upright, which being done he

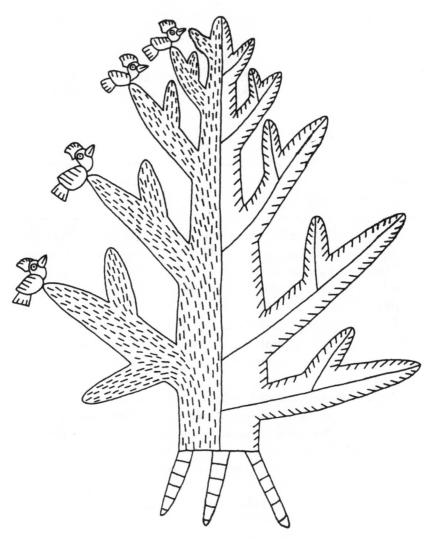

FIGURE 2.9. The Day/Night Tree from Spiro (adapted from Phillips and Brown 1984:Pl. 236).

brought out a basket containing six rattles, which were taken out thereof and placed at the foot of the staff. Another old man came in and set up a howling like unto a mighty dog, but beyond him for length of breath, withal making a proclamation. This being done and most of them having painted themselves, some red, some black, some with black and red, with their bellies girt up as tight as well they could girt themselves with ropes, having their sheaths of arrows at their backs and their bows in their hands, being gathered together about the staff, six of the chiefest men in esteem amongst them, especially one who is their doctor, took up the rattles and began a hideous noise, standing round the staff with their rattles and bowing to it without ceasing for about half an hour. (Swanton 1946:763–764)

While it is useless to speculate on the meaning of this long-extinct ritual, two things deserve mention—the description of the striped pole and the leg effigy so reminiscent of some of the Plains Sun Dance paraphernalia. This appears to be another manifestation of the axis mundi as encountered in tribal ceremonial life. Just as there are extensive possibilities of world axes in ritual, it must be pointed out that the Hixon style striped pole is not an isolated phenomenon in the art of the SECC. There are so many examples of it, in fact (in at least five different contexts in the Spiro shell engravings) that it clearly is beyond the scope of this chapter to pursue the shifts in meaning or reference.

FIELD 3. The looped square of the Cox Mound style cosmogram is here seen as simply a disk as viewed from the side—a bar. The Middle World has become merely a bar across the lower part of the image. There has been a good deal of discussion about the meaning of the lowering of the crosspiece of the cross, but from the viewpoint of the cosmological model, the horizontal bar is not part of the striped pole, but is instead one of the planes which is connected to the whole by the pole. It can thus be judged to be lower for artistic purposes—there is no "cross" needing a centering to protect its meaning, and the artist needs some space for his birds. So the Middle World becomes a footing for the birds.

FIELD 4. The birds have undergone a transformation in several ways. For one thing, they now appear in full body, and that body has two major artistic forms. In one presentation the wings are folded alongside the body, emphasizing the avian shape. In the other, the feathers are flared into a fan, but whether this is intended to be a tail fan or a wing fan is not clear. It is this latter artistic form which has led to the identification of the birds as turkeys, but that is by no means an unarguable conclusion. It is, on the contrary, quite possible that the feather fan is the result of artistic license which has as its purpose not the identification of a naturalistic model of the bird, but the creation of an iconographic pun, or kenning. Those feather fans bear a strong resemblance to fans which are held in the hands of human (?) dancers in other SECC designs, as well as to the form of the "lobes" of some of the bi-lobed arrow designs. When a different figure is seen in the same posture, but holding peculiar fans somewhat like bat wings, it becomes clear that the posture and the fan shape comprise a standard artistic convention of the SECC corpus. In light of that pattern, it may be that the Hixon feather fans (present on only some of the gorgets, it will be recalled) should be understood as an artistic technique for communicating to the knowledgeable some iconographic "subtext" which cannot at present be read. Until there are workable interpretations for all those designs that are part of the "fan complex," it is fruitless to speculate about the ways in which kenning might operate in this art. For present purposes, it is enough to suggest that there is an alternate way of looking at those feather fans other than to make a naturalistic leap toward turkeys.

The suggestion gains strength from an additional fact—the identifying characteristics of the Crested Bird in the Cox Mound style (the straight sharp beak and the head crest) are both present in the Hixon birds. If attention is not diverted by the feather fan, then the identification of these full birds as the same as the Crested Birds is a reasonable step. One further problem in the identification is the number of birds—how did four birds become two? The answer is simple, but not provable. In the drawing of a side view of the cosmogram, it is just not artistically feasible to attempt to draw four full birds. It would be difficult to do, and the result, even in expert artistic hands, would probably be an unreadable mess. To put it even more simply, the heraldic design of the Crested Birds flanking the striped pole is aesthetically pleasing, with its balance and clarity. If the viewer already knows the meaning of what is being portrayed (the four Winds/Thunders), then the reduction to two is successful. For those who don't know the referent to begin with, the reduction is obfuscating.

FIELD 5. The final transformation in the change from the plan view to the side view is of great significance in moving from this study to further examination of other iconographic images. The problem is that turning the cosmos on its side removes the shell disk from its double-meaning position; since it is no longer the "bottom" of the cosmos, it cannot serve as the symbol of the Beneath World. It should be noted that in most versions of the Hixon style there is an engraved frame for the design, even if the design laps across it; in the Cox Mound style the edge of the gorget was the frame, because the gorget was part of the design. The Hixon style shell may (and probably does) retain its significance as a power object with connections with Mishebeshu, but only in the same sense that all shell gorgets do. It has, however, lost its role in the iconographic image itself. That means that some other symbol had to be introduced to represent the Beneath World in the cosmogram. That symbol appears in the vast majority of the Hixon style gorgets as two sets of curved lines which connect the bottom of the Middle World to the bottom of the gorget. In a few of the designs it takes the form of a series of vertical lines. Fortunately, in three of the Hixon style gorgets there is a naturalistic variation which provides the essential information for decoding the mysterious lines (Fig. 2.10).

FIGURE 2.10. The Hixon style's Beneath World in several symbolic variants.

The Crested Birds stand upon a pot, and in at least one of the gorgets they do so without benefit of the Middle World disk. In other words, the rim of the pot can either be the support of the earth-disk, or itself represent that disk. The identification of the pot in the naturalistic gorgets makes it clear that what is offered as a shorthand symbol for the Beneath World in the others is a cross-section of the rim of a pot. That equation thus makes it clear that the Beneath World can be symbolized as a pot, an image which is fairly reasonable in light of the facts that water is the key and that it must be contained in something (what is holding the dirt that the Earth Diver recovers from the "bottom"?). The something—the metaphor—is a pot. The pot is also the structural complement to the solid sky vault, completing the circular cosmogram. In this connection, it is significant that the Choctaw specifically compare the pot in which the green corn is cooked to the sky—the pot is even called *shoti hikiya*, "sky standing" (Kenneth York, personal communication, 1997).

The circles on the naturalistic pots in the Hixon gorgets resemble eyes, and it is possible that the Beneath World is being personified. There may thus be here a reference to a personage not yet identified, or perhaps to Mishebeshu himself. This is not a particularly surprising revelation, because similar stylized designs from Florida have been discussed as possible symbolic pots, and a similar analysis of Cahokia pottery designs as cosmological structures has been persuasively argued (Pauketat and Emerson 1991). This current insight into the Hixon style pot as metaphor for the Beneath World is consistent with those earlier observations and adds to the evidence that pottery may possess a high level of symbolic content.

Conclusion

As observed at the beginning of this chapter, only the denotative meanings of the two gorget styles are the subject of this exploration. The evidence for their interpretation as the symbols for various aspects and powers of the cosmic structure has been presented. If the reader finds that evidence persuasive, then there may be agreement on the referents of the symbols and on the overall argument that the Cox Mound style and Hixon style gorgets are cosmograms. That set of assignments of conceptual content of several widely used symbols in the SECC corpus will provide the basis for further explorations and connections. What is missing from this interpretation, however, is a functional understanding—the answers to questions such as: Who had the right to wear a picture of the cosmos on his or her chest? Why wear such a cosmogram anyhow? If it was an object of power, what did it do? Was that sort of function related to the abilities of the wearer, or was it a cultural artifact referring to someone else's power? Did such gorgets serve simply as status indicators, marking membership in some important clan, lineage, or association? Knowing that the gorgets are cosmograms serves to heighten the possible importance of the object, but it does not go very far toward any of the functional answers.

That omission indicates future tasks which await the researchers. One hint as to the possibilities for exploration lies in testimony regarding the religious usage of such objects. A Kansas informant told of how one gorget, probably a "mask" gorget and clearly not one of the cosmograms, was used. As they prepare for a military raid, the leader smokes a disk pipe: "He must hold it in his right hand, blowing the smoke into the clam shell [human face], which he held in his left. The smoke is supposed to ascend to the thunder-god, the god of war, to whom it is pleasant" (Dorsey 1885:674). Such a practical use for a gorget suggests a conceptual category that was recorded from the Shawnee, a group of divinities whose pragmatic role is to function as "witnesses."

> Such beings act as intermediaries between man and the Creator, but are set upon the earth by the Creator in their various stations for man's benefit. They include the deities of the four quadrants of the earth, the Thunderers, and an unidentified list of associates of the Creator which is not readily specified. Certainly Fire occupies a major position as a mediator or witness, as does the Sky, Tobacco, Smoke rising to transmit messages to the Creator, and the like. Subsidiary witnesses including Thunderbirds, sacred bundles, cedar in peyote meetings, the stars, all uncultivated plants used as medicinal herbs, and such. (Schutz 1975:106–107)

Since some of these "witnesses" are the very characters encountered in the examination of these cosmograms, consideration of their role in the religious life of the descendants of the makers of the gorgets may yet suggest ways of understanding the functions of these enigmatic works of art.

3. The Petaloid Motif: A Celestial Symbolic Locative in the Shell Art of Spiro

F. Kent Reilly III

The Petaloid Motif is not listed separately in the "Glossary of Motifs" contained within *Pre-Columbian Shell Engravings Vol. 1*. The petaloid border is described as a common motif in Craig A and B style engravings (Phillips and Brown 1978). The petaloid derives its name from its resemblances to the vegetative petal-shaped leaves found on flowers. However, iconographic investigations of the art of the Southeastern Ceremonial Complex illustrate that the "Petaloid Motif" is derived from feathers. The same investigations demonstrate that the Petaloid Motif could function symbolically as an event locator or locative. Specifically, a Petaloid placed around individuals, objects, or supernaturals would identify their location as celestial. Within the corpus of Spiro shell engravings, the prominence of the Petaloid Motif, executed in the Craig style, strongly suggests that the motif set can be linked to a stylistic chronology and perhaps a specific linguistic group.

During the Mississippian Period, A.D. 900–1500, particularly between A.D. 1200 and 1450, the native peoples of the Mississippi River Valley and other areas of the Southeastern Woodlands of the United States produced beautifully executed art objects that were often embellished with a complex symbol system comprised of abstract images as well as anthropomorphic and zoomorphic designs. Many of these art objects are on par with the great artistic renderings of the Post-Classic cultures (A.D. 900–1521) of Mesoamerica. Stylistically, these art objects and their accompanying symbol system were identified originally as objects existing within an ideological framework that researchers named the Southeastern Ceremonial Complex (Waring and Holder 1945:1–34). More recent investigations of the Southeastern Ceremonial Complex (SECC) have shown clearly that such objects can be better understood as the artistic production of a series of ideological complexes that existed within several style regions during the Mississippian Period (Brown 1989, 1991, 1996; Muller 1966, 1989). Therefore I propose that the designator *Mississippian Ideological Interaction Sphere*

(MIIS) aptly describes the specialized artistic output of the Mississippian Period as well as the belief and ritual system that these objects and symbols visualized (see Chapter 1).

The presence of some degree of unity among the several Mississippian style regions and their ideological underpinnings is demonstrated by their contemporaneity, as well as by the fact that a certain number of the symbols and zoomorphic images cross style regions. This shared imagery may reflect the existence of a common ideological source or sources for the style and its symbol system. Current candidates for such MIIS points of origin include the art styles of the Woodland Period (1200 B.C.–A.D. 600), particularly the imagery appearing on the pottery of the Weeden Island Gulf Coast Culture (Jenkins, personal communication) and the art and imagery of the Hopewell Culture, which developed in the Ohio Valley during the same period.

Among the numerous motifs and symbol sets found within the MIIS, several can be demonstrated to function as symbolic locatives (Chapter 2, this volume). Specifically, information is presented for the existence of a critical locative within the corpus of shell engravings from the Craig Mound at the site of Spiro, Oklahoma. The term *locative* designates a linguistic identifier applied to a word or phrase that carries the location of an action within a narrative. Within art historical analyses, locatives are important categories of motifs in systems of symbolic communication within literate and nonliterate societies. In such symbolic systems, locatives provide the initiated viewer with a visual key to identify the location of narrative imagery depicted in a work of art. Specifically, symbolic locatives in ancient artistic systems are used to identify the cosmological realm in which a certain action unfolds (Schele and Miller 1986:45–55; Reilly 1995:120–123, 2004:129–131).

Returning for a moment to Mesoamerica, it has been repeatedly demonstrated that locatives functioned importantly in the art of the Classic Period Maya as well as the art of the Post-Classic Aztec and Mixtec cultures. An excellent example of such a symbolic locative in Classic Period Maya art is the "Ground Line" used to represent a palace floor on painted vessel scenes. This band, sometimes a single black line, functions in this instance as a locative, signaling to the viewer that the action unfolds within a structure that exists in the earthly realm. In marked contrast to these earthbound scenes, an additional locative has been iconographically identified as the "Sky-Band Motif." The sky-band, on which deities can be seated, locates these activities in the celestial realm.

Now that I have illustrated how locatives function in Maya art, the question arises, "Do locatives exist in the symbol system of the Southeastern Ceremonial

a   b

FIGURE 3.1. Craig style gorget: (a) two anthropomorphic figures dancing on either side of a center pole (Phillips and Brown 1984:Pl. 130); (b) a three-dimensional rendition of the same Craig style gorget, drawn by Jack Johnson.

Complex?" The answer is: "Undoubtedly, yes!" Within the corpus of Mississippian shell gorgets, one certain and obvious symbolic locative appears as an unadorned double line that forms the circular frame on certain gorgets (Fig. 3.1a). The action takes place on top of, or within, these double- or multiple-lined circular frames. Therefore, we may conclude that, in some instances, these gorget frames function as ground-lines. If this interpretation proves correct, the recognition of a ground-line (perhaps the rendering of a dance circle) allows us to understand such scenes as actual depictions of a specific ritual moment within a Mississippian ceremonial dance. The recognition of ritual-specific ceremonial actions may also prove instrumental in the recognition of the dance and medicine societies that were undoubtedly critical elements of the MIIS. Taking these insights a step further, we may productively apply the art historical principle of multiple perspectives, or horizons, to such objects as a means for interpreting the formal qualities of certain thematic representations in the art of the MIIS (Reilly 1995:32 and n50).

Using a multiple-horizons technique has the advantage that it creates a visual field in which an oval orientation—as in a dance circle—is shown with a vanishing-point perspective, while the individuals within the circle are shown in profile (Fig. 3.1b). In other words, the one-dimensional surface on which the scene was carved is perceived in three-dimensional perspective much as our Western technique of using a vanishing point creates the illusion of three-dimensionality for us. With this particular Craig style gorget, when we apply this "cut out and fold up" technique, the surrounding double-line border assumes the shape of a dance or ceremonial circle, within which two individuals in profile perform a ritual on either side of a striped center pole. Thus, the modern

researcher using the "cut out and fold up" technique slightly shifts expectations
to view the entire scene in the familiar Western three-dimensional manner. The
fact that these two flanking individuals are depicted in dance postures underscores the meaning of the frame as a dance circle, anchored by the double-line
of the ground. Certainly, the raised position of these individuals' feet strongly
suggests dancing. In several of the Native American dance and medicine societies of the nineteenth century, objects—either worn or held by individuals—
identified society membership and in some instances rank within such a society.
Possessing such a gorget in the MIIS also could have identified the wearer as a
member of a specific dance or medicine society. If this is the case, then we should
also be able to argue that in some instances, MIIS works of art functioned to visually manifest and validate rank within Mississippian Period dance and medicine
societies.

As we can see in the above instance and after testing these findings on other
shell carvings, there is strong iconographic support for the existence of an earth-
band locative within the MIIS. Logically, we may posit that similar locatives undoubtedly must identify the celestial and beneath-world realms which figure so
prominently in the belief systems of the Eastern Woodlands (Chapters 2 and 5,
this volume). Indeed, this search has been successful, leading to the interpretation of certain scenes as narrative actions unfolding in the celestial realm. In
demonstrating the existence of just such a celestial locative, I limit my examples
to the corpus of Spiro shell engravings rendered primarily in the Craig A and B
styles (Phillips and Brown 1978, 1984). By limiting my initial investigation to
the Craig style, I will be able to link this particular celestial locative to a specific category of imagery. It will then be possible to test the locative hypothesis
on the broader categories of MIIS art. More specifically, closely examining this
Craig style material has led to the development of the following hypotheses:

Hypothesis One: The Feather/Petaloid frames, enclosures, borders, or car-
touches that appear on Craig style shell engravings functioned as symbolic locatives, which identify the action as unfolding in a celestial location or realm.

Hypothesis Two: The Feather/Petaloid motif is derived from feathers. A close
examination of this motif set reveals that such surrounds may actually signal
two locatives—a feather whose petaloid shape is derived from avian downy
feathers and the feather motif itself. In this case, the feather symbol more generally denotes a celestial realm. Petaloids, on the other hand, visually identify
locations *within* the celestial realm. However, as a minimal conclusion, I interpret most motifs and symbols surrounded by petaloids as indicating that they
function within a celestial location.

Hypothesis Three: With further examination, the Feather/Petaloid motif can perhaps be linked to a specific style and hence to a specific linguistic group—ultimately to specific nineteenth- and early twentieth-century ethnographies in which specific mythic concentrations, though separated by geography and language families, can be shown to have a common origin within a temporally distant Mississippian Period cultural matrix.

To test these hypotheses, I have restricted my corpus of artistic material to the medium of carved shell. Stylistically, I have focused on the carved shell in the Braden style and more particularly in the Craig styles from the Craig Mound at Spiro, Oklahoma. These styles employ high concentrations of this particular symbol set. After isolating the motif within this select stylistic corpus, the location of the motif within the overall composition is examined. When the structural analysis of the motif is completed, then, and only then, an interpretation can reasonably be developed. When possible, the interpretations of these hypotheses are corroborated further with ethnographic evidence.

The Petaloid Motif

Although the petaloid motif figures prominently in the overall corpus of Craig style engraved shell objects, at least twelve examples also exist within the corpus of Braden style engraved shell objects. Space constraints will permit only one illustration, a Braden A example of the petaloid motif (Fig. 3.2). This image has been selected for two reasons. First, it clearly illustrates the fact that within the Braden corpus, petaloids generally are not associated with narrative action or anthropomorphic imagery. Nevertheless, they do appear with such symbolic representations as disembodied skulls, broken bones, separated body parts, and supernaturals. Second, this scene also contains a band bearing stripes and ovals that is identical to the striped-pole motif—a motif that has been shown to function as the center pole used in ritual activities. In this instance, the band or pole is not upright and overlies the petaloid motif.

However, one of the clearest proofs that feather and petaloid share a common avian origin is seen on the famous "Birdman" engraved shell cup at the Museum of the American Indian (Fig. 3.3) identified as Craig B in style (Phillips and Brown 1984, Plate 203). The wings of this so-called Falcon Dancer are outstretched fully on either side of an anthropomorphic figure that has been identified as the mythic hero Morning Star. This winged figure is also referred to in the ethnographic literature by his epithet "Red Horn" (see Brown, Chapter 4, this volume). But in this case, the wing feathers descend from a wing-bar, as if dropping behind a row of petaloids. These petaloids relate to the overall wing configuration as flight feathers do to the downy feathers of birds, in that the long flight feathers overlie the soft downy feathers. In other words, the downy

FIGURE 3.2. Braden B style shell cup fragment. Snake, human heads, skull, broken bones interlaced or positioned above a striped pole and petaloid ground line (Phillips and Brown 1978:Pl. 57).

FIGURE 3.3. Braden B style shell cup fragment. American Indian Birdman or Falcon Dancer, most likely a representation of "Morning Star" (Phillips and Brown 1984:Pl. 203).

feathers tend to be placed on the interior of the wing underneath the wing-bar. Note that the tail feathers of this "falcon dancer" also are petaloids, except that they are topped by a distinctive excised spine, or quill.

Plate 165 in Phillips and Brown (1984) illustrates all three of these incised Craig style feather types (Fig. 3.4a). This Craig A shell cup shows wing feathers, downy petaloids, and tail feathers with prominent quills (Fig. 3.4b). Phillips and Brown (1984:plate 165) point out one distinctive characteristic of these tail feathers in the Craig A style: they carry a semilunar eye-motif within each

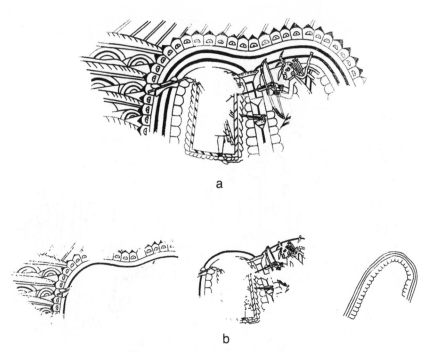

a

b

FIGURE 3.4. Braden B style shell cup fragments: (a) possibly an early depiction of the Pawnee "Morning Star Arrow Sacrifice" (Phillips and Brown 1984:Pl. 165); (b) a structural analysis of the petaloid and feather motifs (Phillips and Brown 1984:Pl. 165).

feather. Within the overall scene there appears to be a specific reference to a historically known Native American ceremony. Some researchers have interpreted the frame centered within a surrounding cartouche of feathers and petaloids as the scaffolding on which a Pawnee Morning Star "sacrificial victim" would be tied (Murie 1981:114–136). This specific area of the shell engraving is badly damaged but if indeed it is a rendition of the Morning Star sacrifice the victim is surrounded by inwardly pointing petaloids, while the tail feathers and the wing feathers point outward, as Phillips and Brown have observed (1984:164). Note that the petaloids in this example seem to be attached to a frame or border composed of bands or stripes. The fact that they are attached to such a frame or border strongly suggests that they also functioned as material ritual objects.

The carving on another Craig A style shell cup, illustrated in Phillips and Brown as Plate 164 (Fig. 3.5), also bears the petaloid motif as a frame. Within the frame, a figure walks holding a staff adorned with a raccoon bindings motif (Phillips and Brown 1978:154). Phillips and Brown suggest that the same artist who created the cup illustrated in plate 165 (see Fig. 3.4a) also carved the cup illustrated in plate 164. As on the first cup, the scene on this cup is surrounded by a band of inward-pointing petaloids attached to a border of bands or stripes. The tail feathers, again, are arranged to point outward. The central anthropomorphic figure appears to be walking on top of the inward-turning petaloids.

The scenes on these two cups are remarkable in that they appear to illustrate

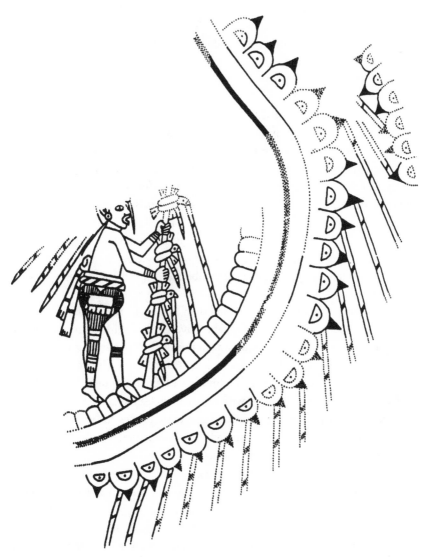

FIGURE 3.5. Braden B style shell cup fragment. A probable depiction of a journey on the "Path of Souls/Milky Way" (Phillips and Brown 1984:Pl. 164).

a series of celestial locatives that are derived from two separate feather patterns. In this mythic depiction, the overall use of feathers and petaloids certainly suggests that in this instance, these feathers function as two aspects of the same celestial locative. Since the figure walks on the petaloids, they visually alert the viewer that the narrative scene they circumscribe unfolds within the celestial realm. The tail feathers with semilunar eye-motifs may be a less specific metaphor depicting the celestial realm. In fact, further research may demonstrate that this motif may serve as the symbolic metaphor for the earth's-eye view of the starry firmament or a specific domain within the sky such as the "cloud region" (Bailey 1995:40).

Ethnographic Analogy

To review, I have suggested that the petaloid motif derives from the soft downy feathers under the wings and breasts of many birds. Feathers and feather headdresses undoubtedly had celestial connotations for Native Americans. What do the ethnographic data specifically tell us about Native Americans' use of down in rituals? The literature is extensive, and only a few select examples are presented here. Among the Osage, eagle down was ritually important. For instance, in one of the "Songs of the WA-XO-BE" it is noted that "on the face of the old man roughened and wrinkled by time; the aged man who in councils sits clothed in ceremonial attire, his head [is] covered with eagle down, a sacerdotal insignia." This eagle down head covering symbolizes the old man's closeness to the sky powers (Bailey 1995:166).

The Pawnee are Native Americans who belong to the Caddoan linguistic family. A majority of the scholars who have worked with Spiro material are convinced that the original inhabitants of the site belonged to the Caddoan linguistic family. Recently, James Brown has associated the Greater Braden style Spiro engraved shell work with the Southern Siouan linguistic family (Osage and Omaha) and the Craig style with the original Caddoan inhabitants of Spiro (Chapter 9, this volume). If Brown's hypothesis proves to be correct, then it makes sense to use Caddoan ethnographic sources (Pawnee, Caddo, Wichita, etc.) to look at Craig style engraved imagery.

The Skidi, or Skiri, and other branches of the Pawnee assign a celestial locative value to downy feathers. According to Maurie and Dorsey, the downy feathers these Pawnee wear in their hair identify the celestial supernaturals: "In the decoration of the different chiefs an eagle feather is placed upon downy feathers—the whole symbolizing Tirawa standing above the white fleecy clouds" (Chamberlain 1982: Appendix 1, n.15:222). A further reference notes, "Sometimes you will see a star in the southeast with a downy feather on its head" (quoted in Chamberlain 1982:164). Further, "A star which stands in the south is said to have a white headdress which gives it somewhat the appearance of a comet, and it is called Opirikiskuhka (star-with-the downy-feather-headdress)" (Chamberlain 1982:60, n.2).

Plate 161 from Phillips and Brown shows six matching shell cup fragments. Joined, they depict three club-bearing anthropomorphic figures, each emerging from within a rectangular petaloid frame (Fig. 3.6). Their postures remind one of a specific ritual episode in the Skiri Morning Star sacrifice in which the four star beasts (Bear, Panther, Wildcat, and Wolf), or anthropomorphic companions, after having guarded Evening Star, are overcome by Morning Star. The fact that there are only three figures in this grouping of shell fragments instead of four may be explained as the loss of the fourth figure due to the fragmentary nature of the original shell cup. Petaloids perform a prominent ritual function in order to ritually illustrate this specific mythic episode.

> In addition, another element of the ceremony dramatically portrayed the destruction of the guardian star beasts. Four rings, about the size of a fireplace, were marked on the floor in semi-cardinal directions, and the grooves of the rings were covered with delicate downy feathers. These rings represented the celestial homes of the four stellar powers or star beasts. The great male star (Morning Star) had to travel through these regions and overcome the star beasts to reach the female (Evening Star). The star beasts had guarded the female from the male stars who sought to possess her. (Chamberlain 1982:64)

Later in the ceremony, the Morning Star priest destroyed these circles and scattered their downy feathers with a club. This ritual action meant that the Morning Star had overcome the star beasts and conquered their celestial lodges. In this ritual reenactment the downy feathers function as locatives in a ritual episode which unfolds in the celestial realm. The downy feathers surrounding the metaphorical celestial lodges of the star beast clearly suggest the linkage between sky and downy feathers. This mythic episode is linked to the Skiri Pawnee variant of the morning-star story and thus further supports the hypothesis of downy feathers serving as a celestial locative.

Future Directions for Locative and Ritual Object Research
In almost all cases of iconographic analysis, when an interpretation is substantiated by both structural analysis and ethnographic analogy, then additional iconographic explanations are revealed. Recently George Lankford (Chapter 8,

FIGURE 3.6. Braden B style shell cup fragment. Possibly an early depiction of anthropomorphic companions or beast gods of "Evening Star" (Phillips and Brown 1984:Pl. 161).

FIGURE 3.7. An engraved winged serpent from a Hemphill style clay vessel, Moundville. From a photograph by David Dye. Drawn by Kent Reilly.

this volume) has argued convincingly for the function of wing motifs on the depictions of Moundville winged serpents engraved on Hemphill ceramics (Steponaitis 1983). A close examination of winged-serpent imagery makes clear that, in the case of this supernatural, the wing locative itself is composed of two motifs—a series of stylized feathers that are attached to a striped pole (Fig. 3.7). Here the celestial function of the striped pole readily reveals itself when one sees it forming the wing-bar of the wing locative on the Moundville winged serpent (Lacefield 1995).

The identification of the striped pole as a wing-bar in winged-serpent imagery presents important implications for any discussion of the ceremonial objects that were used in rituals of the SECC. The striped pole, often depicted in the SECC art, appears to have been a material ceremonial object. If the wing-bar is a ritual object, then images of the winged serpent may well represent actual important ritual moments. The ethnographic literature records that in the Pawnee medicine men's annual ceremony, ceremonial participants constructed a sixty-foot-long image of the Underwater Monster out of wood, cane, and animal hides (Linton 1923:67). Lankford interprets this effigy as the Underworld variant of the Moundville winged serpent (Chapter 5, this volume). At the conclusion of the ceremony the underwater monster effigy, as well as those of other supernaturals, was paraded through the village and deposited in the shallow water of a nearby stream (Linton 1923:70–71). The winged serpent actually existed in these three-dimensional objects that functioned ritually with great significance. Unfortunately, the climate of the Southeast has yet to allow recovery of any specimens of such objects; hence, the critical evidence of the ethnographic archive.

Another example of the corollary benefits from successful iconographic interpretation is Phillips and Brown's reconstruction of a Craig B style winged spider (Fig. 3.8a). A wing locative identifies this spider as inhabiting the celestial

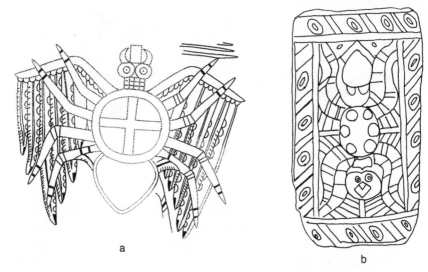

a

b

FIGURE 3.8. Spiders: (a) Braden B style shell cup fragment—a winged spider representation (Phillips and Brown 1984:Pl. 248); (b) a carved wooden tablet from the central Tennessee River Valley. This tablet may very well illustrate a Native American stellar vision. Drawn by Kent Reilly.

realm. The Osage "Rituals of the Chiefs," in the songs describing the symbolic identification of the Ga-Tsiu People, as Francis La Flesche recorded them, includes a chant that seems to describe just such a spider, which exists in an above or celestial world, and ensnares and draws up all living creatures to itself. The chant intones:

    4. We have nothing fit to be used as a symbol,
    5. The isolated earth people replied: O little ones,
    6. You say you have nothing fit to use as a symbol.
    7. I am one who is fitted for use as a symbol.
    8. Verily, at this time and place, it has been said, in this house,
    9. He set up a house,
  10. And then he said: I have not set up this house without a purpose.
  11. I have set it up so that within it the necks of living creatures shall be
       broken.
  12. I have not set up this house without a purpose.
  13. I have made it to represent and to be a symbol of the spider.
  14. Verily this house, like a snare draws up to itself
  15. All living creatures, whosoever they may be.

16. Into it they shall throw themselves and become ensnared.

17. When the little ones use its power to make the animals appear

18. Even before the break of day. (La Flesche in Bailey 1995:240–241)

Engraved on the Spiro shell fragment, the placement of the wing locative on this spider strongly suggests that this arachnid dwells in the sky. Although currently no spider constellation is known in the Eastern Woodlands Native American ethnographies, the iconographic and ethnographic evidence suggests that such a starry image may well have existed in the Mississippian Period zodiac.

To support this hypothesis, we return to Fig. 3.2. At the bottom of this carved shell fragment is a band with stripes and ovals that is identical to the striped-pole motif that functions as a wing-bar in Moundville winged-serpent imagery. In this case, the striped-pole motif overlies a row of petaloids. The position of the petaloids below the striped-pole motif indicates that the viewer is to understand that the striped pole exists in the celestial realm. Elsewhere, I have argued that the striped pole plainly functions as a celestial locative (Reilly 2000). Not only does the wing-bar function as a wing-locative, but it also is directly associated with the petaloid motif. Examining the striped pole in light of a unique wooden tablet from the central Tennessee River Valley, one can argue that this motif may function analogously as the spider house/lodge does in the Osage literature quoted above (Fig. 3.8b). On this wood tablet, a spider sits in a web, bordered by a frame formed of striped poles. Jim Knight suggested that this might depict a spider supernatural seated in its own sky lodge (Knight, personal communication). The arrangement of the striped pole as a framing device convincingly reinforces Knight's hypothesis. The association of the center-pole motif and petaloid locative in Fig. 3.2 also underscores the multifunctionality of motifs such as the striped pole.

If the petaloid motif functions as a celestial locative, then this hypothesis may be applied to interpret other MIIS objects. For instance, the petaloid frame surrounding certain gorgets may well signify that the motifs it encloses are celestial in origin or meaning. The petaloids bordering a stone palette from Moundville suggest that this palette was used to grind paint with celestial connotations (Fig. 3.9a). Just as with the shell-cup examples, the petaloid surrounds on this palette are associated with a double-line border. It may prove productive if iconographic research demonstrates that the notches on the Moundville rattlesnake disk likewise are a variant of the petaloid border (Fig. 3.9b). If this were the case, it would support Lankford's identification of the hand-and-eye motif as a celestial locative (Chapter 8, this volume). The petaloid surrounds on bi-lobed arrows that are depicted on a clay vessel from Moundville help to iden-

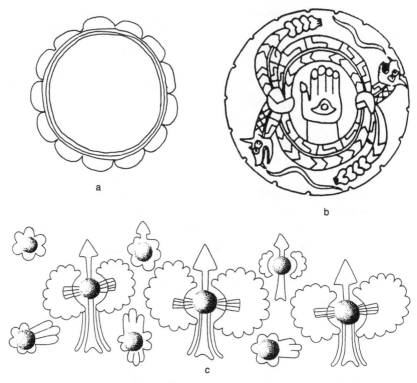

FIGURE 3.9. (a) A carved Moundville palette with a petaloid surround border. Drawn by Kent Reilly; (b) a carved Moundville palette (rattlesnake disk) with a notched or petaloid-like surround border. Drawn by Kent Reilly; (c) roll-out of a ceramic vessel from Moundville. This vessel carries a series of bi-lobed arrow motifs. Each of the bi-lobes is bordered by a petaloid surround (Moore 1905:FIGURE 88).

tify the lobes themselves as feathers and perhaps as celestial markers (Fig. 3.9c). The petaloid lobes on these arrows also support the hypothesis that interprets the bi-lobed arrow motif as a Mississippian ancestor of colonial Calumet ceremonialism (Hall 1997). This is a most appropriate association when one considers the Calumet in its variant as the eagle dance. In this dance, the Calumet Pipe's winged lobes are symbolized as the wings of the dancers when they assume the identity of eagles and ritually fly into the upper reaches of the heavens (Reilly 1999).

Conclusion
I have demonstrated that iconographic evidence supports reading the feather motif as a symbolic locative that identifies the celestial realm. More specifically,

the corpus of symbols on shell engravings, particularly in the Craig styles, confirms that petaloids visually identify locations within the celestial realm. Generally, I suggest that most motifs and symbols surrounded by petaloids have celestial associations. The identification of locatives within the corpus of the art of the MIIS has great potential for recognizing and categorizing cosmological imagery within this symbolic system. The existence of locatives within the MIIS also demonstrates that the artists who created these objects were encoding and manipulating symbolic messages with profound and breathtaking significance.

4. On the Identity of the Birdman within Mississippian Period Art and Iconography

James Brown

The falcon is one of the more conspicuous images in Mississippian Period iconography, and in its incarnation as Birdman the theme has assumed prominence as a central theme in the Southeastern Ceremonial Complex (SECC). Images of this bird have given rise to more interpretive interest than perhaps any other (e.g., Brown 1975, Emerson 1997, Strong 1989). However, the scope of that interest has remained limited to traits intrinsic to the living hawk. Missing is serious consideration of ideological associations independent of the bird's biological or ecological attributes. It is these ideological associations that connect importantly with Mississippian Period political economy.

We need not look far to find a rich source of culturally constructed meanings. A particularly useful case comes from the Osage of the Prairie Plains, where the sacred *Wa-xo'-be* is the "symbolic hawk." This hawk or falcon is simultaneously an avatar of warriors in combat and an object for supplication, not merely to ensure success or failure on the field of battle, but more essentially to ensure a lengthy life, a healthy family, and a long line of descendants (La Flesche 1939:9–13, 85–86). As reinforcement for this symbolic bird's less-than-obvious significance, its origin is placed supernaturally in the sky among a pantheon of the sun, the moon, and four stars (La Flesche 1921:63, 1930:603). There is nothing intrinsic about these heavenly connections. Nor are they arbitrary; rather, these associations are an essential part of a carefully articulated cosmology. For humans the hawk is a symbolic source of supernatural gifts of health, longevity, and a long line of descendants. The bird is merely an exemplar of the theme, not the theme itself.

What follows is an attempt to transport the ideological essentials of the falcon theme of recent, post-contact time back six hundred to seven hundred years earlier, to a seminal period in the history of Cahokia when the falcon imagery found elaborate figural expression. The burden of the iconographic argument is to stress the logical durability of the falcon theme as a charter for key social statuses in a range of different political economies. Signature characteristics of the theme are its association of life's chances with high-stakes gaming, the triumphant return of life with the pre-dawn appearance of the morning star, and the flight of the arrow as a metaphor for the succession of generations into the future. All or a combination of these constitute essential features of the theme in Southeastern myth.

Background

The present chapter follows a lead created by Robert Hall (1983a) when he drew attention to what appears to be a reference in the Red Horn myth cycle of the Winnebago (Radin 1948), another tribe of the Prairie Plains, to a distinctive prehistoric archaeological object, the long-nosed god maskette. A placement of the Red Horn cycle deep in the past received a boost with the archaeological discovery of another revealing image. This time the connections were provided by a detail on one of the painted figures on the back wall of the Gottschall shelter in southwestern Wisconsin. Distinctive "axe-head" marks detailed around the nipples are sufficiently like the outline of long-nosed god maskettes to recall a physical attribute of the younger brother of Red Horn (Hall 1983a, 1989, Salzer 1987, Salzer and Rajnovich 2000). In the Red Horn myth this brother wore his human head legacy on his chest. Whereas his older brother inherited human heads in the same position as his father's—that is, in his ears—the younger brother was distinguished by displaying these marks of Red Horn's power on his chest (Radin 1948).

Bob Hall's identification of imagery in the form of distinctive human head maskettes, together with the painted detail at Gottschall, retains a great deal of appeal. His identification was promoted by a more than incidental likeness between the Winnebago myth cycles collected by Paul Radin in 1912 and a tableau of diminutive figures painted probably around 1200 on the back wall of a small shelter. A number of additional correspondences between details in the myth and archaeological images supply more details to reinforce the identification. But before we can develop a pre-contact version of the Red Horn ideology, uncomfortable obstacles to the credibility of such a project require due consideration.

Challenges to Continuity

The first of the challenges to cultural continuity consists of technical issues having to do with the qualifications of the archaeological and ethnographic evidence. The reference material drawn upon here belongs to the Braden style of the thirteenth century. The falcon iconology first attains prominence in the Braden style of the early Mississippian Period. The expressions of interest here are solely those belonging to the Braden style, which historically has been so central to the definition of the SECC. It is described and provided with an archaeological context in Chapter 9 (this volume). The primary locus of production of the Classic version of this style is the site of Cahokia and its cultural environs in the greater St. Louis region. A large number of engraved shell cups of this style, however, were recovered from the distant site of Spiro in eastern Oklahoma. Although the Spiro site corpus defined the style, it was not the ultimate source. On a number of grounds the style had to have been produced elsewhere (Brown 1989). This style is present on local pottery at Cahokia and on pictographs in the region (Brown and Kelly 2000, Diaz-Granados and Duncan 2000). Independent data support such a source in the same general region for the shell gorgets that have gone under the rubric of the "Eddyville style" (Muller 1997a:373–374). Benchmark copper repoussé plates likewise found in scattered locations throughout the Southeast are from Cahokia as well (Chapter 9). Even the carved red pipestone sculptures can be related to this tradition. In short, the Great Braden style compasses a diversity of media, including engraved work, copper embossing, painting, and stone sculpture.

The post-contact ethnic groups who are the most likely heritage bearers are ones with the strongest historical connections to the Prairie Plains borderlands. The Southern Siouan speaking people should provide the stock of material that is the best starting point for finding linguistic and mythic connections. The ethnography of the Southern Siouan groups is rich in textual resources on the falcon. For instance, symbolism may have carried meanings that were specific to particular languages or related languages. Even in the same basic narrative, characterizations, motifs, and symbolism are likely to have specific meanings not shared with other languages.

Available information points to peoples who spoke Dhegiha and Chiwere-Winnebago Siouan languages as having the clearest claim to pre-Columbian occupation of this area. According to glottochronological calculations these have only arisen as distinct languages in the interval since A.D. 1000 (Springer and Witkowski 1982). Origin myths of the Dhegiha, also known as the Southern Siouan, make specific reference to a common homeland at the junction of the Ohio with the Mississippi (Dorsey 1886, Eggan 1952). The Dhegiha conceived of themselves as "downstream" people and the Chiwere as "upstream," conceptually representing their post-dispersal locations. Although the mouth of the Ohio River is somewhat south of the Prairie Plains, it is nonetheless remarkably nearby.

Likewise, there seems to be a basis for thinking that the Chiwere-speaking Ioway and the Winnebago, from both of whom a Red Horn myth has been collected, were inhabitants of the eastern Prairies for many hundreds of years, stretching back to a time well before the Mississippian Period. The archaeological continuity of both groups can be documented in the Eastern Prairies. That of the Ioway can be documented in detail. Their movements before initial French contact can be traced to the Red Wing area of Minnesota around 1100 (Sasso 1993). The Winnebago are usually traced to antecedents living within the state of Wisconsin (Overstreet 1995), although Hall (1993, 1995) alternatively has placed their forebears in northeastern Illinois. In either case the homeland of the Winnebago is situated adjacent to the western shore of Lake Michigan and well within the Eastern Prairies. Thus, the Ioway and Winnebago, the two contributors of the Red Horn myth cycle, have had a long prehistoric presence in the Eastern Prairies.

Cultural groups that have had a long-term connection with the grassland edge of the Eastern Woodlands may appear to be a tangential point of departure into ancient beliefs and practices of pre-contact groups seated in the Deep South. But the practices of one of these—the Osage—nonetheless speak forcefully to the potential for the falcon to be both a symbol for success in war and a vehicle for acquiring much-desired life-assuring gifts among a broader circle of Southeastern peoples. The Osage are not so geographically remote when the history of complex life in the Southeast takes into consideration the early expression of the SECC at the site of Cahokia, located on the edge of the prairie forest in the Mississippi Valley.

The theoretical challenges are more serious. No matter how brilliantly suggestive, the extrapolation of the Red Horn myth cycle into pre-Columbian times raises important issues having to do with the stability of an image's attachment to a specific set of meanings. Six or seven hundred years extends over a period in which significant changes have taken place in social organization, economy, depopulation, and Christian missionary pressure—to say nothing about the impact that the general loss of political autonomy has had. Are we to believe that mythic integrity will prevail over these changes?

Continuity of material culture, which has been the mainstay of the direct historical approach, typically has borne the weight of supporting arguments for long-term continuity in meaning. In advocating claims for pre-contact beliefs, Prentice (1986) has offered a conservative approach to the problem by relying on commonalities of beliefs among the broadest collection of ethnic groups. This is the "common ground" approach. But such continuities in material culture have provided misleading guides to the stability of beliefs (Kubler 1970, 1973). At best, the direct historical approach can only inform us as to the historical integrity of a particular tradition of cultural forms; continuity in content is not assured. While such formal continuities are a necessary precondition for proffering continuities in ritual meanings, associated mythic narratives, and iconographic representations, they cannot assure us of the stability of iconic meaning. Information independent of the imagery itself is required. Direct assessment of the social, political, and economic structures pertinent to a specific cultural tradition provides a more secure route, particularly in the absence of substantial textual documentation.

The Amerindian experience with drastic depopulation in the wake of European colonization raises the problem of that depopulation's impact on cultural memory. If sacred lore was the possession of ritual specialists, a sudden loss of crucial officeholders and custodians of important bundles could be particularly devastating to the preservation of this lore. However, this social-truncation argument can be more effectively placed in the fifteenth century during a period of noticeable decline in craft skill, well before the transfer of disease across the Atlantic. A decline set in without recovery when chiefdoms could no longer provide reliable economic support for high-level craft skills. As for specialized ritual knowledge, its future was largely assured among the Southern Siouans by the parceling out of knowledge among all clan bundle holders.

Two other objections raise related points having to do with fidelity of intergenerational transfer of cultural knowledge. Given the distance in time involved, it would be easy to assert that the Red Horn myth of 1912 had to have differed significantly from any supposed ancestral myth of 1200. It is an error to read the Red Horn cycle directly into imagery of the thirteenth century. For this reason, counterarguments have to be advanced to rationalize any continuity. Independent support has to be generated for any system of ancient beliefs. Ronald Mason (2000) has cast the preservation of cultural knowledge and beliefs in terms of an intergenerational transfer problem. With each transfer, new material will be taken up and older material dropped out. For Mason the consequent drift ensures an unrecognizable outcome after many transfers. But this assumes that the power-defining logic of a particular myth does not actively construct the cultural context that nurtures it (cf. Pauketat 2003). It is this "recursive" relationship between ideology (myth) and society that allows an argument of continuity to be advanced under specific conditions.

Long-term persistence of ritual practices in the pre-contact Eastern Woodlands appears in other material (Harrod 1995, Pauketat 2003, von Gernet 1993).

The stability of platform mound architecture and associated mortuary ritual for hundreds of years implies at least minimal continuity of associated beliefs. Even longer runs can be identified. Two of these are the 2,000 years of specific deer butchery practices connected with feasting (L. Kelly 2000, Martin 1998, Styles and Purdue 1991) and the specific modules for organizing ritual space (Rolingson 1994). The persistence of these and other practices leads us to inquire as to the circumstances surrounding their alteration.

Largely ignored is another obstacle. The richness of mythic material has to exercise some limitation on the number of connections we can potentially posit. When the sources are meager, there are few alternative assignments to be made. Without a stock of alternatives, we fall into the less than comfortable position of merely taking advantage of what is available ethnographically and argue around the inconveniences of disparate locations and, above all, transformations that must have accompanied the passage of time. Because the ethnographic record is so imperfect, we do not know what the distribution of relevant myths might have been if coverage were more complete. In the spirit of fostering an even-handed approach to the questions, we must ask a more basic question. Do we choose the most appealing, or those we judge as most relevant to pre-contact imagery?

An Art Historical Approach to Continuities

Lastly, Panofsky (1939), Kubler (1970), and other art historians have offered another perspective on the change in meanings that images take over the course of many centuries. When major religions make their appearance, the impact leads to abrupt change in meaning with minimal alteration to the imagery itself (Graham 1998). Any attempt to bridge this gap through uncritical attribution of meanings to much earlier images provides an opening for endless dispute. To make the argument additionally problematic, a baseline is lacking in the Southeast for image and textual correspondences. Unlike the case with Mesoamerica, where early texts are supplied with images having pre-Columbian antecedents, Southeastern texts are disassociated from imagery, at least in forms that can be extrapolated into pre-contact times (Townsend 1979).

Nevertheless, parallel equations of form and meaning have been so pervasive throughout the Eastern Woodlands that it is difficult to believe that cultural interconnectiveness at such a scale is entirely recent and without significant pre-contact roots. That, together with the persistence of ritual forms across the Columbian timeline, encourages the thesis that meanings documented in post-contact times are likely to have had deep historical connections extending back into pre-contact times as well (Knight 1986). In the end, the issues of meaning become a matter of just what dimensions have changed and which have remained constant.

The Social Contexts of Image Production

A provocative article by George Kubler (1970) critiqued the archaeological preference for uncritical dependence upon the ethnohistoric record to interpret Classic Period Mesoamerican imagery. Gordon Willey (1973) responded to this challenge by advocating an analysis of patterns of continuity in demography, ecology, technology, and social institutions after narrowing the possibilities of iconographic interpretation through general comparative analogy. He posed the problem of cultural continuity in terms of the kind and scale of discontinuities.

> . . . moving from these ranges of general analogical reasoning, we should go to specific historical cultural continuities. How are these expressed regionally and chronologically? In what media or what aspects of culture are these continuities best revealed? When disjunctions occur in these media, how do these seem to correlate with disjunctions or lack of disjunction in other media? (Willey 1973:161)[1]

Gordon Willey's programmatic recommendations tell us that any kind of serious discussion of pre-Columbian iconography in the Eastern Woodlands has to consider the impact of social and political discontinuities upon the history of image meanings. The weight of this argument shifts our inquiry to an examination of discontinuities in iconic meaning within a continuous history of material form.

For example, Richard Townsend (1979:13–15) relied on telltale discontinuities to pose the problem of uncovering the source of meaning behind Aztec sculptural conventions. Were these meanings drawn from those embodied in ritual and calendric conventions established hundreds of years earlier throughout Mesoamerica, or were they significantly altered? His argument in favor of retention rested on the degree to which Aztec sculptural conventions were self-assured from the inception of this craft tradition and showed no sign of the kind of experimentation (using Kubler's own Islamic example) that would surely manifest itself when old conventions required reworking to satisfy new meanings.

It is important to stress here that abrupt change in material culture is not necessarily the focus of inquiry. Rather, as Willey has indicated, discontinuities are to be sought in markers of fundamental social, political, economic, and religious change. For this reason, classic applications of the direct historical approach fall short by rarely focusing on the telling discontinuities. Typically, ascertainment of ancient meaning rests primarily with the integrity of ethnic traditions tracked mainly on the strength of slowly changing material culture. But as Kubler (1970) argued, such ethnic traditions have sometimes survived in the face of fundamental religious change. In his example of the replacement of Christianity with Islam, a dramatic shift took place in meanings attached to imagery despite continuity of form. In general, change in the sacred is more likely to be tied to challenges to the ultimate sacred propositions of Rappaport (1999). Small changes are more likely to be contested and to be associated with the ideological and political ambitions of factions, whereas change to central or core meanings is likely to be stepwise and directed rather than subject to drift. Continuity of the sacred can be expected to overrule the impact of small incremental change because of the legitimacy issue.

Ideology and Political Economy

Improvement on Willey's program can be achieved by recasting his economic, demographic, and organizational factors into a political economic model. By focusing on an analysis of political economy, one can construct an argument linking the ideology of any political economy to the verbal, performance, and material means used to express that ideology. A consideration of the political economies, or rather a historical sequence of such, has the advantage of focusing on the political and economic interests of class and faction (Brumfiel 1992).

Ideology is expressed in myths and rituals. Even the layouts of principal settlements emphasize the derivation of various powers and rights (Earle 1997:8–9). Rites and other practices operate at all levels of cultural complexity, and as such can be expected to specify rights and obligations essential to the working of a particular society, including the order of precedence for specific authorities. Petty rights and authorities coming under constant challenge and subject to ever-present renegotiation typically make use of cosmically ordained order to place the political and economic benefits of a privileged group beyond the reach of ordinary challenge. Thus, ideology in the sense used here can be expected not only to have a historical tie to particular myths but also to have its ultimate sacred propositions rendered concrete by myth (Rappaport 1999).[2] Although myth and icon can support ideology, this does not prevent some degree of independence. Nor is the relationship between ideology and myth simply reflexive. What is important here is that ideologically sanctioned myths and imagery are actively maintained in order to support key statuses and institutions. What I am advocating is a line of argument that emphasizes the construction of ideological meanings in imagery produced within social and political contexts.

Control over the access to the supernatural typically has been identified as an important means for achieving centralization of political power (Chang 1983, De Marrais, Castillo, and Earle 1996, Helms 1998). This control is achieved in numerous ways, and in the end the strength of chiefly authority rests a great deal upon public reception of a leader's claims. In staking claim to control, leaders can ensure their success by asserting their unique position through descent from a godhead. This descent allows them to embody heavenly forces through their exclusive bloodline conduit. The effect is to personalize the leader's control through his or her liminal spiritual role—in effect blurring the distinction between the leader and the supernatural. This declaration of priestly function can also be accompanied by public performance as well as graphic representation of supernatural support. Through thematic reiteration both performance and graphic art become an ongoing culturally framed argument justifying the power and central importance of the elite.

As strongly identified with the justification of elite power as ideology is, it plays an equally important role in collectively oriented "egalitarian" societies. In systems in which sacred power predominates, the power over action is "structural power," to use Wolf's (1999:5) important conceptualization.

> By this I mean the power manifest in relationships that not only operates within settings and domains but also organizes and orchestrates the settings themselves, and that specifies the direction and distribution of energy flows. In Marxian terms, this refers to the power to deploy and allocate   .
> social labor. (Wolf 1999:5)

Without formal materialization, performance in public ritual works out the same dynamic. As Wolf observed—

> Participation in ritual, Roy Rappaport has argued, also obviates discussion of belief and publicly signals adherence to the order in which one participates. Requiring people to take part in ritual or abstaining from ritual thus signals who has power over whom. (Wolf 1999:57, citations omitted)

This insight allows us to find lines of ideological support in egalitarian societies that parallel those in hierarchical ones. The forms of materialization are likely to be different.

Ideology and Image Production

The approach adopted here is to interpret politically charged imagery in terms of the political economy in which images are produced and deployed. This is a who, what, and how question that steps outside the image and requires due consideration of social matters of motive and intended effect. We need to ask the questions of who benefits, and who is in a position to commission these potent images. Archaeologically it should be asked why anyone should want or need to materialize beliefs respecting the hawk. These productions are technically refined and relatively expensive to produce, and their fabrication tends to promote the development of exclusive craft-working expertise, to say nothing of invoking, through graphic imagery, dangerous powers that are better left alone. How is a benefit derived from making and disseminating the images? In short, what does the imagery control? In Eastern Woodland studies, the question that needs to be asked is what rite and what social position(s) do these particular images charter? After all, individuals have produced these images, selecting out of a spectrum of subject matter those that are politically suitable.

One can conceive of image production as a social act. It exemplifies social agency on a number of levels, of which the mere fact of materialization is the least problematic. On a subtler level, agency is exemplified by "all ideologies enshrin[ing] an aesthetic of sign communication in their very mode of construction" (Wolf 1999:57). Choice of subject matter is another element. It has great importance because of the leverage the subject potentially exercises over a conventionally acknowledged set of connected meanings. With this choice comes power over the deployment of the imagery through special knowledge and insight. But there is hardly any inherent correspondence between any particular political economy and the kinds of images over which some power is exercised. But knowing the subject matter connected with one set of imagery, there can be general expectations as to what the potential range of meaning might have been. Likely candidates can be drawn from the common stock of images, myths, and rites present on the subcontinent at contact times and later. While narrowing the field of potential iconographic expression, the requirement that imagery work to underwrite and support chiefly status has the even more desirable result of fixing the range of imagery over which chiefs have chosen to support their claims irrespective of time and place. We need to ask what icons the chiefly elite might choose to charter their powerful status positions. After all of these questions have been addressed, we need to pose the final question—How does mythic narrative and imagery prevail over the forces of change produced by the passage of time?

The Osage Falcon Political Economy

Let us explore the operation of falconid ideology in the political economy of the Osage. Here and elsewhere in the post-contact Southeast this case illustrates the power that the sacred power of an older narrative might retain long after any connection with a formerly powerful elite had passed away. In so taking for my case a tribe from the Prairie Plains, I can illustrate the ways in which falcon symbolism works in the context of a nineteenth-century tribal society. For the Osage of the mid-1800s, access to various supernatural powers was widely available to men and women alike from all clans and groups. But access to the most powerful of these powers was institutionally constrained.

The tribe was divided into five autonomous villages, each of which was governed by two chiefs, drawn from the sky and earth moieties respectively (Bailey 1995:49). They exerted leadership over basic day-to-day affairs in the village through their personal authority as representatives of the most prestigious clans of their respective moieties. These chiefs were highly visible in coordinating village-wide subsistence activities. A very different sort of power was exercised by the clan priesthoods. Not only did they control access to major sectors of the supernatural, but they also used their access to mediate military initiatives and to impose requirements for induction into the seven priestly grades. Each of the twenty-four patrilineal clans supported a priesthood, although certain privileged clans monopolized control over specific village-wide rituals (namely, the sacred pipes, the Great Bundle, and the Great Medicine Bundle). Custodians of the *Wa-xo'-be* bundles hold in severalty the totality of the tribal religion.[3]

> Each clan symbolically represented part of the cosmos. . . . In other words, the ritual knowledge and authority of the tribe, relative to the visible world, was divided into twenty-four separate parts, and each part was controlled by the priesthood of a particular clan. (Bailey 1995:49)

This conception of ritual control recognized the importance of a completely dispersed authority, the very opposite of monopolization. As a pattern of distributive power it expressed the ethos of complementary collective control over the means by which the supernatural could be accessed—with the object of securing the blessing of Wakanda.

The elements to an ideology in the sense used herein begin to become more explicit in the Osage legend of its tribal history. This myth lays out an implicit order of precedence by seniority. According to Bailey (1995:74), it structures the various authorities taken under the tribal control and distinguishes them by source, either from this world or the other world. Ontologically the sacred pipes (*Wa-wathon*) pre-existed the tribe and make possible its founding. Logically, this precedence confers upon them the highest authority. The tribe then established one House of Mystery for naming children and another for the declaration and prosecution of war. The clan bundles were created next, and lastly two chiefs were chosen from each moiety to manage the daily problems of secular village life. But unlike the socially derived origins of authorities up to this point, the powers of the Great Bundle and Great Medicine Bundle were derived through direct revelation. It was through the vision quests that the Gentle Ponca and Gentle Sky chiefs acquired the knowledge represented by the Great Bundle and Great Medicine Bundle respectively.

One might respond by positing that the priest of the Elder Water clan held a monopoly over the sacred pipes (Bailey 1995:54). But they were only symbolic custodians of the sacred pipes. Each set of pipes or pipe stems was created for a specific occasion. The various clans who held the rights to make parts to these pipe stems and their stands collaborated in their production. Again we see distributed authority in action. However, neither the collaborators nor their order in the production sequence were arbitrarily assigned. The part that completed the pipe stem was a tuft of owl feathers contributed by the Deer or Deer Lung clan to the distal end of the stem (La Flesche 1930:205–208, 254). The contribution of this particular clan turns out to have significance in another Siouan context that will be introduced later. Although the ethos of complementary duties pervades this and other ritual performances, one must look to how a collective ceremony, the "Songs of Wa-xo'-be," possessed the power to deploy and allocate social labor.

Control over military powers, such as they were, was made subordinate to ritual authority. Military action taken against another tribe was a power vested with a council of all clans. The performance of the "Songs of the Wa-xo'-be" was the key rite that initiated military action. War honors were the social and political benefit of success at war. These honors "were bestowed upon men only for their actions as members of organized war parties—that is, war parties organized under the authority of a clan priest or the collective authority of priests acting in unison" (Bailey 1995:220).

Economics came to the fore with the obligatory transfer of scheduled payments to priests and the serving of food to a large number of witnesses during ceremonies that lasted from three to seven days.

Every clan priesthood was in turn divided into seven degrees or stages. To become a clan priest, a man had to be formally accepted and initiated into one of the seven degrees of the priesthood of his clan. Although theoretically any man could become a priest, only a small minority of men actually did so. Becoming a priest was costly. Gifts had to be collected for presentation to all the participating priests, and food had to be found to feed the visiting priests and their families during the three- to seven-day initiation rite. The expense of initiation varied with the degree taken. (Bailey 1995:49)

To see how structural power is produced, one need go no further than the performance of the "Songs of the Wa-xo'-be." This rite restated themes central to tribal concern—that authority emerges from tribal unity and is legitimated through clan organizations (Bailey 1995:220). The rituals were "group efforts that required the participation and support of every clan, phratry, and moiety. The ritual served as a social paradigm communicating the idea that the individual, like the clan, was not independent but merely part of the larger unit and therefore dependent upon others" (Bailey 1995:220). Even "war had to serve the unified objectives of the people. Spontaneous acts of aggression were dangerous . . . [and] had to be controlled and directed" (Bailey 1995:220).

The rite becomes "the introductory part of the ceremonies that attend the organization of a war party. The rite is continued by the man thus chosen, not only during the ceremonies, but throughout the entire expedition, both when going and returning" (La Flesche 1925:41). The cosmos was symbolically re-created in the seven songs and the six songs. "Sacred Warrior who was to lead the party was chosen and made ready, the eight commanders were selected, the warriors were prepared, the party moved against the enemy, etc." (Bailey 1995:220). Ideological control extended beyond the ceremony to the actual ritual conduct of the war parties. The Rite of Vigil was the ceremony for which the Sacred Warrior was chosen. The sacred war leader actually carried his clan's hawkskin[4] suspended on his back, and the eight subordinate *Xthe'-ts'a-ge* officers had theirs as well (Bailey 1995:79).

The key individual in the ceremony was a priestly sponsor, *Xo'-ka*, who assumed the "persona" of the spirit at specific steps of the ceremony. He started out mainly representing the sun and ended by embodying the "symbolic man," i.e., the tribe (Bailey 1995:77–78). For rites leading to war he wore a skin of the puma as a symbol of destruction (Bailey 1995:78).

The *Xo'-ka* gains power by sponsoring a recruit and imparting to him some of his ritual power. Priests attain authority through their ritually sanctioned access to the supernatural. By moving up through each of the seven ranks, a priest gains additional ritual knowledge. One has to bear in mind that the totality of ritual knowledge is divided by priestly grade and clan. Traditionally, promotion

required certain war honors that were acquired through skill, luck, and opportunity. Ritually, they were advanced in grade through gifts that the spiritual
power awarded the priest—long life, war success, etc.

Discontinuities

The task of decoding the SECC Birdman is an order of magnitude more difficult
than that of decoding the Aztec sculptural one. Here the gap of about five hundred years stands between the period in which the Mississippian Period images
were current and the time when an ethnographic record began to accumulate.
But it will be helpful to cast the Birdman problem in terms of the impact that
historically known discontinuities in political economy could have had upon
ideology.

During this five-hundred-year period a number of potential discontinuities
can be identified. First of these is the simplification of chiefly economies after
1400. Production of all kinds of imagery declined dramatically during this century, along with craft production in general. For instance, all stone mortuary
statues were produced before 1400; none can be securely attributed later in time
(Brown 2001). During the 1400s, shell gorget production became restricted to
the Southern Appalachians. Images engraved on ceramics of the Moundville III
period remained, but the sphere of image production was constricted to relatively small areas. In short, contrary to the thesis of Brain and Phillips (1996),
image production is uncommon after 1400.

The second of these discontinuities is the shock from depopulation that struck
the interior during the centuries of European contact following the entry of the
Spanish. Continued penetration into the interior by colonial powers and sub-
sequently by Americans ensured no letup. With depopulation and subsequent
removal came a loss of specialized offices and the personnel that staffed them,
together with the specialized knowledge they were entrusted with. Devastating pandemics continued into the early nineteenth century. In 1805 a smallpox
epidemic on the Plains was particularly devastating for the Osage. Most sce-
narios select depopulation as the factor that was most damaging to the enduring
context of myths.[5]

Other discontinuities were to come. The third of these impacts is that of
Christian missionary efforts. Their effects were subtler. Christian missionaries
were generally antipathetic, if not downright hostile, toward defleshing and secondary burial of the dead, particularly in association with shrine figures and
other signs of "devil worship." By the first quarter of the eighteenth century
all mortuary shrines were either emptied of their offending contents or abandoned (Brown 2001). The ascendancy of Christian tenets created a hegemony

over native belief systems. This influence led to the introduction of new myths to charter new roles (as in the Midé ceremony) and led to deliberate alteration of existing myths and beliefs. Radin (1948, 1954) argued that a number of mythic narratives bear signs of having been reworked along lines that were influenced by Christian models. For instance, life and death dualism took on features of the heaven/hell distinction foreign to autochthonous native cosmologies.

The final disjunction was the loss of autonomy that accompanied resettlement on bounded reservations and the cessation of warfare. They proved fatal to the ancient associations. The entire raison d'être of the chartering myths no longer had any anchor to the realities of reservation life. It is not surprising that the challenge to these ancient associations came with the religion of the Native American Church (Bailey 1995). The old myths became desanctified and the keepers of these charter myths turned their back on them. In the case of the Osage and probably other groups, these myths were no longer told. Only desanctified excerpts gained some currency as cautionary tales (Radin 1948). In the case of the Winnebago, the curators of these myths decided to memorialize them by committing them to writing for Radin's benefit.

All told, this list amounts to a formidable sequence of disjunctions. Yet the effects of each bear on our problem in potentially different ways. While it is customary to attribute the main change to political simplification upon depopulation, the nature of each disjunction entails a more nuanced approach to consequences. The disappearance of the chartering role of the Timucuan myth cited above was argued by Keyes (1994) to be an instance in which change followed the movement from hierarchical to egalitarian society. Although the impact of depopulation cannot be minimized, the way in which myths chartering falcon symbolism have been adapted to new social and political circumstances points to the resiliency of powerful, highly specific beliefs concerning life-forces.

We now have become acquainted with the role that this symbolic complex has in the egalitarian social context of late nineteenth-century Osage and even Winnebago life. As the detailed excerpts from Osage rites demonstrate, the continuity of life with the falcon, the morning star, and warfare is not an association that is confined to chiefly societies but one that has a quiet, successful place in simpler ones, whether it be the pan-tribal ceremony chartering the Great Warrior among the Osage or the clan war bundle charter of the Winnebago.

Another way to model the sequence of disjunctions is to suppose that the falcon symbolism had commonplace meanings that were far more widespread than the distribution of Southeastern chiefdoms and reach back to a time before these political formations existed. Such commonly held conventional meanings would then have merely reasserted themselves in response to the waves of colonially induced change. In support of this line of thinking is the widespread distribution, on an almost subcontinental scale, of key narrative elements in the Red Horn myth. Those that have achieved categorical status are the "Star Husband" and "Children of the Sun" themes. But many miscellaneous myths in addition testify to the importance of the falcon theme generally and its cosmological place (Radin 1950, Reichard 1921).

Whatever the case, this chapter has argued that the falcon complex associations have remained remarkably durable in post-chiefly societies. The range of contexts in which this complex appears speaks to the durability of the "conceptual theme." On the other hand, the "visual theme" is less easily traced. This durability can only be due to the ease with which the falcon complex has adjusted to new lifeway circumstances.

The conceptual theme that this chapter has identified with the Birdman is a very special set of allegories that makes this hero-deity representative of the mythic combat of life against death. Although everyone must die eventually, life is the victor through the survival of one's descendants. The avatar of this struggle of life to reassert itself in the face of inevitable death is the falcon, and one of his guises is the Morning Star. In the pre-dawn light the Morning Star beats back the darkness to make way for the life-sustaining sun. The fact that the myth has embedded within it the diurnal progress of night and day, the passage of the heavenly bodies, and the cardinal directions tells us that they are properties of a particular cosmology. These elements are not loosely connected.

Myth as Political Charter

In a work of great relevance to this chapter, Greg Keyes (1994) brought to bear Malinowski's (1926, 1936) insight into his interpretation of the Appalachian ball game of the early historic time period. Malinowski argued that myths not only charter social positions but also contain subjects and actions that facilitate this chartering role through dramatic illustration. Keyes found that certain hierarchical relations were described in the richly detailed Appalachee Ball Game foundational myth collected in the 1670s in Florida. In comparison with later Southeastern versions incorporating much of the same thematic content from the nineteenth- and twentieth-century Tunica, Yuchi, and others, these hierarchical elements are completely absent. From his analysis he concluded:

1. The major characters are deified and are clearly elite in the mythic society;

2. The myth chartered at least one real social position in the Appalachee power structure; and

3. Ceremonies performed by the Appalachee had their origins accounted for by these mythic characters. (Keyes 1994:110)

In short, Keyes (1994:114) concluded that "legitimizing ideologies of the elite vanish when the elite vanish. The stories may persist, but stripped of the special context and details that made them what they were. The motifs, informed by a new society with new needs, are reshuffled and restructured." In the instance of a single myth salient to the matter at hand, Keyes' argued that important narrative elements were present because they chartered elite power specifically mentioned in the text. First, he showed that the power-chartering functions of myths are described and encoded in the plot and the cast of characters. Following Malinowski (1926, 1936), critical powers were assumed to necessitate a sacred charter. Furthermore, the scope and importance of that power will be encoded directly and unambiguously into the narrative. The myth can be conceived of as a narrative describing the actual course over which power and authority were transferred. Second, he showed that narratives persist long after they have been remodeled as stories stripped of their power-chartering functions. This means that myths collected in the nineteenth and twentieth centuries must be regarded as ones that, potentially, had been used to charter social statuses at one time in the past.

Third, one can expect that myths and liturgies will draw upon pre-existing myths to strengthen their legitimacies. Because of the aura of certitude that pre-existing ideologies often retain, new mythologies can be expected to incorporate much that retains this authority. The resistance to abandoning time-honored legitimating logics can be expected to be high, particularly when the subject is divine or supernatural favor. For this reason, particular narrative themes will persist with requisite modifications to plot, motive, and behavior necessary to logically underwrite whatever position requires charter. Paul Radin (1948) made this point after studying the unprecedented corpus of texts he was privileged to have collected from the Winnebago. He pointed out that the longer myths, in particular, possess key plot turns that fulfill the logic of the myth. The characters and their actions likewise fulfill this logic.

Before we finish with this topic we need to expand on Keyes's thesis by extending it into the arena of visual representations for the purposes at hand. In light of Keyes's observations, a leader's claim to supernatural access is likely to be stated visually through an interposition of the leader into the cosmology. An archetypical method is for the leader to anchor him- or herself to the ultimate naturally based symbols of heavenly movements. These have the premier standing as immutable and predictable means, in contrast to the risks and misfortunes of ordinary life.

One would expect that the subject given the fullest and most complete visual realization would mark, exhibit, and display the core mythic identities that these elites are concerned with controlling through their role as exclusive intermediaries with the supernatural. By such an imposition the leader represents himself as one of the gods. His authority to do so is signaled by his visual depiction on artifacts instrumental to that political authority, including in extreme cases the emblazonment of images on public architecture.

Falcon Ideology

The falconid theme in the following example of the tribal priests possessed the kind of power that Eric Wolf (1990) called "structural." Following the Osage case are examples where exclusive rights to authority are reserved to a particular clan, and then to a particular apical lineage (or subclan).

The rite is so central to war making and war honors that it becomes a prime subject in itself for chartering status. In the Osage case this status is nonhereditary, strictly speaking. It is an achieved status open to all and is not exclusive to any one clan. In practical terms, key members of only a select group of subclans could accumulate the war honors necessary to qualify or even to be able to muster the large number of material goods necessary to pay for induction into each one of the seven grades. When one considers that the reward conferred upon the inductee is precisely the long life, battle success, and many descendants that make future inductions even possible within the subclan, it is easy to visualize how continued elevation into these grades tends to be self-fulfilling within certain subclans. What we have here is a charter for an aristocracy, a group of individuals that always includes a certain number of "new men."

The position of the powerful Sacred Leader (*Xthe'-ts'a-ge*) is chartered by an important Osage narrative. According to La Flesche, it "narrates the experience of a man who had been chosen to be leader of a war party and who, during his [seven days and nights of] fasting, witnessed a night scene which he regarded to be a response to his supplications" (La Flesche 1939:9).

Each night of the fast the man heard two birds swiftly chasing each other. When they joined in fight, he recognized their cries as an owl and a hawk. They kept alternately fighting and chasing each other.

As the morning star appeared in the east[6] the faster heard again the sound of the approaching combatants, like the blowing of the wind through the forest. They came near, then with marvelous quickness the hawk darted under the man's bent knee, while the owl sped on, clattering his mandibles with rage. The hawk spoke to the man, and said: "Protect me against my enemy; it need be for a little time only, until the break of day. The darkness of the night puts me at a disadvantage, for my strength is in the broad light of the day. Give me protection till the pale light of dawn appears in yonder sky, then in your sight I shall vanquish my enemy, and I will reward you by giving you that dauntless courage with which I attack my foes."

The owl returned, alighted upon the ground near the man, and demanded in an angry tone, "Give over to me that person, that I may put him to death. I also can give reward. I attack my foes in the darkness of night in their sleep and vanquish them. You shall have the same power that I have to see in the night. This I offer to you as a reward. Push over to me that person."

The man moved not, for the power to attack a foe when he was deep in slumber did not appeal to him as the right sort of courage and made the man's sympathy incline toward the hawk, but he spoke not, neither did he move.

Soon a pale streak of light appeared along the eastern horizon, then the hawk spoke to the man, saying: "You have rendered me a service. Now, as a reward, take from my left (the man was a *Tsi'-zhu*) wing the shortest feather there, and when you are about to attack your foe attach it to your left shoulder, so you will do to him what I am about to do to yonder person. I go to attack."

The hawk, without effort, rose in the air, and when he had reached a certain height, he paused. At that moment the courage of the owl seemed to depart from him and with much flapping of his wings he took to flight. Like an arrow released from a strong bow[7] the hawk shot downward in attack, struck the fleeing owl in the head, severing it from the body.[8] With an exultant cry the hawk soared around a few times in the light of the rising sun, alighted on a tree near by and spoke to the man: "Fail not to remember me when you attack the foe."[9] (La Flesche 1939:10–11)

In sum, this text declares two ways in which the falcon exerts its power to win on the battlefield—with the directives not to forget and to "wear this feather."

When the faster in the above song murmured to himself on his way home, "Thus the power of day overcomes the power of night"[10] (La Flesche 1939:10–11), he was articulating a deeper significance of the falcon theme. Osage beliefs also reach deeper by attributing powers to the falcon that do not emanate from the hawk's behavior, its life cycle, its habitat, or anything else having to do with its biology or ecology. Are these beliefs completely arbitrary and idiosyncratic, or do they have something to do with a culturally conferred role for the falcon? If so, how is the connection logically constructed?

The chartering principle applies to other myth cycles. One of the mythic narratives that come to mind is that of the Winnebago Red Horn. I think that the most convincing line of argument for this myth being a suitable socially charged ritual charter rests on the importance of the Red Horn myth's content, which at the core is the story of life's triumph over death. This underlying message is encapsulated by the deadly gaming of the heroes against representations of the life-taking forces. By having the two sons recover the head of their slain father, this myth reaffirms the vigor of the principle of life through a chain of lives. Loss of life to death may be inevitable even to a god, but one's "life-force" continues in the bodies of one's progeny. This message is one that has great resonance throughout the Southeast and the Prairie Plains. An issue that is left unresolved is the warrior status of Red Horn and his companions. It is clear from the cultural context in which life triumphs over death that it is conceived of as a deadly contest in which the outcome is basically uncertain.

Ideology and Iconography

At the beginning of this chapter I argued that the most secure route by which the public, nonintrinsic meanings of pre-contact Birdman[11] can be reconstructed requires that we forgo the logic of identifying meaning through isolated image matching. No matter what the iconic links between pre-Columbian images and ethnographic texts might be, they remain potential connections only, whether in the form of ancient myths or in other formats. For image making to carry conviction in general, it has to be logically compelling as a means for representing mythic charters legitimating elite power. Any such compelling identification rests on multiple correspondences, and in the instance where various representations are frames within a sequence, that sequence has to make sense as a narrative, in particular as a narrative dealing with powers that elites might have an interest in controlling.

At the most obvious and substantive level, verbal imagery from mythic sources needs to be identified on a wide range of objects and dress known through ethnohistorical and archaeological sources. Essential to this kind of analysis is a satisfactory identification of specific motifs, together with pertinent details that are key to their recognition. This level is one commonly worked at in iconographic analysis. For example, what is the nature of the "heart-shaped apron" hung from the waist of Birdman? What is the nature of the "bi-lobed arrow" and so forth. Such elements require close attention because logically they function to denote the essential activities in these compositions, something that comes close to its functional meaning. There is a kind of naming function implied here that is emically important in precise and unambiguous identification.

The activities communicated by these images have an important role here because they provide a link with narrative action. Although the activities involved are often obscure, where they do exist these activities are key to the narrative. Vigorous "gaming" is one such activity that is prominent. Of all the multiple correspondences that potentially might be present, the greatest importance should be attached to those that point to a narrative sequence of particular protagonists. The freeze frames of diverse, but iconically linked, compositions allow multiple sequences of arrangements. But only a few make sense in terms of their post-contact connection with sacred and other powers. Just such a narrative is advanced to support the model for identities advanced herein.

Specifically, variations and transpositions of the images should relate plausibly to scenes spelled out in the myth. Thus correspondences in motifs and in the various contexts in which the motifs are placed imply a parallelism in narrative. That is, do the various ways in which the images of falcon are represented, to take an example that will be explored below, link in ways that provide a plausible narrative? The final step is to inquire whether any mythic narrative exists that follows a visual sequence and involves protagonists engaged in similar activities and dressed in ways and carrying items bearing resemblance to verbal descriptions.

This is a kind of semiotic analysis. Although the task is one usually thought to be beyond the grasp of archaeological investigation, nevertheless, what I have in mind here is a modest approximation, in which meaning can be approached descriptively and in narrative form. It is a kind of conventionalized meaning that emerges from the interpretive space created by the spectrum of the ways in which a specific image is shown in varying activities and in specific juxtapositions with people, animals, and objects. This is very much like all the ways in which a specific word can be cast in a sentence. The meaning of the word thus emerges from the multitude of different sentences in which the word has been used.

The establishment of meaning is the subject of a distinct operation focused on iconographic analysis. The subject material for analysis becomes the range of expressions in which, say, the Birdman is deployed in a single historical style. The notion embodied in this pattern of expression is that it describes an aspect or level of meaning in the combinations, activities, and contexts the imagery is subjected to. Hence to approach the meaning of Birdman it is essential to examine the various activities in which this theme is given visual expression, together with the bodily stances, costumery, environmental setting, and articles employed in each activity.

The Birdman Corpus in the Braden Style

Following Panofsky's (1939) schema, we need to establish the artistic framework we will work within. The Braden style is an obvious choice for two reasons — the clearly narrative power of very detailed imagery, often in explicit activities, and the all-important historical and geographical connection of this style with the site of Cahokia, the Eastern Prairie geographical area, and with the Dhegiha Siouan speaking peoples or Southern Siouans (Omaha, Osage, Quapaw, Kansa, and Ponca) inhabiting the surrounding Prairie Plains area. Focus on the Braden style also avoids any distraction with contemporary styles from other regions with differing organizational principles.

Now that the subject matter has been established, the stage is set for an analysis of Braden style Birdman imagery over a specific span of time. These dimensions include stylistic format, the archaeological contexts of production, and relationships to post-contact ethnic groups.

In accordance with Panofsky's (1939) program, formal consideration of figural composition, costumery, and activities will occupy our attention before we move on to address various issues of meaning. In the analysis to follow, what we will be looking for is not simply a correct identification of various motifs, but a search for patterns of consistency in deployment, patterns of substitution, and manner of "performance" in complete compositions.

The Birdman corpus will be divided into four separate sets to parcel out this imagery into coherent groupings. These sets focus on the Classic Braden phase of the style (see Chapter 9 in this volume). The first two include unproblematic Birdmen on copperwork that are marked by a backdrop of falconoid "angel wings" (Figs. 4.1, 4.2). Falconoid eye surrounds are found in all except two or three cases. The Birdmen in the first two sets illustrate an array of activity stances. Three stances stand out, namely the "warrior," the "dancer," and the "chunkey player." These three are plausibly linked because many of the details of dress are present throughout the series. Confirmation of this linkage comes from a single engraved gorget from Spiro (Fig. 4.3) that combines the warrior and chunkey-player themes into a single composition. An engraved cup, in addition, displays these themes in a connected tableau.

With this basic commonality established in the first two sets, I then move onto the third and fourth sets, drawn from engraved shell gorgets and cups in which the same activity-stances are present without the distinctive avian back-

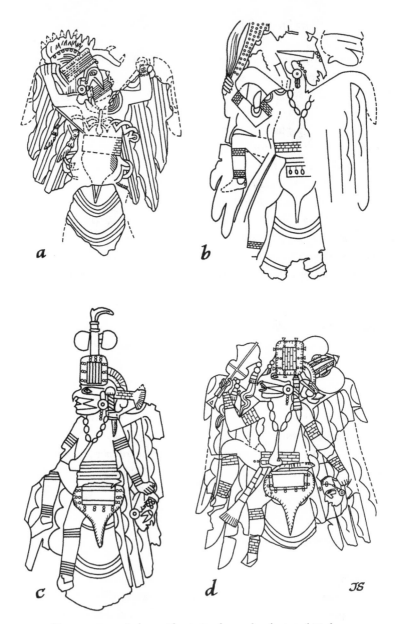

FIGURE 4.1. Copper repoussé plates. Classic Braden style of winged Birdmen:
(a) chunkey player, Mangum plate #1, Claiborne Co., Mississippi (Phillips and Brown
1975:FIGURE 268, redrawn from Roberts 1969); (b) variant on club-wielding Birdman,
Lake Jackson #2, Leon Co., FL (redrawn from Jones 1982:FIGURE 7a, 7b); (c) classic
club-wielding Birdman, Etowah #2 (Rogan 2), Mound C, Etowah site, Bartow Co., GA
(Phillips and Brown 1975:FIGURE 244, Thomas 1894); (d) classic club-wielding
Birdman, Etowah #1 (Rogan 1), Mound C, Etowah site, Bartow Co., GA (Phillips and
Brown 1975:FIGURE 243, Thomas 1894).

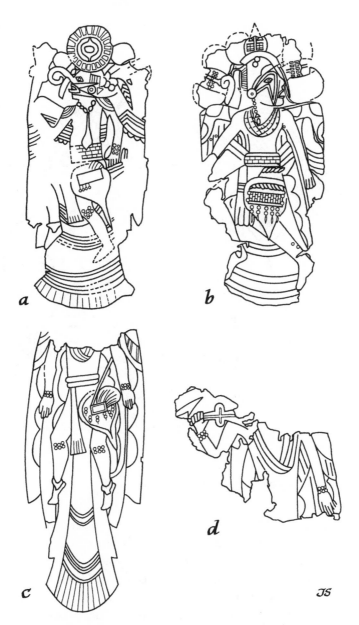

FIGURE 4.2. Copper repoussé plates. Probable Late Braden style of winged Birdmen: (a) classic club-wielding Birdman (winged), Lake Jackson #1, Leon Co., FL (redrawn from Jones 1982:FIGURE 6a, b); (b) dancing warrior, Etowah #3 (Moorehead 1), Mound C, Etowah site, Bartow Co., GA (Moorehead 1932:FIGURE 13, redrawn from Phillips and Brown 1975:FIGURE 245); (c) dancing warrior, Spiro #2, Craig Mound, Spiro site, LeFlore Co., OK (redrawn from Hamilton, Hamilton, and Chapman 1974:FIGURE 69); (d) classic club-wielding Birdman, Spiro #1, Craig Mound, Spiro site, LeFlore Co., OK (redrawn from Hamilton, Hamilton, and Chapman 1974:FIGURE 67).

FIGURE 4.3. Chunkey player shell gorget #7 (Phillips and Brown 1975:Pl. 7).

drop (Figs. 4.4, 4.5, 4.6). These sets assist in extending details in the compositional patterning established in the first two. My rationale for considering the third and fourth sets together with the first two follows my position that figures rendered with the same highly specific details should have linked meanings of some important kind. In the case of both the winged and the "unwinged" Birdmen, parallel forms lacking the bird connection can be readily regarded as the same subject in an alternative guise. This connection is strengthened by the marking with either a columella pendant suspended on a necklace of a single strand of large beads or a multistranded "rope" necklace of small beads usually depicted in a distinctive twisted form. The twisted rope necklace is found on the Etowah #4 plate, on Classic Braden shell cup engravings, and on Eddyville style engraved gorgets (Brain and Phillips 1996:141, Phillips and Brown 1978:180–181). Table 4.1 identifies the members of the four sets.

FIGURE 4.4. Classic Braden style engraved shell gorgets, unwinged Birdmen: (a) club-wielding warrior, Castalian Springs, Sumner Co., TN (redrawn from Phillips and Brown 1975:FIGURE 233); (b) chunkey player, St. Marys #1, Perry Co., MO (Phillips and Brown 1975:FIGURE 231 upper); (c) club-wielding warrior, Douglass, New Madrid Co., MO (redrawn from Phillips and Brown 1975:FIGURE 230); (d) chunkey player near Eddyville, Lyon Co., KY (redrawn from Phillips and Brown 1978:FIGURE 231 lower).

FIGURE 4.5. Dancing warrior, Spiro cup #19, Craig Mound, Spiro site (Phillips and Brown 1975:Pl. 19).

Among these Braden style Birdmen are images that Hamilton, Hamilton, and Chapman (1974) declared to be categorically distinct (Phillips and Brown 1978). However, significant crossovers in figural stances and other details tell us that significant connections exist among them. On copper plates the warriors that are either empty-handed or brandishing weapons have clear stylistic and thematic correspondences with the warriors grasping severed heads.

The first set is composed of three copper repoussé plates that are so similar as to suggest that they were made in the same workshop. These images fall within the Classic Braden style that Phil Phillips referred to as the "Etowah Copper Style." They include the two Rogan plates from Mound C at Etowah (Fig. 4.1c, d) that are archetypical of this "style" and a third variant example from Lake Jackson (Fig. 4.1b). The basic plate outline is relatively broad and conforms to the figure. The angel wings have flared wing tips (Sampson and Esarey 1993). The fourth plate from the Mangum site (Fig. 4.1a) brings into consideration a different assemblage of costume and ritual equipment. But as Phillips (Phillips and Brown 1978:205–206) has declared, it has features of figural stance and other details that essentially conform to Classic Braden style as it is represented on engraved shell. All four copper plates of the first set belong to what I call the Classic Braden style, and what formerly was set aside as the "Classic Etowah Copper Style."

The second set is a group of copper repoussé plates that are likewise stylistically uniform, at least with respect to format. They belong mainly, if not entirely, to the Late Braden style. In this group the narrow, closed wing outline of the wings and tail compose the "backdrop" for a superimposed human figure. Only two of the many plate fragments from Spiro (Fig. 4.2c, d) are of interest since they are the only examples of the Birdman theme preserving sufficient detail to undertake the comparisons that follow. One of these is the Lake Jackson plates (Fig. 4.2a). Moorehead recovered two other plates from Etowah (Fig. 4.2b)

FIGURE 4.6. Chunkey player, Spiro cup #20, Craig Mound, Spiro site (Phillips and Brown 1975:Pl. 20).

Table 4.1. List of Images Used in Iconographic Comparison

Set #1
Classic club-wielding Birdman (winged, forelimb style)
1. Etowah (Rogan #1) #1, Mound C, Etowah site, copper repoussé plate. Classic Braden, arms and grasped head (Phillips and Brown 1978:Fig. 243, Thomas 1894)
2. Etowah (Rogan #2) #2, Mound C, Etowah site, copper repoussé plate. Classic Braden, arms and grasped head (Phillips and Brown 1978:Fig. 244, Thomas 1894)
Variant on club-wielding Birdman (winged, forelimb style)
3. Lake Jackson #2, copper repoussé plate. Classic Braden, raised arms (Burial 16, Jones 1982:Figs. 7a, 7b)
Chunkey player (winged, forelimb style)
4. Mangum plate #1, Mangum site, Claiborne Co., MS, copper repoussé plate. Classic Braden, raised arms (Phillips and Brown 1978:Fig. 268)

Set #2
Classic club-wielding Birdmen (winged)
5. Spiro #1, Craig Mound, Spiro site, copper repoussé plate. Late? Braden (with coverts), arms, and possibly a grasped head (Hamilton, Hamilton, and Chapman 1974:Fig. 67)
6. Lake Jackson #1, copper repoussé plate. Late Braden (with coverts), arms and presumably grasped head (Burial 7, Jones 1982:Figs. 6a, 6b)
Dancing warrior (winged)
7. Spiro #2, Craig Mound, Spiro site, copper repoussé plate. Classic? or Late? Braden (coverts), lowered arms (Hamilton, Hamilton, and Chapman 1974:Fig. 69)
8. Etowah (Moorehead #1) #3, Mound C, Etowah site, copper repoussé plate. Late Braden, lowered arms (Moorehead 1932:Fig. 13, Phillips and Brown 1978:Fig. 245)

Set #3
Club-wielding warrior (unwinged)
9. Castalian Springs, Castalian Springs site, Sumner Co., TN, engraved shell gorget. Classic Braden (Myer 1928, Phillips and Brown 1978:Fig. 233)
10. Douglass, New Madrid Co., MO, engraved shell gorget. Classic Braden (Phillips and Brown 1978:Fig. 230)
Chunkey player (unwinged)
11. Eddyville, near Eddyville, Lyon Co., KY, engraved shell gorget. Classic Braden (Phillips and Brown 1978:Fig. 231)
12. St. Marys #1, St. Marys site, Perry Co., MO, engraved shell gorget. Classic Braden (Phillips and Brown 1978:Fig. 231)

Set #4
Dancing warrior (unwinged)
13. Spiro cup #19, Craig Mound, Spiro site, engraved shell cup. Classic Braden (Phillips and Brown 1978:Pl. 19)
Chunkey player (unwinged)
14. Spiro cup #20 (Lightner cup), Craig Mound, Spiro site, engraved shell cup. Classic Braden (Phillips and Brown 1978:Pl. 20)

Unassigned
Dancing warrior (unwinged)
15. Stack 4, Spiro site, copper repoussé plate. Late Braden (Hamilton, Hamilton, and Chapman 1974:Figs. 8, 9)
16. Stack 13, Spiro site, copper repoussé plate. Late Braden (Hamilton, Hamilton, and Chapman 1974:Figs. 24, 25, Phillips and Brown 1978:271)
17. Okahumpka, Old Okahumpka site, Lake Co., FL, copper repoussé plate. Late Braden (Moore 1895:543, Goggin 1949, Hamilton, Hamilton, and Chapman 1974:Fig. 97, Phillips and Brown 1978:271)
18. Jones, unknown site, Jackson Co., AL, copper repoussé plate. Late Braden (Hamilton, Hamilton, and Chapman 1974:Fig. 96, Phillips and Brown 1978:271)
Dancing warrior (winged)
19. Etowah (Moorehead #2) #4, Mound C, Etowah site, copper repoussé plate. Late? Braden (Moorehead 1932:39, Fig. 12; Byers 1962:Fig. 3)

that are transitional to the Late Braden style group. Although they are the more aberrant stylistically, they have to be placed within the Classic Braden style.

The third set of marine shell gorgets bears engraved human figures in the same activity poses as the copper plate Birdmen. However, none has wings of any sort. Again, two poses are available. The pose with warriors brandishing a weapon in one hand and holding a severed head in the other is found on the Castalian Springs and Douglass gorgets (Fig. 4.4a, c). The chunkey player pose is represented by the Eddyville and St. Marys gorgets (Figs. 4.3 b, d). These are principal members of Muller's (1966, 1989) "Eddyville style." At least three fragmentary gorgets of this pose have come from Spiro (Brain and Phillips 1996). Although no wings of any kind are present, the activity stances are so similar to the ones found on the first two sets as to compel direct comparison.

The fourth set is composed of two engraved shell cup surfaces (Fig. 4.5, 4.6) that are drawn from the Classic Braden corpus of the Spiro site (Phillips and Brown 1978). The two cups display multiple figures in associations that broaden the iconographic connections. In fact, they compose the core of Phillips's "Multiple Figures in Motion" theme. This set provides an alternative way of making the connection between the "Birdman," "dancers," and "chunkey player" through multifigural compositions rather than the single-figure focus found in the other three sets.[12] Despite the absence of wings, the secondary figures and ancillary objects on the cups are brought together in a way that is highly useful for the analysis that follows. As in Set 3, none of the figures is winged; however, good Eddyville style–like warriors brandishing weapons are present. Elaborately costumed warriors having their empty fists raised high or placed down parallel to their body are present on Classic Braden cups from Spiro (nos. 1, 2, 3, 4, 5, 6, and 9) (Phillips and Brown 1978). Note that in cup 6 both a rope necklace and a forked eye surround are present on a single figure. A severed head is grasped in the hand on a gorget fragment (cup 23A), and a more complete shell gorget features a figure doubled in court-card symmetry that grasps severed head, chunkey stone, and striped pole, thereby combining warrior and chunkey player themes (Fig. 4.3).

Birdman-Associated Motifs

The first step is to establish the identity of specific motifs. In terms of Panofsky's (1939) principles, what he calls the pre-iconographic analysis focuses on form alone. In the case of the Birdman it is necessary first to make an avian taxonomic identification with the peregrine falcon (*Falco peregrinus*). This matter was reviewed at length by Byers (1962) and again by Brown (1975, 1996). In the Osage example to which I have devoted some attention at the beginning of this chapter, the falcon or hawk in general, terms seemingly used interchangeably, is central to the representation of intertribal conflict.

> The choice of the hawk to symbolize the courage and combative nature of the warrior proved satisfactory to all of the people, for the courage of the hawk was considered as equal to that of the eagle, while the swift and decisive manner in which the smaller bird always attacked its prey ever excited the admiration of the warrior. (La Flesche 1921:63)

Among the Osage this avian symbol, along with the sacred pipe, the war club, and the battle standard, constitute the essential ritual equipment for successful pursuit of intertribal conflicts. A number of beliefs about the efficacy of the hawk draw upon and make obvious reference to the duck hawk's behavioral characteristics—its swooping aerial dives that knock much larger birds out of the air. The image thereby created is one of a courageous bird suddenly striking with lethal force against a larger and potentially stronger adversary.

Other images require identification, although, strictly speaking, pre-iconographic analysis recognizes no icons or identities. Where Panofsky (1939) invokes literary sources to confirm the identity of specific details of imagery, we bring in archaeological evidence of pattern consistency over time, in addition to connections of broader sociocultural context. Of course, on another level, the kind of support that Panofsky receives from literary sources has to be deferred, since the meaning of these details may have shifted over time.

Objects and costumery detailed in the images can be recognized as specific material objects recovered archaeologically (Brown 1975, 1976; Waring and Holder 1945). The correspondences are remarkable in detail. These are the bi-lobed arrow, earspools, bead in the forelock, necklace beads, columella pendant, and mace-shaped club. Many of these objects are found bedecking individual burials, particularly in the graves at Mound C Etowah (Larson 1971). They are easily identified in the archaeological or ethnological record for the Southeast—for example, the chunkey roller (stone discoidal) (DeBoer 1993), various forms of axes and ax heads (Brain and Phillips 1996:376–379, Brown 1996:477–481, Larson 1971), the mace (Brown 1996:474–477), columella pendant (Brown 1996; Larson 1971), earspool (Brown 1996:156–173), and bi-lobed arrow (Brain and Phillips 1996:136, 141, 158). The chunkey pole is one of the few artifacts scarcely noted, although the copper sheath next to chunkey stones in the main collective burial at Cahokia Mound 72 appears to be an exception (Brown and Kelly 2000).[13] Another element is the single long braid of hair suspended at the left side of the head. Such an item of dress cannot be expected to have been preserved, but nonetheless it is one whose significance we will return to later. The iconographic significance of the bi-lobed arrow and the single braid of hair will be deferred until a low-level semiotic analysis is completed.

One object needs further discussion, since this motif, which is of great significance, has only recently been provided with identification. This is the heart-shaped apron. Analysis shows that it represents a scalp whose only connection with an apron is its position at the belt (Brown n.d.). Neither, the "heart-shape" name that is a legacy of Spinden (1913:244) nor its "bellows-shape" name variant (Phillips and Brown 1978:98) implies anything more that its overall shape. And that shape comes from the victim's hair, short in front and long in the back. The term *fringed*, used by Waring and Holder (1945:15), keys onto the "fringe-like" margins of flowing hair. The peculiar oblong device, often with suspended beads, found at the upper center of the apron is an important detail to this motif. It represents the tablet headdress mounted at a forehead position (Brown n.d.). Significantly, the tablet worn on the central figure is of the same shape and type as the one on the scalp suspended at the belt. But the decorative infill is always different, signaling a distinction in identity. As a point of confirmation, the kind of twillwork weave chosen for the fill in the tablet worn on the central falcon-backed figure in two cases (Fig. 4.1c, d) was used again on the scalp tablet of another plate (Fig. 4.2b).

Birdman Activities

The next step is to identify the activities that are represented. This requires an examination of the various ways in which Birdmen are depicted. For this we need to accept a simple assumption that enables the analysis to proceed. And that is the human figures marked by hawk wings and other distinctive falconoid features refer in a basic sense to the same individual or the same category of individuals. The objective in the following analysis becomes, at its basic level, an argument showing that the figures brandishing a weapon are in some important, nontrivial sense, the same as the weaponless figures in the same or identical costume—and, for that matter, they are the same as those figures grasping severed heads in one pose and grasping chunkey-playing equipment in another (DeBoer 1993).

The four sets illustrate the carryover from winged to nonwinged figures of the three activities marked by distinctive equipment, or lack thereof (Table 4.2). The first is the "falcon-warrior stance," well known through the two Rogan plates, in which a club is wielded in an upraised arm and a severed head grasped in the other. In its winged form this stance is commonly known as the Birdman (Phillips and Brown 1978).

Table 4.2. Distribution of the Four Sets among the Iconographic Themes

	Themes		
	Warrior	Dancer	Chunkey Player
Set 1:			
winged, forelimb style	Etowah 1		Mangum 1
	Etowah 2		
	Lake Jackson 2		
Set 2:			
winged, draped covert style	Spiro 1	Spiro 2	
		Lake Jackson 1	Etowah 3
Set 3:			
wingless	Castalian Springs		Eddyville
	Douglass		St. Marys
Set 4:			
wingless		Spiro Cup 19	Spiro Cup 20

The two Rogan plates from Set #1 provide us with significant details. Attached to the belt is a "bellows-shaped apron" that is none other than the scalp of another supernatural (Fig. 4.1c, d, Brown n.d.). One detail here is very important. The eye marking on the severed head differs from that on the main figure. This "forked eye" references the very bird whose wings are used as a backdrop to the main figure. The hair dressing of both the main image and the head are likewise similar. Both images stand in contrast to the decorative markings of the bead-laden hair of the scalp. The resulting lineup has the main figure and his grasped head belonging to one kind of imagery and the scalp to quite a different one. A third example is exemplified plausibly by the Lake Jackson #2 plate (Fig. 4.1b, Jones 1982:Fig. 7a, 7b), but if this is the case, both arms are upraised. Although the left hand holds an item acceptable as an axe (not a mace in form), the large object grasped at one end by the right hand is bereft of recognizable detail. In size and shape it could be a severed head.

The Lake Jackson #1 and Spiro #1 plates carry through with the theme even though they are divergent from Classic Braden and may belong to the Late Braden style (Fig. 4.2a, b). They embody all of the essential features present in the Rogan plates, although the presence of a hanging braid may be an exception.

The second activity pose of the chunkey player is well known through the Eddyville and St. Marys shell gorgets (Fig. 4.4). The diagnostic implement is the striped chunkey pole, usually shown snapped and splintered, and three of the four examples herein have a chunkey roller grasped in one hand. The figure is in the act of tossing the roller, but his staff is broken, plausibly signifying the end of the game, if not defeat itself. Two of the players in the four examples are dressed in a distinctive spool-shaped hat and loop-ended broad-belt that Phillips has called the "Mangum Flounce" (Fig. 4.1a, 4.4b, Phillips and Brown 1978:178).

In the ethnohistoric record the game of chunkey is well attested to as associated with heavy betting (Adair 1930:430–431; Swanton 1946:682–684). Because we are dealing with a game that supports an important social position, it is safe to say that its stakes are ones of cosmic proportions. The seriousness of the game is signaled by such images as a decapitated head and the broken chunkey pole. In the corpus of Classic Braden shell engraving, images of decapitation and breakage alternate with whole bodies and complete weaponry in such a way as to suggest that someone's defeat is being communicated by the difference. From this simple distinction between whole and broken, winners and losers, we can gather that a high-stakes game of chunkey was played in which the protagonist or protagonists lost. The price of defeat was the loss of their heads.

The third activity pose is characterized by the absence of gaming implements or weapons. Instead, a large bird-wing fan is in the hand of the figure in Spiro cup 19 (Fig. 4.5). Although the figures are in a dancing posture, both arms of each figure are down-stretched and empty-handed, as if at rest (Fig. 4.2 b, c). This is what Henry Hamilton has called the "dancing warrior" (Hamilton, Hamilton, and Chapman 1974). The arms take a position that opposes the highly engaged arms that are either upraised or holding an object.

Birdmen as Narrative

A specific thematic complex remains to be pulled out of the iconography and examined as the visual underpinning of elite authority. Just such a charter can be constructed from a set of images marked by the hero's possession of falcon wings. The activity stances of these Birdman images can be arranged into a narrative. The wings identify the personas of the narrative and the forked eye-surround facial painting marks off a certain subset.

Activities depicted convey important information about the narrative. The chunkey-player group focuses on a game and the falcon warrior group focuses on a decapitated head grasped in the hand of the warrior. Is decapitation the outcome of loss in a high-stakes game? Now, this image is routinely cited as an instance of the Mississippian imagery of war, with the decapitated head as a trophy taken from a fallen enemy (e.g., Brown 1976). The triumphant pose of the central dancing figure is thought to suggest a return from combat of some kind.

But what about the object suspended from the belt? This, the so-called "heart-shaped apron," has long been thought to have been an article of costumery. But a far better case can be made that it is nothing less than a scalp with a full head of hair and a decorated, status-declaring headdress tablet. The evidence lies in the form of iconic detail, in stylistic history, and in iconographic references, summarized above.

This scalp represents the enemy. Note how the details of imagery contrast with the decapitated head that lacks the fancy headdress. Since the scalp at the belt already signals trophy taking from an elite enemy, is not the severed head redundant with the scalp image? The severed head could be other than that of a fallen enemy. In support of this point, the face of the severed head bears a forked eye surround that refers to the same bird imagery of the central figure, albeit in different form. The falconoid marking has significance in the sign language of these images. Hence the central figure and the severed head should be regarded as belonging to "the same team."

To take a leap of interpretation, the two images, that of chunkey player and severed-head grasper, can be conceived of as two parts of the same sequence of action. Loss of the game is first, followed by a display of the chunkey player's head upon its recovery by the hero. The intermediate step in which the chunkey player is beheaded is skipped over. Thus, the severed head in the hands of a triumphant dancer makes sense as a consequence of a lost game, not as a battlefield trophy.

From the way in which the party of protagonists is portrayed it makes sense then to reconstruct the narrative as a game against a deadly adversary, defeat with loss of head(s), and rescue by an unaffected hero. In this light the famous imagery of the Rogan plate warrior expresses triumph over the protagonist's adversaries, who might have won the first round, but ultimately lost through heroic intercession. If we think of the various poses in the Birdman tableaux as composing a narrative, then it is plausible to regard one of the surface meanings as having to do with gaming.

This leaves unassigned the dancer with downcast arms—arms arguably ones that signal the absence of action. In the one shell cup engraving (Fig. 4.5) featuring this dancer, he is framed in what I would label as a star band, assuming that the roundels represent a special kind of star.[14] From this association, one might conclude that the dancer with the lowered arms either comes from the stars or is about to become one. One might even suppose that this figure is the fallen hero undergoing some sort of apotheosis as a star himself.

A linkage between the chunkey player and the "Multiple Figures in Motion" theme is established by cup 20 (Fig. 4.6), in which one of the three dancing figures with downcast arms grasps a broken chunkey pole in one hand. This figure bears the forked eye surround marking of the falcon and wears a bi-lobed arrow headdress borne by classic Birdmen images. Another point of connection to the copper plate forelimb style is the presence of the heart-shaped apron (cup 1) on one of the four figures, with the others wearing an off-center kilt. The aproned figure wears a bi-lobed arrow headdress.[15]

The last question has to do with the identity of the adversary. We need go no further than cup 20 from Spiro to answer this. In the corner of this composition is an antlered snake quite recognizable as a plausible embodiment of death, or rather the forces controlling death, known ethnographically in the form of the "underwater serpent" or "underwater panther." If we accept this obvious candidate for cosmic confrontation, our gaming heroes are portrayed as confronting death, only to lose, and then become "rescued," in a fashion, by an unaffected ally of the protagonists.

One piece brings these elements together in a striking composition. Spiro gorget #7 of the Classic Braden style contains a chunkey player holding a tasseled staff and roller (Fig. 4.3). The player is tattooed in closely spaced vertical lines with a hint of the "T-shaped" terminals. The face has the falconoid eye surround. In the staff hand is an isolated head with long hair. A curious appendage meets a row of arrowheads lined up on the radial axis. Philip Phillips identifies this appendage as bird talons. Uniting this falcon dancer/chunkey player image is a serpentine vortex marked with distinctive trilobate markings.[16] All of these motifs are compressed within this image: falcon dancer with trophy head, chunkey player with gaming implements, a band of stacked arrowheads, and an all-encompassing serpent. Conceptually uniting the human activities is the bird-talon hand grasping the chunkey roller.

The Falcon as Symbolic Rebirth

The chain of reasoning I have been employing leads us to recognize in our Birdman narrative the elements of a contest between the forces of life and those of death, in which there is no clear-cut winner, only an alternation of winners in a continuous cycle of defeat followed by victory. The courtcard symmetry of the above-cited Spiro gorget #7 reinforces the notion of continuous repetition. This form of symmetry Phil Phillips identified by analogy with figural representations on playing cards (Phillips and Brown 1978:67–68). To cite our Osage example, symbolic rebirth is expressed most pervasively by the falcon, which, as I have emphasized, is the avian identity of the Birdman.

This interpretation finds support in the climax to the "Songs of the Wa-xo'-be" with the "Songs of Drawing His Arrows," through the manipulation of the hawkskin and the symbolic deployment of a little bow and two arrows that were specially prepared for the ceremony by the Sole Owners of the Bow clan. During the initial song the sponsor is readied by having the hawkskin hung around his neck and the little bow and its two arrows placed into his hands. The guests have already moved away from the bowman's line of sight. The action begins with the third line of the first stanza of the second song. The sponsor "takes two or three steps forward, fits the black arrow to the cord of the bow, and as he pulls the cord he utters the magic cry. But he does not release the arrow. Before turning around to come back to this place the Xo'-ka takes pains to remove from the cord the arrow, in order to avoid bringing its point into line with the Non'-hon-zhin-ga sitting on both sides of the lodge" (La Flesche 1925:234). He repeats this action three more times.

From this we learn that the arrows have a magical significance in conferring life at the expense of taking life—hence the concern not to place anyone in the assembled House of Mysteries or the village at large in jeopardy.

> By these symbolic acts the initiate is not only assured that he will be protected by the Black Hawk [Wa-zhin-ça-be], the Gray Hawk [Gthe-don-xo-dse], the Little Hawk [Gthe-don-zhin-ga], and the Consecrated One [Do-don-hon-ga, i.e., the Sacred Warrior, who was chosen by the people to act as their messenger to Wa-kon'-da when they organize their warriors to move against the foe (La Flesche 1925:365)], as all of these represent the warriors of the tribe, but that he will have a line of descendants that will continue through all time.
>
> The Songs of Drawing His Arrows and the ceremonial acts accompanying them express a desire that the initiate shall not only have a successful military career but that he shall also have an endless line of descendants, a lineage that shall continue as long as day and night continue. (La Flesche 1925:233–235)

In the second song, the Xo'-ka begins by impersonating the blue-backed hawk (La Flesche 1925:367). Then "the Xo'-ka impersonates the successful Do-don-hon-ga who comes home to his village in triumph with his commanders and warriors, having battled with the enemies of the tribe and overcome them" (La Flesche 1925:368). The final act of the Xo'-ka is the Laying Down of the Wa-xo'-be. He removes the bird from his back, places it on his upturned palms, sings the song of Laying Down the Wa-xo'-be and drops it. If the birdskin lands breast upward it is a sign of success (the initiate will prosper and enjoy the full length of his life; La Flesche 1925:370), and if not, it indicates defeat or death. From the second song and concluding acts we learn that the Xo'-ka sends the arrows and re-creates the successful return to the village as an impersonator of the falcon. The final act is one of divination.

The bow and arrows themselves are painted with special reference to the diurnal succession. "The breast of the bow is painted red as a symbol of the recurrent day and the back is painted black, a symbol of the night that ever follows the day. One of the arrows is painted red and the other black, so that both together symbolize day and night" (La Flesche 1925:234). These arrows assume a magical significance in the ritual when an arrow becomes fitted to the bow string.

> When the Songs of the Arrows are about to be sung the people whose houses happen to be in the line over which the arrows are to be set in flight move out, even the horses that happen to stand in the way are driven aside, for there are many persons who believe that any man or beast over which the magic arrows make their flight will die within the year. (La Flesche 1925:239)

It takes no great leap of thought to see that control over life-preserving rituals and their associated falcon imagery is of utmost interest to those who have an investment in the deployment of social labor. The very individuals who dominate the economy have an interest in controlling the magical means for its increase. Their continued proliferation is key to their ongoing capacity to fund these ceremonies of increase. Hence, they are the principal beneficiaries of the magical benefits of the ceremonies.

Morning Star Myths as Potential Status Charters
Up to now I have relied on the Osage exclusively. But to reinforce my claims I will cite a myth from the Winnebago, another Siouan-speaking tribe from the Prairie-Plains region, one that provided Hall's exemplary narrative in the first place. All of the themes cited up to now are plausibly linked through the story line of the Winnebago Red Horn myth cycle. When this myth was taken down in 1912 under Paul Radin's stimulus it had been the charter for the war bundle powers of the Thunderbird clan. That it is a suitable socially charged ritual charter rests on the importance of the Red Horn myth's content, which at its core is the story of life's triumph over death. The context in which this triumph takes place clearly is conceived of as a deadly contest in which the outcome is subject to the fortunes of chance. Just as clearly, the protagonists are regarded as warriors whose prowess in combat can save ordinary mortals from destruction. But once dead, the hero is reprieved by coordinated action of his two sons. By having the brothers recover the head of their slain father, this myth reaffirms the vigor of life as a chain of generations. Loss of life may be inevitable, even to

a god, but one's "life-force" continues in one's progeny. This is a message that has great resonance throughout the Southeast and the Plains.

The power of Red Horn is graphically described in the narrative. Red Horn and his companions engage in a deadly contest with the Giants who are harassing and eating humanity. They win one match with the Giants after another. In their first game of stick ball, Red Horn is matched against a giantess (chief?). After much close gaming, Red Horn gains the upper hand by having "the little faces in his ears stuck out their tongues at her and the eyes winked at her" (Radin 1948:125–126). The giantess laughs and lets down her upraised stick. By so disarming her, Red Horn scores the fourth and decisive goal, whereupon the mother of the giantess exclaims, "The good-for-nothing woman, she is smitten with him! She will make the whole village suffer on her account!" (Radin 1948:126). After a rematch that repeats the same decisive wins, the losing team demands the sacrifice of the chieftainess, whereupon Red Horn steps forward to claim her as his and to marry her. That she has the same red-colored hair as Red Horn's evidently indicates an underlying bond between them (Radin 1948:126).

For the persona of Red Horn to stand for the vitality of life requires a clarification and elaboration of Red Horn's identity and behavior. On his identity the narrative uses elaborate means to inform us that the protagonist goes by three names. The protagonist explains that "Red Horn" is the name by which he is known to humans. The hair has regenerative powers that are highlighted by combing. In the Osage language, which I refer to in the absence of other dictionaries, the meaning of the word *horn* can include a lock or braid of long hair (La Flesche 1932).[17] That a long braid is a possible referent for *horn* is found in a myth of "Blue Horn's Nephews" (Radin 1954:82). His jealous lovers, who take the step of tying the strands of his braid to four interior posts of his lodge while he is sleeping, undo the protagonist in this short myth. A connection of sexual favors with a long male hair-braid is unmistakable. Enlarging on this generative connection, a broken bowl is repaired that emphasizes the same power in different terms.

Red Horn tells us that a name conferred upon him by the gods is "He-who-wears-human-heads-as-earrings." All of this is by way of highlighting the significance of the third name, "He-who-gets-hit-with-deer-lungs," which was given him by his oldest brother, and fellow hero god, Kunu. The significance of this name was highlighted by the inappropriate action of Kunu's wife, who upon drawing the wrong inference from his sobriquet acts doubly inappropriately by throwing deer lungs at Red Horn. Kunu admonishes her for disrespect of Red Horn, and by implication, he may be reproaching her (as a woman) for mishandling the physical object of deer lungs as well.

Red Horn is marked with certain important avian characteristics. First of all, Radin tells us in his commentary that Red Horn has an identity as a kind of thunderer, providing Red Horn with avian characteristics. In the narrative he joins "Storms-as-he-walks" in flying to their destination. Of all the avian possibilities, a hawk would be an appropriate bird form considering Red Horn's leadership in aggressive battle. This attribute takes on added significance with Radin's (1948:165) observation that "Red Horn was associated with war powers but no particular war weapon is ever mentioned as particularly his." A separate weapon is not required of a falcon, since his aerial combat capabilities would be sufficient unto themselves. To further complete the correspondence of Red Horn with the falcon in Osage belief, Radin tells us that he represents or embodies the morning and/or evening star.[18]

Red Horn's actions communicate a message of vitality that closely corresponds to the flight of the Osage mystic arrow. In a trope on the flight of the Osage arrow, Red Horn wins a footrace among the gods by casting himself as an arrow that he magically manages to shoot ahead of himself. Upon materializing himself at the end of the arrow flight, he repeats the magical shots two more times to emerge the front-runner. Red Horn's regenerative power also rests in the "deer lungs" by which he is known. The nose and other parts of the face come into play. At creation the heavenly gods conferred upon him the generative power represented by the long nose. Each of these graphical images has to do with the life-force, in particular the male procreative force.

The Calumet and Rebirth

The incident with the deer lungs needs to be enlarged upon. Two points are declared. One, being hit or touched by deer lungs has a vital significance. The other is that the name refers to some kind of "deer lungs" other than those found inside a flesh-and-blood animal. To the listener the answer was probably easily understood in terms of the symbolism of the Calumet in the old and important ceremony of that name among tribes of the prairies and plains (Hall 1997).

Among the Osage the Calumet ceremony or Wa-wathon requires two *Wa-xo'-be*/sacred items, two peace pipes (Bailey 1995:53–54) made for the ceremony. The pipe stems are straight sticks termed "arrow shafts." Attached to these shafts are skins of the heads of ivory-billed woodpeckers, tail feathers of the golden eagle, large downy feathers from the undertail of an eagle, fat from the back of a buffalo, large downy feathers from the undertail of a yellow-tailed hawk, and owl feathers. The completed pipes are supported by forked sticks. The eagle tail feathers make the conspicuous feather fans suspended from the stems. The owl feathers are located at the distal end (La Flesche 1939:205–208).

The Deer Lung clan contributed the finishing touch of a bunch of owl feathers. Furthermore, the location of the owl feathers at the distal end of the stem comes close to the point of contact with its human subject during the ritual of re-naming, which, as Hall has amply argued, is an act of spiritual revivification. By being touched by the calumet stem in this heavily freighted ceremony, the person who is undergoing a rebirth stands to be brushed by the owl feathers provided by a member of the Deer Lung clan.

The association with the magical flight of the arrow is well entrenched in the narrative. Although Red Horn as the youngest brother is the implicit underdog, his qualifications for leadership are established by winning a foot race against Turtle after repeatedly projecting himself forward as a arrow. Later in the narra-tive the deer-lungs name is explained. In short, we have the conceptual basis for both the calumet stem and the second name of Red Horn. Although the name is mainly an alternative moniker for Red Horn, in the past the consistent asso-ciation of the bi-lobed arrow with Birdman offers the prospect that the bi-lobed arrow is also a possession of his!

We find again a symbolism strongly associated with revitalization, albeit without the sexual overtones of the first. In conclusion, being struck by deer lungs is tantamount to being touched by the life-giving force of the bi-lobed arrow.

Material Markers

By bringing the Winnebago narrative to bear on our Birdman, we can bring together similar themes of contest and combat, life and death, and assurance of longevity in one's descendants, in ways that complement the Osage example. The gaming motif, which is far stronger in the Winnebago narrative, provides an even stronger connection between the theme of the victorious falcon/Red Horn and the narrative structure that can be re-created plausibly from our sets of archaeological images. The fit becomes more compelling when specific marker details are pinpointed linguistically among these and other images linked to the Birdman theme. I have in mind three identifying attributes that have to do with dressing the head: (1) long-nosed maskettes worn in the earlobes; (2) the long braid worn over the left shoulder; and (3) the bi-lobed arrow mounted in a hair pin. Other details bear mentioning, although their meanings are obscure: a rope of shell beads appears as a necklace that alternates with a columella pendant in a necklace of large beads.

Robert Hall (1983a, 1989, 1991, 1997) has identified the first name, "He-who-wears-human heads-as-earrings," with the twelfth-century ear ornaments known archaeologically under the name of long-nosed god maskettes. The significance of these maskette faces is graphically narrated in the Winnebago myth of Red Horn referred to above. When the top-playing giantess threatened to beat Red Horn, the hero diverts her attention by making his ear faces' wink and stick out their tongues—thereby scoring on her error and winning the game. To lose on a trick is one thing, but to be accused by her mother of having fallen in love with Red Horn suggests that more than mere winking and ear wiggling is involved. The theme takes on new dimensions when the giantess is rescued by Red Horn, who has a son by her. Only if the long nose is admitted to the facial attractiveness of Red Horn does the symbolism makes sense as a sexual one. The connection is underscored by the appearance of these maskettes on Classic Braden figures.

The second name dwells on the meaning of "Red Horn." *Horn*, here, refers to long hair that is likened to the long horns of bison and other animals. The length of the hair is laden with meaning. In Winnebago myth a theme of sexuality is disclosed in the activities of men with long, braided hair of different colors. Red Horn's hair should then be visualized as long and braided, in addition to having a trademark redness that was later inherited by his sons. The connection of the word "horn" in his name to hair is shown in the Winnebago myth, "Blue Horn's Nephews," in which the warrior in question had a scalplock stretched in the form of a queue that was very long and very blue (Radin 1954:81). The power to repair inanimate objects with a stroke of his hands could also increase the size of his and other people's hair. In sum, we have established two material markers, the first being the long-nosed god maskettes and other being a long braid of red hair.

The long braid of hair is consistently portrayed in our sets. It is also displayed on a sculptured figure known as "Big Boy" wearing long-nosed god maskettes from his earlobes.

Deer Lungs and the Bi-lobed Arrow

Now that it has been established that the term *deer lungs* in this context references the calumet stem, we need to look for an ancient material precursor of the post-contact form associated with the Calumet ceremony. This ceremony, developed from the Pawnee Hako rite, constitutes an important line of continuity with a primary emblem of hierarchical, chiefly society of the thirteenth and fourteenth centuries. This continuity is a compelling document for the continued place that highly sanctified, power-laden artifacts from previous cultural contexts can have in new post-contact ones.

The Osage have provided detailed symbolic evidence for the magical belief in the ritual power of the hawk's bow to project one's descendents as far into the future as an arrow can be shot. Now we need to seek the presence of arrow symbolism in pre-contact imagery. This is not difficult to find in our Classic Braden materials. An arrow fitted to a strung bow happens to be the archetype for the bi-lobed arrow motif that is mounted in the hairdos of images belonging to each of our four sets. Phillips and Brown (1978:148) have been able to derive the bi-lobed arrow image iconographically from an arrow set in a drawn bow through a series of images. The "lobes" are simply elaborations of feather fans attached to the tips of the bow.

This subsidiary motif is more than a token symbol. Robert Hall (1989) has argued that the bi-lobed arrow is the prototype of the post-contact calumet, or what the Osage called the *Wa-wathon*. What is significant about the calumet is its use as an instrument for ritual adoption through a symbolic resuscitation of the dead (Hall 1997).

The resemblance these pipes bear to the bi-lobed arrow is informative of a long and ancient connection between them. These ceremonial staffs or pipes (they can be either) are traditionally supported by a forked stick that raises the proximal end and allows the effigy head to rest on the ground. When the sacred staffs of both moieties are displayed together, one arrives at an image of the sort painted on a Qawpaw bison robe of the mid-eighteenth century (Horse Capture et al. 1993:136–137). The heads of the staffs converge to form a figure "V." The assemblage looks amazingly like a bi-lobed arrow once the staffs are collapsed together. The eagle-feather fans suspended from the staffs thereby become the two "lobes."[19] As Hall (1977, 1989) has pointed out, the ceremonial staffs are called "arrowshafts," and they are fletched with eagle feathers using precisely the same technique as with utilitarian arrows.[20]

In short, the pairs of calumets held at rest resemble an upside-down bi-lobed arrow in which the arrow stem is split between the two calumet stems and the "lobes" are the feather fans suspended from each of the calumets. In the transition from the bi-lobed arrow device to the historical ceremonial pipe, the principal changes have been the elimination of the bow string and bow.

Iconographic Associations in Pre-Contact Art

At this point in the analysis it is important to acknowledge that the Red Horn myth cycle contains a rich set of iconographic details that go well beyond the two that Bob Hall has singled out with great insight. For this reason it is intriguing to pose the question of just how much of the detail can be plausibly ascribed to material objects and various depictions attributable to the 1100–1300 period at Cahokia and elsewhere in the Eastern Prairies.

The distribution of individual elements having plausible reference to one of the three major protagonists in the Red Horn myth has been cited already. It remains for this section to examine the patterns of mutual association among these elements in an effort to seek further confirmation for the Red Horn/Morning Star theme in pre-contact times.

In the case of elements associated with Red Horn, himself, the task poses remarkably few difficulties. Red Horn has three specific material attributes that are cited in each of his three names. Red Horn refers to his long hair, which as we have seen is conventionally depicted worn beside his head in a long braid. His name at creation, "He-who-wears-human-heads-as-earrings," has reference to long-nosed god maskettes (including short-nosed versions as well). And his third name, "He who is hit with deer lungs," refers to a possession of Red Horn's, the bi-lobed arrow.

Where are these details found iconographically? In the first detailed depiction of the Red Horn type identity known, that of the converted statuette of Cahokian claystone passing under the name of "Big Boy,"[21] the maskettes are carefully depicted attached to the figure's ears. His hair is hung in a long thick braid over his left shoulder. Three other details are present that we will have reference to later. None is indicated in the narrative, but each is important. First is the distinctive headdress with what looks like a copper plate mounted at an angle to the facial plane. Of particular interest here is the device that the plate bears. The ogee, oriented vertically, has a strong resemblance to a stylized vulva.[22] Second is the rope of beads worn around the neck, and third is the long cape that is worn over the shoulders. The cape bears feather-like elements that are interpretable plausibly as scalplocks. The red ochre packed around these elements carved in relief reinforces the red hair associations. All told, we have in this figure a remarkable combination of the very elements by which the Red Horn hero-deity of the Winnebago is identified in myth. Although this might suggest that the Red Horn identification can be extrapolated into deep antiquity, caution is dictated because of the inherent ambiguities attendant upon the sources of our information, to say nothing of the time spread involved. For the archaeological expression a new name is called for. "Long Braid" is appropriate.

These early sculptures are very unembellished in comparison with the Classic Braden style. Consequently, these stripped-to-the-basics sculptures can be regarded as sculpted ideographs. Each detail of dress and external association can be thought of as an iconic marker. For instance, the deer head held in the left hand of the red pipestone pipe from Spiro (LfCrI B99-3) takes on new meaning as an iconic identifier (Brown 1996:Fig. 2-97). It certainly makes no sense as a representation of a physical object known archaeologically or in engraved shell art. Thus, finding that the name "deer head" (*ta-pa*) is used to designate the constellation Pleiades among the Omaha and Osage raises the plausibility that the central figure given representation also has a specific name and a core association to go along with it (La Flesche 1939:138).

A signal feature of the Osage arrow and falcon trope as well as the Red Horn narrative is the very universality of the themes. Life's triumph over death through one's descendants has an appeal that does not owe anything to the sources of sustenance, whether it be maize agriculture, bison, or other foodways. This vision of the ultimate victory over death has its counterpart in an analogy with life's prospects with gaming and gambling. In other words, one's chances for prolonged life and a survival of one's descendants depend as much upon luck as they do skill and forethought. And it is the chanciness of life that leads humans to seek out the aid of supernatural heroes and gods. Hence the supplication of these heroes.

As confirmation of this conception of life we need only refer to the *Okipa* ceremony of the Mandan, who represent another branch of the Siouan linguistic family (Bowers 1950). In this ceremony the human impersonator of death, dressed as a black panther, is driven away from the village upon a staged confrontation with "Lone Man" holding aloft a pipe bundle (Catlin 1967). This ritual instrument is a clear embodiment of the life principle. Women who fled in fear of the approach of *Oxinhede* (Foolish One) turn upon him as he flees from the calumet and drive him into the water. This public performance takes on significance in the context of widespread Prairie-Plains beliefs. Women and children are commonly singled out as the favored victims of the underwater panther. Disappearance and death in general were widely attributed to the stealth of this deity. But the deaths of women and children, a very vulnerable component of the population, plausibly could be regarded as particularly acute ones because they were central to reproduction.

What we can take from the history of iconographic representation of Long Braid and related mythic heroes is a record of continuity in the association of specific forms, namely the long braid, Birdman/falcon representation, the long-nosed god maskette, and the bi-lobed arrow. The record extends from about 1100 to at least 1400. From this record of three hundred years of continuity we are in a position to examine the proposition that there has been a continuity of meaning. Although the total set of meanings may have changed or shifted over this period, a certain core will remain.

Alternative Models

The foregoing has to be conceived of as a model, if for no other reason then because no necessary association exists between imagery and meaning. A compet-

ing model already exists, although it has not been developed to any extent beyond the identification of the winged beings as including both men and women.
The latter are marked iconically by the breast-like protuberances on the profiled
chests of certain bird "man" figures (such as the two Rogan plates, see Fig. 4.1c,
d).[23] If this identification holds up, then either one of two conclusions can be
drawn. One, the identification of the Birdman theme with the key logic of male
procreation embodied in the post-contact falcon imagery is incorrect. Significantly different allegorical references had to be present in the thirteenth- and
fourteenth-century past. Two, the commonplace meanings connected with male
procreation are correctly applied to the past, but special meanings incorporating
female procreation were developed by elites and overlaid as secret knowledge.
The passing of elites brought to an end this layer of meaning. The identification
of female breasts certainly opens up the distinct possibility that this marks an
identification of sex distinct from the garb and combative action.

The protuberances are not without alternative identifications, however. A
widely held folk belief exists about how the falcon managed to stun or kill much
larger birds in midair. Although fast photography shows that the falcon kills or
wounds its prey by engaging its claws at the last minute, the action is so swift
that the unaided eye often cannot detect this action (Johnsgard 1990). One folk
idea was that the telling blows were accomplished by stabbing prey with a sharp,
prong-line projection on the bird's breastbone (Grossman and Hamlet 1964).
As for relative priority, neither these two nor any other identification has any
"natural" authority; it remains the task of inter-object pattern analysis to sort
out the identification issue.

But commonly held beliefs among post-contact societies that are the subject
of this chapter identify the morning star as male and the evening star as female
(although the Winnebago may have thought the evening star to have been male
according to Radin [1948]). According to Reichard (1921), where stars belong to
opposite sexes, they play an important role in origin myths as the progenitors
of humankind.

The falcon associations among the Osage expose a weakness manifest in
many studies of SECC imagery. In concentrating on intrinsic attributes, or what
Panofsky (1939) would call "naturalistic meaning," we shut ourselves off from
productive pursuit of a semiosis of nonintrinsic meanings. The Osage example
underscores the way in which obvious elements composing an image can sometimes be those that are least essential. This perspective is essential to the problem
of archaeological interpretation of pre-Columbian "Birdman" imagery.

Given the length of time involved, it would be easy to stand by the position
that the Red Horn myth of 1912 had to have differed in detail from any supposed

ancestral myth of 1200. The contrary has to be rationalized by counterarguments, which in this case require starting with the single most detailed instance.
While the Red Horn myth remains a model for generating an independent system of beliefs, it is not practical to transpose names from the Red Horn cycle
directly into imagery of the thirteenth century.

Summary and Conclusions

The fragmentary nature of both the archaeological and the ethnological source
material drives this involved and complex argument for continuity of certain
essential, commonly held meanings for imagery over many centuries. Despite
claims to the contrary, it is one thing to trace individual objects of ritual or
sacred value to ancient archaeological images and artifacts; it is quite another
to believe that the narratives and beliefs presently associated with these forms
remain consistently attached as one moves back in time.

To advance beyond an ad hoc argument, this chapter rests its case on a proposition that mythically chartered statuses and ceremonies are concerned to build
logically consistent narratives and enduring cosmological identifications. As
long as these statuses and ceremonies remain anchored to the reproduction of a
political economy, the adhesion of meaning with icon will persist, particularly
in its widely held and conventional senses. As a consequence this analysis has
been drawn to a search for myths and attendant meanings that comply with such
status-chartering functions. Particularly helpful are the narratives commonly
present in these mythic allegories. When one turns to the imagery, the narrative target directs attention to different activities of the same figure and away
from the interesting image ensemble or the motif level of detail. Although these
details have a place in this analysis, it remains one of confirming the thrust of
the narrative.

These stipulations become all the more compelling given the gap in time
between the different source documents. Within this gap countless incidental
changes are possible, but little in the way of change of logically interconnected
meanings for the iconic representation of statuses that have enduring vested
interests. The solution to identifying reorganization of these interests takes its
cue from Willey's application of Kubler's principle of social and religious disjunctions. The nature of the sacred falcon/morning star allegory with its cele-
bration of the triumph of life-force over death has an appeal that is transfer-
able from egalitarian to hierarchical societies. The examples of this 'complex's
enduring role in Osage ceremony and Winnebago clan bundle rights point to
its robustness under the stresses of most disjunctions. With this in mind, the

most compelling disjunction affecting the conventional meanings attached to the morning star/sacred falcon complex remains arguably the period of the nineteenth century after the Civil War, when autonomy was surrendered and intertribal warfare no longer was allowed. This transition lay within the time-frame of key ethnographic informants.

The substance of the archaeological end of the argument focuses on the Classic Braden style connected with the town of Cahokia and plausibly linked historically with Dhegihan-speaking Siouan peoples known from the Prairie Plains in post-contact times. A kind of narrative is constructed from overlapping images in which key elements of the Birdman image are prominent. In addition to the classic Rogan plate type of Birdman image, the chunkey player and the dancing warrior play a decisive role. Uniting these thematic types, crosscutting iconic details (e.g., forked eye motif, angel wings) and different recombinations make possible the construction of a plausible narrative. This narrative of gaming with loss and defeat is followed by the return and triumph of the hero. An eventual apotheosis is implied by the dancing warrior theme. Gaming and defeat are paired with revenge and triumph.

When we turn to rituals and myths recorded at the beginning of the twentieth century, one theme stands out. From the Osage we have the sacred hawk complex and from the Winnebago (and Sauk) we have the Red Horn narrative. Each identifies the hawk and its hero-deity self with the Morning Star and prowess in combat, and also as a guardian for one's life-force. Even more compelling is the appearance of specific mythic imagery (e.g., "long hair or braid of hair," "ears with faces," and the "deer-lungs") in thirteenth- and fourteenth-century images of the series (e.g., long braid of hair, "long-nosed god maskettes," and the bi-lobed arrow). These images are about supernaturals, and their portrayal is not about how power was achieved in reality, but how it was represented allegorically.

In view of this argument for the effectiveness of the political economy to maintain the logic embodied by the Morning Star trope, Birdman in antiquity has to represent a metaphor of social continuity through the regeneration of human life.

Notes

1. Reprinted in Willey (1990:301).

2. Following Eric Wolf (1999:55) we can say that "ideology is a complex of ideas selected to underwrite and represent a particular project of installing, maintaining, and aggrandizing power in social relationships."

3. *Wa-xo'-be* were ritual objects (literally "made sacred") of which the primary ones "were sacred objects from which ritual authority was derived," for instance, clan bundles (*Wa-xo'-be zhin-ga*), peace pipes (*Wa-wathon*), the Great Bundles (*wa-xo'-be ton-ga*), and the Great Medicine Bundles (*mon-kon ton-ga wa-xo'-be*) (Bailey 1995:46–47). "Each priesthood was associated with a particular primary *wa-xo'-be*."

4. It is not clear whether this hawkskin had to be that of a specific species, although the spectacular diving strike or "stoop" of the falcon as well as its ability to kill prey much larger than itself would commend the peregrine falcon above other hawk species.

5. It would be a mistake to conceive of this reduction as merely simplification and subsequent drift in content, something implied by Keyes (1994). Although these two processes are undoubtedly relevant, they must share place with the resurgence of alternative rationales that had been present from early on, but had not achieved canonical status as chartering myths. This is possible because the imagery in itself was and continued to be inherently multivocal in meaning.

6. An important association of the falcon.

7. Note the analogy made to one of the principal ritual symbols.

8. This is an explicit reference to the objective of clubbing as the collection of an enemy's head.

9. Here, as throughout, the two birds are treated as if they had human capacities.

10. This is one of the more forthright declarations that the falcon constituted the means by which the power of daytime was restored in a perpetual conflict between day and night.

11. Use of the gendered term *Birdman* follows the precedent established by Phil Phillips (Phillips and Brown 1978). Although this male identity has been challenged (Brown 1982, Koehler 1997, Levy 1999), the dress remains male-marked. For that reason I find it less confusing to retain Phillips's terminology. The gender of the bird person is an issue taken up at the end of the chapter.

12. Note that the isolated head theme and the falcon theme (either naturalized or anthropomorphized) are explicitly not considered, although both of these themes can be related to the human figural ones mentioned above by making use of the same substitution grammar.

13. Although views of the rod-shaped copper sheath and the adjacent and seemingly attached large-sized disc beads support this view (Fowler et al. 1999:137, Fig. 1.8), Fowler (Fowler et al. 1999:170) specifically rejects these rod-shaped chunkey poles without explanation (Brown 2003).

14. This identification of such a roundel as a special kind of "star" sees some support in the costume of the individual dressed as a sinister, cat-like *Oxinhede/Okehéede*

figure in the Mandan *Okipa* ceremony (Catlin 1967). Oxinhede is a kind of cat with large jagged teeth painted over his face in Catlin's painting. Roundel stars are painted in white upon a blackened body. The white-on-black ensemble suggests a reference to the night sky. The corresponding puma figures of the Mississippian Period east are routinely depicted with such roundels, including the fierce Piasa figure on the 1678 Franquelin map attributed to Marquette (Jacobson 1991). From these correspondences it follows that Oxinhede is a version of the dreaded Piasa or wife-and-child-taking underwater monster.

15. Note that a cup fragment classified as Classic Braden (cup 35B) is a ventrally viewed spread-winged falcon with a spotted forelimb and covert feathers. In the Craig style sequence that parallels the Braden one, Birdmen are present with barred oval spots on breast and wing forelimbs. Covert feathers are indicated by parallel lines (cups 165.1, 166?).

16. A possible alternative to the annular markings on the Piasa puma? See a Perrault pipe from the Emerald Mound (Phillips and Brown 1978:204–205).

17. The connection also exists for the Osage, for whom *he-ga'-xa* means scalplock or horn. Otherwise the basic word for horn is *he*, just as in the Winnebago (La Flesche 1932:59).

18. In one statement on the subject, Radin (1948:45) identifies Red Horn with the morning star, in another with the evening star (Radin 1954:13), and in a third he equivocates (Radin 1948:41–42).

19. Hall (1989:250) states,

> The bi-lobed arrow has been interpreted as a bow and arrow (Phillips and Brown 1978:148), and an atlatl with its dart (Howard 1968:26–27), as a war club (Hudson 1976:247), and as an explicit symbol of male generative power (Waring 1968:38). One example pecked into stone as a petroglyph resembles a face, with the arrow as the nose and the lobes as the eyes. Other petroglyphs resemble a dart in an atlatl with lobes as the finger holes of the atlatl. This combination also resembles male genitalia. I believe myself that the motif originally represented an atlatl with its dart, but that by Mississippian times the motif sometimes came to look more like a bow and arrow, since the atlatl and dart was an obsolete weapon system. (figure references omitted)

20. The significance of this usage is important to the point at hand. When a lungs-and-trachea image is combined with an arrow-tipped breath passage, the result is an arrow/trachea flanked by lungs. The resemblance of this image to the bi-lobed arrow motif is striking. Indeed, the iconic origin of the latter according to Phillips and Brown (1978) is that of an arrow set in a drawn bow in which the feathers at the ends of the bow are greatly enlarged. The resemblance of the enlarged feather fans at the bow tips to the lungs, and the arrow to the arrowhead on trachea, merely points to the attempt to make the bow and arrow conform to a biological lungs-and-trachea set combined with an image of the arrowhead as focus of animal force.

21. Carved in the twelfth century but deposited for the final time in the Great Mortuary of Spiro early in the fifteenth century (Brown 1996).

22. This identification was suggested to me by Kent Reilly. This identity was advanced even more broadly in Diaz-Granados and Duncan (2000).

23. The secondary argument of Koehler (1997) that a Classic Braden figural engraving from Moundville was "feminine" follows from a misunderstanding of the codes of the Classic Braden style established by Phil Phillips and Eliza McFadden (Phillips and Brown 1978).

Acknowledgments: This essay is dedicated to the memory of Eric Wolf. It has benefited from critical reading of an earlier draft by Tim Earle, Gil Stein, Mary Weismantle, and Robert Launay. However, I alone am responsible for my statements.

5. The Great Serpent in Eastern North America

George E. Lankford

One of the more striking images from the iconographic collection known as the Southeastern Ceremonial Complex is the winged serpent (Fig. 5.1). The image takes several forms, but the U-shaped serpent with horns and peculiar wings was apparently particularly important at Moundville. In the only published inventory of Moundville ceramics, the winged serpent is the most numerous design (thirty-three examples), rivaled only by the hand-and-eye design (thirty-one examples) (Steponaitis 1983). This preponderance is confirmed by another scholar from his own studies of Moundville ceramics (V. J. Knight, Jr., personal communication, 1996). Other examples of the same design have been found in the ceramic collections in the Central Mississippi Valley near Memphis (Childs 1991; David Dye, personal communication, 1996). There are other forms of the winged serpent (and its variants) known from Spiro. The Moundville design, however, will serve as the particular focus for this study.

The major argument is that the winged serpent is a well-known mythological figure from the religious worldview of the Eastern Woodlands and that the wings, rather than being a part of the essential form of the creature, are an indicator of location in the celestial realm. To lay out this argument, it will be necessary to survey the lore surrounding the horned serpent and look at the relevant ethnoastronomy, which is not well known for the Eastern Woodlands. The astronomical orientation of Pawnee mythology and ritual has long been recognized, but there are indications that other peoples of the Eastern Woodlands and Plains also encoded astronomical lore in their myths (Chamberlain 1982; Williamson and Farrer 1990). That wider distribution, however, may have been more than random occurrences of ethnoastronomical beliefs. This chapter and Chapter 8 argue that a set of astronomical beliefs encoded in myths and iconography constituted a symbolic complex which in earlier centuries was widely known in North America. Further, the cross-cultural nature of this belief com-

FIGURE 5.1. Some of the "winged serpent" designs from Moundville (Moore
1905:229, 374).

plex was probably due to the fact that it was rooted in an even more widely
accepted cosmology (see Chapter 2).

For people who believe that the cosmos is basically a layer cake of worlds,
the relation of the layers to each other becomes an important cosmological concern. Among the various Native American groups in the Eastern Woodlands
and the Plains, those layers became identified with particular powers, enabling
discussion of the relationships to take on mythic form with various "persons"
interacting with each other in the various eras of mythic time.

That mythic identification also permits the casting of structural principles in
terms of the types of relationship in which each person participates. One of the
primary mythological principles is the opposition of the forces of day and night.
The diurnal opposition becomes expressed as tension between the powers of the
celestial vault and the powers of the waters and caverns beneath the earth-disk.
Central to this cosmology is the prior existence of the primeval water, which
is separated from the Above World only by a deliberate act of creation—the
earth, which is made to float upon the water. The primeval water is not a neutral
backdrop for human life in this scheme, for it is the domain of many different
species, both those which are recognized in modern science and those which
are far more powerful—mythological creatures who rule the water world. As
is customary in Native American myths, those water powers were prevalent
and visible in primordial times, but even in modern times they are occasionally
seen by humans—but only if they wish to be seen. "These manitous often come
upon earth and pass among the people; they are not always visible to the eyes of
everybody" (Jones 1911:214). More frequently, only their works are seen, and
their presence is simply supplied by the common worldview.

When they do take visible form, they are described in different ways. In a
variety of myths there are references to a giant fish, but while there are hints that
this form was of considerable importance in former times, it is difficult to make
much more of it now than just to acknowledge its existence. A more important
image in the central Woodlands and the Plains is the Underwater Panther, and
there are graphic illustrations of a panther, probably cognate with that figure,

which come from at least as far back as Hopewellian times. The most widely recognized form of the underwater powers, however, is the Horned Water Serpent. It is frequently referred to as a single creature, but more careful reading through the collections indicates that the Underwater Panther/Horned Water Serpent is really understood to be a race of people, representatives of which may be encountered in any large body of water, whether seas, lakes, or rivers. Even so, there is still frequent reference to a "master" of the underwater powers. (See Emerson 1989 for an excellent study of this figure in relation to Cahokia.)

> The Indians say that this earth has four layers. The bottom layer does not look like the one we are on now. It is night there all the time. That is where the manitou is who is the boss that rules the bottom of the earth. He rules all four layers . . . (Barnouw 1977:41)

It is this "boss" of the Beneath World who is the subject of this chapter.

Since each of the specific labels—Underwater Panther, Horned Water Serpent—points to a particular visual form, this chapter will use the convention of "Great Serpent" whenever the subject is the total concept, regardless of form. This study will first sample the range of descriptive opinion about this figure, in regard both to appearance and function, then attempt to place it in a larger cosmological context that will help interpret various expressions of this concept, both mythic and iconographic. The basic argument is threefold: (1) the Great Serpent was a universally known figure in the Eastern Woodlands for many centuries, despite its many forms; (2) the Great Serpent was located not only in the water world, but also in the celestial realm; and (3) the Great Serpent appears not only in myth, but also in graphic designs, both prehistoric and historic.

The Forms of the Underwater Powers

Although a survey of the formal attributes of the Great Serpent can begin with any group of peoples of the Plains or Eastern Woodlands, the Central Algonkian tribes are a likely source for a broad vision, because the master of the Beneath World is a well-known and important figure among them, a personification known as "Mishebeshu," to use the Ojibwa name. A recent study by Smith (1995) provides a useful summary of past research and adds her own insights. She makes it clear that the appearance of Mishebeshu is complex. The early European observers did their best to find the correct image and translation for the term. Allouez (1664–1667) called it "fabulous animal," Perrot (1654) called it "The Great Panther," Charlevoix (1761) referred to "the great tyger," and current Ojibwa describe it as "a sea tiger on which they put fins"

(Pachot) and "a huge, brown cat" (Redsky). After summarizing these, Smith affirms the standard image: "[C]urrent firsthand experiences are invariably of a water serpent, usually horned and always of an immense size" (Smith 1995:97–98). The horns seem especially characteristic. "The horns here, as in all traditional Ojibwe drawings, are signs of extraordinary power. In the mnemonic scrolls of the midewiwin, a powerful shaman is easily identified by his horns . . . while horns may be affixed to any figure in order to denote power, only Mishebeshu *always* has them" (Smith 1995:103–104). And the horns are often placed upon a snake:

> As a serpent Mishebeshu appears, again, in traditional pictographs, mide scrolls, and contemporary artwork. The portraits are very much like those found among both the Eastern Algonquians and the Plains tribes, often resembling an elongated lizard with a spined back, a huge tail, and horns. However, while his form may appear to be that of an amphibian, Mishebeshu is always described as a reptile. All snakes, it is said, were originally derived from him. (Smith 1995:106)

Even so, Smith was careful to point out that:

> My consultants extended the name [Mishebeshu] even further to include not only these great water dwelling lynxes but water serpents and monster ground snakes . . . To the Anishnaabeg [Ojibwa], Mishebeshu is at once a manitou and a class of manitouk, the ogimaa ["boss"] of all underwater and underground creatures, and any of these creatures that might be termed extraordinary. He is not a person with a plurality of forms like Nanabush but a kind of "plural person" who is met with in a complex of symbols and realities. (Smith 1995:97)

In a Shawnee myth of the Great Serpent, the Algonkian name makes it clear that it is the Underwater Panther that is being referred to. Schutz discussed this myth in detail, and he found a bewildering array of descriptions of the Underwater Panther:

> This creature seems to be a combination of the Cyclopean buffalo with one green and one red horn, as indicated above, and the double-headed sacred water panther—two of the four messengers, along with the sacred fish covered with a turtle shell and the sacred monster turtle. C. F. Voegelin (1936:456) describes their function in reference to the stag-serpent: "this

monster attracts human beings as his victims . . ." using his four messen-
gers. In other versions, as the one collected by Voegelin in 1933, above, and
that which I collected in 1972 (JB), the sea serpent is regarded as a multiple-
headed monster with one green and one red horn—the servant in the 1934
version immediately above. The informant for both of these versions was
MW, who described the monster to me in the summer of 1973: "The giant
water snake had four heads, one facing each direction, with two horns on
each head, one blue (green) and one red." She had her information from
her grandfather, but her mother described the serpent as having two heads
and twelve horns, six horns on each head, all colored red with no legs (EW).
(Schutz 1975:154–155)

In the eighteenth and early nineteenth centuries, on a sheer bluff high above
the waters of the Mississippi River was a painting of a composite creature which
is surely Mishebeshu. Fr. Hennepin took note of it and preserved the local legendary explanation:

> There is a common tradition amongst that People, That a great number of
> Miamis were drown'd in that Place, being pursu'd by the Savages of Matsi-
> gamea; and since that time, the Savages going by the Rock, use to smoak,
> and offer Tobacco to those Beasts, to appease, as they say, the Manitou.
> Legend says that Miamis were at Alton and Mitchigameas were at the
> mouth of Illinois River; two monsters lived between. (English 1922:154)

Although the pictograph was gone by the end of the nineteenth century, its
presence was noted by several observers and its name remembered: "Piasa." That
word derives from the Algonkian-speaking Illinois assumed to have occupied
the area in late prehistoric times. Gatschet summarized the nineteenth century's
knowledge of it, referring to the Peorias' "true tiger" as an "animal of the dragon
species" (Gatschet 1899:257–258).

The "pizha" or "pissi" is better translated "panther" than as an alien "tiger,"
but neither word catches the real meaning of the creature. It had the body of
a panther and four legs, but there was more, including a human head (sometimes), an impossibly long tail, and horns. Eyman described the Ojibwa figure
this way:

> Michibichi, the Ojibwa Underwater Panther, was second in the hierarchy
> of deities. A curious combination of cougar, rattlesnake, deer and hawk, he
> is a central figure in an Orpheus myth which explains the origin of death,
> of the hereafter, and of the Medicine Lodge. (Eyman 1962:233)

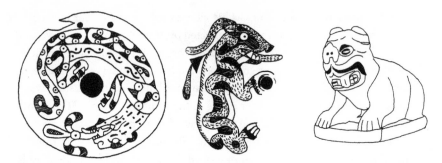

FIGURE 5.2. Some representations of the Underwater Panther: two Hopewellian shell gorgets from Missouri and Texas, and a limestone pipe from Moundville (adapted from Phillips and Brown 1978:214 and Moore 1905:234).

Hoffman noted the Menomini name "mi'shikine'bek, the mythic water monster" (Hoffman 1896:328), and Michelson recorded the Fox and Cree cognates of "me'cigenepigwa" and "misikinapik." Michelson pointed out that a clear case of linguistic error had resulted in the translation of these terms as "hairy serpent," the origin of which he demonstrated to be "great serpent." Moreover, he argued, the animal referred to was not a serpent: "Far from being a snake, the latter represents a horned underneath-monster; both [snake and panther] occur in my unpublished Fox texts" (Michelson 1935:198). The Siouans also know this figure, as Dorsey pointed out: "The water monster which the Thunderers fought resembled a rattlesnake, but he had short legs and rusty-yellow fur" (Dorsey 1889:136) (Fig. 5.2).

Among the Muskogee of the Southeast the water panther is not described in detail, but the myths mention the same figure so well known to the north. A man from Hilibi gave Swanton an account of the destruction of the Muskogee mother-town of Coosa. A water-tiger (*wi katca* = water-panther) mated with a woman from Coosa, and her children were disliked by the townspeople. She reported their threat to kill them to the water-tiger, and "that night the water-tiger brought on a great inundation which covered Coosa, with its square ground and all, but for years after people could see there the main timbers that braced the old tcocofa [ceremonial lodge]" (Swanton 1928a:70; Swanton 1929:69; Lankford 1987:94–96). Unfortunately, while the Southeasterners believed in the Underwater Panther, there is now no record of significant ritual or artistic usage of the figure.

As this brief survey shows, the Underwater Panther is a figure which does not have universal distribution, and that makes it of special interest in determining its antiquity. It appears to be restricted to the central area of the continent. Howard, focusing on the Prairie Potawatomi, did a recent study of this mythological beast and commented, "I have personally secured descriptions of the creature from Arikara, Eastern Dakota, Middle Dakota, Delaware, Fox, Mandan-Hidatsa, Ojibwa, Omaha, Plains-Ojibwa, and Ponca informants" (Howard 1960:217). To his listing should be added the Winnebago, the Illinois, the Miami, the Shawnee, the Iroquois, the Creeks, and the Natchez (Schutz 1975; Swanton 1929). Eyman simply commented that the Piasa was "a major deity to Creeks, Iroquois, Delaware, Ojibwa, and many others" (Eyman 1962:35). This distribution links the Underwater Panther to the Central Algonkian and Siouans, with marginal extensions to the Iroquois and the Muskhogeans. It thus appears reasonable to see the particular form of the Underwater Panther as historically related to the tribes in the heartland, especially the Central Algonkian, but only a subset (or oicotype, to use the folklore term) of the larger category of the Great Serpent.

In other areas of the Eastern Woodlands the Great Serpent is known primarily in its form as a horned serpent. Brinton early noted that the "great water serpent" is found in the beliefs of almost all of the peoples in the Eastern Woodlands (Brinton 1976:117–126). The Central Algonkian also share the vision of the water serpent, despite their emphasis on the Underwater Panther. One serpent form seems to be a way of referring to a specific functional aspect of the Underwater Powers. The south has a directional manitou, Cawana, which is understood to be a great serpent, part of the Beneath World manitouk, who "was desired as a dream guardian" (Jones 1911:212–213, quoted in Jones 1939:16; Skinner 1923a:34–36).

The Northeastern Algonkian also knew the Horned Water Serpent; its name was "abichkam" (and variants). The Micmac lore is characteristic.

The chepichcaam is a horned dragon, sometimes no larger than a worm, sometimes larger than the largest serpent. In one Micmac legend he coils around a man like a constrictor, and seeks to crush him to death. He inhabits lakes and is still sometimes seen. (Hagar 1896:170; see also Parsons 1925:60–61; she also includes additional references for the Micmac, Passamaquoddy, and Penobscot)

These descriptions, ambiguous though they appear (the range of size varies from a worm to fifty yards long), are backed up by personal experience narratives.

Its body, at the neck, was about the size of a stovepipe, and its head was about the size of that of a small dog. Its head was raised high in the air . . . I do not like to be in a canoe on a lake back in the woods. One of those large snakes might pull you under, and you could not help yourself. (Wallis and Wallis 1955:347; see also 113–114)

In the Southeast the unusual mixture of peoples, their many languages (even though Muskhogean was the primary family, there were many isolated representatives of other families), and the early date at which they began reacting to European influences have left the cultural traditions difficult to interpret. The Iroquoian-speaking Cherokees, for example, believed in the Uktena.

In ancient times [say the Cherokees] there lived great snakes, glittering as the sun, and having two horns on the head. To see one of these snakes was certain death. They possessed such power of fascination, that whoever tried to make his escape, ran toward the snake and was devoured. Only great hunters who had made medicine especially for this purpose could kill these snakes. It was always necessary to shoot them in the seventh stripe of their skins. (ten Kate 1889:55).

A creature that is peculiar to the Muskogee nation is the "tie snake." Its origin is unknown, but belief in it seems restricted to that people, and perhaps only to part of them, a possibility which is a reasonable one, considering the multi-ethnic nature of the historic Creek confederacy. One or a few of the participating *talwas* (towns) could well have developed the belief in the tie snake and simply contributed that belief to the larger array of Muskogee lore about the Horned Water Serpent. Swanton summarized the descriptions he obtained:

The "tie snake" is an inch and a half in diameter and short, but it is very strong. It is white under the throat, but black over the rest of the body, and its head is crooked over like the beak of a hawk. It lives in deep water, usually in deep water holes from which it makes excursions into the woods, drawing its prey down into the water to its den. There are many tales told of this tie snake . . .

This snake lives in water and has horns like the stag. It is not a bad snake. It crawls out and suns itself near its hole . . . If any game animal, such as a deer, comes near the place where this snake is lying it is drawn irresistibly into the water and destroyed. It eats only the ends of the noses of the animals it has killed. (Swanton 1928a:492, 494)

When both Creeks and their neighbors share a water-snake legend, the Creek informants tend to identify it as a tie snake (which often has horns), while the others tend toward the horned water serpent. It seems clear that, in myths at least, the tie snake is a Muskogee variant of the horned water serpent and the name is restricted to those people. (For an expanded discussion of the tie snake, see Lankford 1987:Chap. 4.) The Underwater Panther is a separate Muskogee mythic character.

The Siouans of the upper Missouri River apparently elaborated the Horned Water Serpent into four or more different types. In a Mandan myth, Old-Woman-Who-Never-Dies told the twins to call a serpent to take them across the river ("Whale Boat" episode; see below).

> You will see the waves moving, and a large snake with a single horn will come out of the deep water. When he reaches the shore, tell him he is not the one you want. Call again, and there will be another snake with two forked horns but send him back, also, for he is not the one either. A third one will come out, and you will see a growth of young willows and small cottonwoods between his two horns. Tell him he is not the one you want either. Call "Grandfather" again, and there will be large waves along the shore. The last snake will have long horns with cottonwood, willows, grass, and sage growing all over his head. (Bowers 1950:263)

Beyond these four, however, there is the giant serpent who is the consort of the Old-Woman-Who-Never-Dies and is the master of the Missouri River, surely a closer image of the Great Serpent.

The Dakota specify a single horn, but the full description is so un-snakelike that it may more clearly refer to the Underwater Panther.

> Long ago the people saw a strange thing in the Missouri River. At night there was some red object, shining like fire, making the water roar as it passed up stream. Should any one see the monster by daylight he became crazy soon after, writhing as with pain, and dying. One man who said that he saw the monster described it thus: It has red hair all over, and one eye. A horn is in the middle of its forehead, and its body resembles that of a buffalo. Its backbone is like a cross-cut saw, it is flat and notched like a saw or cog-wheel. When one sees it he gets bewildered, and his eyes close at once. He is crazy for a day, and then he dies. The Tetons think that this monster is still in the river, and they call it "Mi-ni-wa-tu," or sea monster.

They think that it causes the ice on the river to break up in the spring of
the year. (Dorsey 1889:135)

Two of the Siouan equivalents are the Dakota "unktehi" and the Winnebago
"Waktceqi." The Dakota provide a nice gender distinction not encountered elsewhere: "These water powers (the males) are supposed to dwell in rivers, while
the females inhabit streams that exist beneath the hills" (Dorsey 1893:233).
Radin's comment on the Winnebago term stressed its untranslatability:

> The meaning of the Winnebago word for this deity, wak'tcexi, is un-
> known. The translation "Water-spirit" does not claim to have anything to
> do with the real meaning of the word, but it was preferred by the Win-
> nebago because this deity is always pictured as a water monster. (Radin
> 1923:239–240)

Ultimately, the complexities of ritual and myth dealing with the Horned
Water Serpent make it quite clear that it is a major figure in the religious and
cosmological understanding of the Woodlands and Plains. The problem of the
variations in the ways of imaging the Great Serpent is greatly augmented by
the difficulty of separating the Underwater Panther and Horned Water Serpent.
Fig. 5.3 presents a list, probably incomplete, of peoples expressing belief in the
two major forms of the Great Serpent, with the overlap of belief in both.

Although Western eyes might readily identify the two creatures as quite different species, the native view, rooted in shape-shifting and symbolic imagery,
seems to find much less distinction between the two. It appears, in fact, that the
two quite different images would be better envisioned as the two ends of a pole,
with various morphs possible between the extremes. As if to demonstrate the
mutability of form of the Great Serpent, two Craig style shell engravings from
Spiro, almost certainly by the same hand, produced almost identical designs, the
major difference being the form of the major figure (Fig. 5.4).

Functions of the Great Serpent

ETIOLOGY

Implicit in these fairly ambiguous descriptions of the Great Serpent is a set of
clear roles. It is above all the guardian of the waters and, by extension, all that
is beneath the surface of the earth. All groundwater is apparently understood
as connected, so that inhabitants of lakes and rivers are also in communication
with those who live in the sea; it is, in effect, a single race of manitouk that gov-

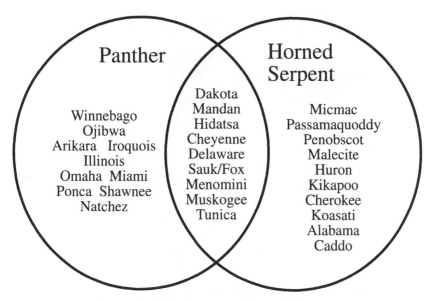

FIGURE 5.3. Distribution of belief in the two major forms of the Great Serpent.

erns the waters. Just as each animal species has a chief, the Great Serpent is the leader of the various races that live in the water, or even, to use Smith's provocative phrase, the "plural person" who represents all the powers of the Beneath World. Since the earth is but a disk floating in the water, however, "the waters" is a shorthand way of referring to the lower half of the cosmos. Any deed done by a water manitou is thus the work of the Great Serpent as one of the major cosmic powers. One deed of great significance to humans is the protection of the water, which is frequently violent; most drownings of humans and animals were (and in some cases, still are) attributed to the Great Serpent. The Potawatomi are illustrative. They called the Piasa "Nampe'shiu," and they were precise as to the manitou's activities:

There is also an evil power in the water, who possesses the ability to pass through the earth as well as its natural element. This is the great horned Water-panther, called Nampe'shiu, or Nampeshi'kw. It is at constant war with the Thunderbirds. When one appears to a man he will become a great warrior. Such panthers maliciously drown people, who are afterwards found with mud in their mouths, eyes, and ears. One of these lived at Mana'wa, now Milwaukee, and sucked people in. The name Mana'wa refers to its den. (Skinner 1923b:47–48)

FIGURE 5.4. A Spiro artist's presentation of the Great Serpent in two guises (a detail from Craig cups 228 and 229, adapted from Phillips and Brown 1984:Pl. 228, 229).

Mishebeshu is the uncanny element in the Ojibwa northern winter world, "the hidden form beneath the ice, which may suddenly crack in winter. He is the one who pulls boaters and swimmers to their deaths and the one who makes the ground go soft beneath your feet" (Smith 1995:100).

Most of the references to the tie snake in the literature from the Muskogee portray it as an objective danger associated with the rivers, and as a legendary figure it serves an etiological function—the tie snake is responsible for drownings and vanished animals and people (See Swanton 1929:Natchez # 16, Hitchiti # 16; Lankford 1987:Chap. 4). It is to the Great Serpent as guardian that tobacco is offered at the outset of a journey on water, a nearly universal practice in the Eastern Woodlands.

The underwater powers have a collateral etiological function: they can explain the fossil bones that are occasionally seen by Native Americans. The bones that wash out along rivers and creeks, particularly those of species not now known, need to be explained, and the Great Serpent provided at least part of the explanation. Gatschet noted in regard to the Siouan figure, "Unktehi, or Unktexi, their Neptune or divine ruler of the waters, whose name also designated a fabled monster of the deep and the whale of the salt-water," that "Unktehi means any large animal, for it is used also to designate some large extinct animal, whose bones are at times found by the Indians" (Gatschet 1899:258).

The enmity between the two polar powers, like the cosmology in general, places humans at the point of intersection, and myths sometimes express the tension of life in the middle, caught between major powers at war. One of the etiological beliefs related to the Horned Water Serpent is that the eternal struggle results in the presence of the storm powers, which can mean rain. Thus humans have developed some ways in which they can turn that fight to their advantage. Among the Ojibwa, "killing frogs and snakes is said to bring on a storm, especially if one lays the snake on its back, thus exposing its belly both as a taunting gesture and as a tempting morsel for the Thunderbirds" (Smith 1995:138).

SOURCE OF POWER

The functional importance of the Great Serpent is far beyond etiology, however. As one of the great cosmic powers, it is a source of power, for good or ill, in human life. It relates directly to the world of humans in wielding power and being willing to give it to people—especially power in hunting, love, and curing illness. That power is demonstrated, in part, in the Horned Water Serpent's ability to cause illness.

> We never kill a snake, because it is a manitou; anyway, it is not safe to kill a snake. The manitous keep watch for the slayer, and hurt him in some way, either by illness or by an accident. A sudden swelling of the arm or leg or jaw, or in any part of the body, is a sign that the manitous are getting in their baneful work. The manitous have a way of prolonging the pain and agony; they bring the person up to the threshold of death, but don't quite let him pass in. (Jones 1911:214–215)

If the serpents can cause illness, of course, then they can cure it. Radin noted that "the Thunderbird is supposed to be at eternal enmity with him, and for that reason he is regarded by most of the Winnebago as a sort of a mixed deity, partly evil and partly good, but always to be feared and capable of bestowing great blessings on man" (Radin 1923:239–240). Those blessings were sought by the daring who wished to establish a vision relationship with the Great Serpent. As the Potawatomi said, "When one appears to a man he will become a great warrior" (Skinner 1923b:47–48). Among the Sauk, "he is personified as a great serpent, and was desired as a dream guardian" (Skinner 1923a:34–36).

If the relationship could be established, the blessings were received in the form of objects. The metaphorical conception is that the Great Serpent bestows power as gifts of his own body. The three major forms the gifts take are horns, bones, and scales (which were considered manifest in the Middle World as shells or copper).

Pieces of the fabled multicolored horns are understood to be an important part of the medicine bag of healers throughout the Woodlands. There are many myths which include the detail of the sawing off or breaking off of part of the powerful horn for use in medicine, but other parts of the body will also serve. In one reference the gift is not the horn itself, but a red object which becomes in human magical practice powdered vermilion (ochre?). An Ojibwa text collected by Kohl tells of an encounter between a human and an Underwater manitou:

> "Dost thou see," the snake said, "what I wear on my head, between my horns? Take it: it will serve thee. But one of thy children must be mine in return for it."
>   The Indian saw between the horns of the water-king something red, like a fiery flower. He stretched out his trembling hand and seized it. It melted away in his finger into a powder, like the vermilion with which the Indians paint their faces. He collected it in a piece of birch bark, and the serpent then gave him further instructions. (Kohl, quoted in Smith 1995:109–110)

Radin skeptically referred to the Winnebago power objects: "The attitude of the Winnebago toward him is full of inconsistencies. He is evil, yet his 'bones' are the most prized possessions of man on account of the remarkable power with which they are endowed" (Radin 1923:239–240). Fletcher described the use of those bones: "He [her informant] says that this animal is but seldom seen— that it is only seen by medicine-men after severe fasting. He has a piece of bone, which he asserts was taken from the animal. He considers it a potent medicine, and uses it by filing a small piece in water" (Eyman 1962:234).

The Cherokees had the same medical practice, but the objects did not have to come as a gift.

> Four days afterwards the Cherokees went to the spot where the snake had been killed, and gathered fragments of bone and scales of the snake's skin. These they kept carefully, as they believed the pieces would bring them good luck in love, the chase, and war. (ten Kate 1889:55)

That seems also to have been the case among the Shawnees. One of their myths told of the slaying of the water manitou and the use of his body as a source of medicine. According to Gatschet's version:

> The snake was brought to the shore, cut up, and the assembled tribe voted as to the use to be made of the snake's body. They resolved to cut it into pieces and to give a piece to every person (to serve as talisman, physic, or

amulet), and then a name was given to the snake, calling it Msi Kinepikwa, or "great reptile." (Gatschet 1899:256–257)

Schutz concluded that the water manitou fills the role among the Shawnee of explaining the origin of certain medicine and bundles. He offered references to the shamanistic tradition associated with the killing of the Underwater Powers: "As early as 1648 the Huron received amulets from the Algonquians . . . Ragueneau said these were called onniont and were a certain kind of charm of great virtue—a sort of a serpent of almost the same shape of an armored fish which pierces everything it meets and hence was called Oky par excellence. Those who killed it or obtained a piece of it brought good fortune on themselves" (Schutz 1975:163–164).

The Northeastern legendary accounts emphasize the size of the serpent and the unusual shape of the head, but they do not say much about the crucial identifying mark of the Horned Water Serpent, the horns. Apparently the abichkam' was understood to have only a single horn, but it was important in the traditions of shamanism. "This horn has magical application and such a horn was part of the outfit of a witch (bu'owin)" (Parsons 1925:6on).

The key characteristic of the horn is its power, usually expressed in the use of pieces of it in healing and other forms of magic. These magical properties of the horns, however, are an important part of the full concept across the Woodlands. Among the Muskhogean speakers and the Cherokee of the Southeast the Horned Water Serpent had horns similar to deer antlers, but they were worth far more.

> The old Creeks sometimes got hold of the horns of this snake, and they were broken up into very minute fragments and distributed among the hunters of the Creek nation. These fragments are red and look like red sealing wax. (Swanton 1928a:494)

Among the more important gifts of Mishebeshu to Central Algonkian people of power were megis shells and copper. The shells, which were the primary symbol of the Midé Society, used by them in rituals as objects of power, were considered to be cognate with the scales of the Mishebeshu and could be found floating upon troubled waters (Howard 1965:125; Smith 1995:185, 187). It is not known whether this emic interpretation was restricted to megis shells or applied to all shell, but it may explain the importance of conch shells in the prehistoric trade networks. The broader range is likely, if the rationale is similar to that for copper, the underwater source for the substance. Mishebeshu's second gift, copper, "belongs" to Mishebeshu because it comes from beneath the water in the Great Lakes region. He is sometimes described as himself covered with copper, and especially his horns. When the French learned of the practice of scraping off some of the horns to place in a medicine pouch, they asked about it and were told that it was copper, "the horns and sometimes the entire body of Mishebeshu being covered in the metal" (Smith 1995:111).

> One often finds at the bottom of the water pieces of pure copper, of ten and twenty livres' weight. I have several times seen such pieces in the Savages' hands, and, since they are superstitious, they keep them as so many divinities, or as presents which the gods dwelling beneath the water have given them, and on which their welfare is to depend. (Allouez, in Thwaites 1896–1901, vol. 50:265)

Copper and shell are thus substances which participate in the underwater world and probably carried that basic meaning in their usage in human life. In this connection it may be significant that a great deal of the Southeastern Ceremonial Complex iconography is found on copper and shell.

One other possession or gift of the Great Serpent is surprising, and there is limited documentation for it. Jones recorded the Fox belief that fire is also under the care of the Beneath World and that even the Thunderbirds have to acquire it from their dualistic opposites.

> Our fire comes from the manitous who live in the world under the earth. They created the fire, and it is theirs. All their time they spend watching after and caring for it. The fire that people use first came from this place under the earth. Even the Thunderers, who keep watch over the people, obtain their fire from the manitous of the underworld. This is the fire one sees flashing from their mouths when they pass across the sky. (Jones 1911:214)

This concept may not have wide distribution, however, for the Southeastern peoples are generally thought to have seen a clear relationship between the Sun and fire, even to the extent of seeing fire as the earthly representative of the Above World. (See Lankford 1987:Chap. 3 for details of this belief.) Even so, the variety in the myths that explain how humans came to have fire may indicate a significant belief in the Beneath World origin of fire. In the Cherokee myth, for example, it is the water spider who brings fire from an island across the water. Further, the notion may explain how both the Thunderbirds and the Horned Water Serpent can shoot lightning, which is a form of fire.

Intimately related to this function of furnishing to humans sources of power is what may be historically the most important locus of all, the Midé Society of the Central Algonkian. In their view, the Great Serpent did not freely give these medicine powers to humans; he was highly dangerous to people and not especially sympathetic to them. There are indications that the outcome from a human attempt to gain power from the sky layers was more likely to be successful than a similar attempt to join in partnership with Mishebeshu. As Smith put it, "Mishebeshu could be courted by shamans eager to share in his great power, but such alliances with the monster carried great risks for human beings" (Smith 1995:109). Possibly because it was considered such a mark of achievement for human spirit travelers to be able to use the power of the Underwater Panther, the Midé Society claimed to harness that power to all other powers to produce a major focus of cosmic force.

In the basic Central Algonkian myth, Manabozho's brother Wolf was killed by the Underwater Panthers. That first death had two general outcomes. The majority of the local versions tell of Manabozho's revenge on the water manitouk, killing several of them through a deception at the water's edge and an impersonation of a doctor, with the Flood as the Underwater Panthers' response. A few of them, however, insert a special episode in which the manitouk effect a reconciliation with the disconsolate Manabozho by sharing their medicine powers, in effect creating the Medicine Lodge; this event is found among the Potawatomi, Sauk, Ojibwa, and Menomini.

> Thus, by pooling their supernatural knowledge, all of the gods compiled the mythology and the rituals of the Medicine Lodge. The most ancient of the gods, those underwater, provided most of the knowledge and most of the ritual forms. Wolf was released, and was the first "to go home by a road that he had never before traveled." The rites and the lore of the Midewiwin have ever since been taught and practiced, to give men the power of dealing with death. (Eyman 1962:235)

Eyman noted generally that in the western Great Lakes area, the Great Serpent/Panther "was the major subterranean deity and played central roles in the mythology of the Midewiwin, the Grand Medicine Lodge" (Eyman 1962:33), and Howard (1960:218) observed that "among the Ojibwa and Potawatomi the monster is especially venerated by the members of the Midéwiwin or Grand Medicine society." That linkage simply makes clear what was implicit in the majority versions—that the Underwater Panther is closely associated with the Midewiwin, as source of power, or even as mythic founder. Assuming different roles of importance from group to group, the Midé or similar medicine lodge was part of the life of all the Central Algonkians, as far as is known, and it is noted even for those peoples whose myths were not well collected.

The Mythic Representations

The presentation to this point has focused on the beliefs that surround this powerful figure, but those beliefs are enshrined in a permanent way in the stories that are told about it. There are at least seven different myths or mythic motifs which detail the knowledge humans possess about the Beneath World powers. Here are brief sketches of the seven plots, all of which are widely known.

THUNDERBIRDS VERSUS HORNED WATER SERPENTS

The fundamental opposition between the Above World and the Beneath World is expressed most graphically in the stories which revolve around physical conflict between the thunders (usually in bird form in these myths) and the Horned Water Serpent. As mentioned above, both can shoot lightning at the other, according to some informants, but the Horned Water Serpent can crush the Thunderbird in its coils, while the Thunderbird can seize a serpent in its talons and take it into the sky, tearing it to pieces and dropping it. In some texts a human is begged by both combatants to take sides and assist.

> Long ago, the Tetons encamped by a deep lake, whose shore was inclosed by very high cliffs. They noticed that at night, even when there was no breeze, the water in the middle of the lake was constantly roaring. When one gazed in that direction he saw a huge eye as bright as the sun, which caused him to vomit something resembling black earth moistened with water, and death soon followed. That very night the Thunderers came, and the crashing sounds were so terrible that many people fainted. The next morning the shore was covered with the bodies of all kinds of fish, some of which were larger than men, and there were also some huge serpents. The water monster which the Thunderers fought resembled a rattlesnake, but he had short legs and rusty-yellow fur. (Dorsey 1889:136)

Even terrestrial snakes are related to the Horned Water Serpent complex, and they may also attract unwanted attention from the Thunders. Thus some tribes found snakes, though sacred and not to be harmed, dangerous because of the ongoing cosmic war.

> Snakes are called Manitu'wuk, or Spirits, by the Potawatomi, as by the Sauk. They are not desired about the lodge, as lightning often strikes places

where they lurk. If seen they are offered tobacco, and driven or coaxed away with prayers for good luck. (Skinner 1923b:48)

WHALE BOAT [R245]

The curious name of this myth comes from the historical fact that Franz Boas first identified the plot in his studies of Northwestern myths, and the major water figure there is a large fish. The name has stuck, even though it does not accurately describe the Eastern mythic figure. The basic plot is simple: the hero needs to cross a body of water, so he asks the Horned Water Serpent to give him a ride. The human is prepared with food, whether corn-balls, dead birds, or pieces of his own flesh, and he feeds the Horned Water Serpent at intervals to keep it moving across the water. He barely makes the shore and leaps off, when (in many versions) thunder from the sky strikes and kills the helpful serpent. In both a Koasati and a Natchez version of the "whale boat" episode, the hero takes advantage of the journey to saw off one of the horns, reflecting the belief in the medicine power of that substance (Swanton 1929:Koasati #13, Natchez #9. There is another Koasati text of the same story, and the Alabamas have a variant: Koasati #12, Alabama #12). The myth is of fairly widespread distribution, being found among both eastern (Naskapi, Micmac, Malecite, and Passamaquoddy) and western (Kickapoo, Ojibwa) Algonkian peoples, as well as the Huron, Arikara, and Dakota. (See Thompson 1956:n.179. Thompson's list is not exhaustive, for the Mandan/Hidatsa and the Chitimacha ought to be added, as well as the Koasati, Alabama, and Natchez texts mentioned [Bowers 1950; Beckwith 1938; Swanton 1907]).

HORNED WATER SERPENT KILLED FROM WITHIN [K952]

A similar episode tells of the swallowing of the hero after a great many other people have been swallowed. He finds many dead, but some still alive. He retains a weapon of some type, in some cases only a flint chip, with which he is able to slice and destroy the serpent's internal organs. When the heart is cut apart, the serpent dies, and the hero is able to cut a hole in its side, through which the survivors escape.

Even more than the preceding myth, this episode has extremely widespread distribution. Although the nature of the monster changes from group to group, the plot is found from the Eskimo throughout North America. In the Eastern Woodlands and Plains, the monster is usually the Horned Water Serpent, and the episode is found among the Siouans, Caddoans, and Central Algonkian, with marginal representation among the Southwestern Hopi and Navaho and the Southeastern Cherokee (Thompson 1956:Note 159).

JOURNEY TO THE UNDERWATER LODGE

Since the Horned Water Serpent is a powerful creature who grants power to humans, legends of the shamanistic journey are to be expected, and the myth collections do not disappoint. Whether a society practiced a universal vision quest or simply reserved the quest for the few courageous religious specialists, they would want to have a model for the encounter between the human and the Horned Water Serpent. Such tales are found throughout the Woodlands, usually posing just as a simple legend of a man's peculiar adventure. A Micmac text included a transformation, and the evaluation of the experience was apparently negative, so the power was not universally acclaimed.

> A man went to a Tcipitckaam lodge underwater and began to change into one. A medicineman brought him back: "With a wooden knife the medicineman cut off the creature's head, and removed the entire body of the man . . . If he had stayed there another day, it would not have been possible for him to come back." (Wallis and Wallis 1955:346)

Others, however, did not see the transference of power negatively, and the myth serves as a charter for shamans who would use power from the Horned Water Serpent. The plot tells of the journey of a young man to the underwater lodge of the water serpents, where he is befriended. After he passes some tests of courage and strength of will, he is granted power and taught the appropriate lore before being sent back to his people. In the Southeast the legend is found among the Creeks, the Hitchiti, the Alabama, and the Cherokees, and in fragmentary form among the Biloxi (Swanton 1929:Creek #28, Hitchiti #18, Alabama #29; Mooney 1900:#73, 83, 85, 87; Dorsey and Swanton 1930:#18).

KILLING OF THE HORNED WATER SERPENT

A variant of the journey to the lodge is the myth of the attraction of the powerful serpents to the shore by human shamans, where the monster is killed and its body broken up for use in medicine. The result is the same as before, but the monster comes to the humans rather than the reverse. This myth is particularly characteristic of the Shawnee, where it was told as the origin of witchcraft. The story begins with the Turtle's taking of some warriors into the water by means of their magically sticking to his shell; because they have been killed, the shamans of the tribe call forth the various water monsters, until finally the culprit comes forth. He is killed and fragments of his body become the source of witchcraft medicine (Schutz 1975; truncated versions of the myth appear also among the Cheyenne, Dakota, and other Plains tribes; see Dorsey 1889:136; Gatschet 1899:68–69, and Kroeber 1900:184).

That outcome, however, is probably best understood as a historical reflection of a negative attitude toward shamanism in general, for the same story is more frequently told to explain the origin of Horned Water Serpent medicine, regardless of the purposes for which it was used. Here is an outline of the same plot among the Creeks.

> The ancient Creek Indians believed in a miraculous horned snake, which at times appeared at the surface of water-holes, and whose horns, used as a war-physic, were prized higher than any other fetish within their knowledge. When the snake was seen in a blue hole filled with deep water, the old men of the tribe sang their incantations, which brought the snake to the surface. They sang again, and it emerged a little from the moving waves. When they sang for the third time, it came ashore and showed its horns, and they sawed one off; again they sang, and it emerged for the fourth time, when they sawed off the other horn. Fragments of the horns were carried along in the warriors' shot pouches on their expeditions, and the song lines of the horned-snake referred to all the manipulations connected with the capture of the snake's horns or tchito yabi. (Gatschet 1899:259)

A slightly different version was found among the Yuchi, where it appears to be a major cosmological myth. It begins with the primeval water of the Earth Diver tale, but it includes an episode of the killing of a water-serpent—even decapitation does not destroy him, until the head is placed on top of a cedar tree: "The cedar was alive, but covered with blood, which had trickled down from the head. Thus the Great Medicine was found" (Swanton 1929:Creek #90).

SNAKE-PARAMOUR

A classic way of portraying the close relationship of humans and powerful others is to tell of a marriage (or mating) between a human (usually a woman) and a member of the other species. The Horned Water Serpent tradition is no different, and there are widespread versions of the basic concept. In some the marriage is broken up and the woman restored to the people, and in others the marriage is stronger and the people are punished for trying to oppose it. (See Thompson 1956:Notes 228, 235, 228a, 231, and 262 for a sample of the possibilities.) As noted above, this myth is also found as the story of the marriage of a woman with an Underwater Panther in the Southeast. The Muskogee used both snake-man and water-panther-husband myths as introductions to the legend of the Coosa flood; in this case they appear to function as allomotifs (motifs which can be substituted for each other). Similar texts, but with the serpent form as the primary image of the water husband, are found among the Iroquois, Menomini, Zuni, Hopi, Tunica, and Caddo (see Wycoco-Moore 1951: Number 571 for references).

MAN WHO BECAME A SNAKE
Another very widely known myth is the story of two men who disagree on the wisdom of eating some unusual food. The one who ate it undergoes a transformation into a water serpent, and he becomes a protector of the tribe from his position as a guardian of a pool which magically expands into a lake. The myth is known in several variants throughout the Plains and Eastern Woodlands. Even the Micmac of the far Northeast have a variant of it, for a boy (identified as Gluskap in one text) gets a horn rooted on his head, and he is freed from it only after his sister undergoes several adventures (Parsons 1925:62).

The basic myth of the snake-man, however, is strongest in the Southeast, where ten texts were collected from the Creeks alone. The same story is found even in Central America, and the myth is best understood as yet another account of how close relationships between humans and the Horned Water Serpent came about. (For a more extensive discussion of the distribution and variations in this myth, see Lankford 1987:Chap. 4.)

The Celestial Great Serpent

Mooney recorded several Cherokee myths about the Uktena, the horned serpent whose jewel in the head provided powerful medicine for anyone who was able to get a piece of it (Mooney 1900:252–254, 297–300, 458–461; see Hudson 1978). The Uktena was described in a way that made its connection with the Great Serpent very likely, but it was also consistently located on the earth. There is a single reference which indicates otherwise, however. In the Cherokee version of the Orpheus myth, "the Uktena grew angrier all the time and very dangerous, so that if he even looked at a man, that man's family would die. After a long time the people held a council and decided that he was too dangerous to be with them, so they sent him up to Galun'lati [the sky], and he is there now" (Mooney 1900:253). The Great Serpent is, surprisingly, connected in some way with the celestial world.

This surmise is supported by a curious Chickasaw note: "Another big snake was called *nickin-fitcik* ('eye-star') because it had a single eye in the middle of its forehead. If anything passed in front of its lair the snake would catch it, but

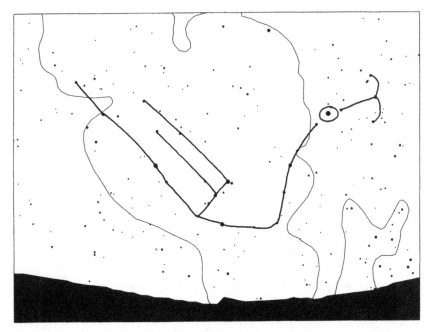

FIGURE 5.5. Scorpio lies across the Milky Way in the southern sky. Voyager II skymap. The constellation is a speculative drawing; the oval is Antares.

none have been seen in the western country" (Swanton 1928c:252). That this snake is cognate to the Uktena with its jewel seems clear, but why is it named "eye-star"? The simple answer, albeit speculative, is that it enshrines an understanding that is no longer current among the Chickasaw, that there is a Great Serpent in the sky with a bright "eye."

The Great Serpent is associated with the sky for a very strong naturalistic reason—there is an important serpentine constellation which is located in the southern sky. Known in the European tradition as Scorpio, it is so far south that in North America it can only be seen in the summer months, when it rises in the night sky just a little above the horizon in the south. The stars comprising the constellation make a clear serpentine shape, and the constellation stretches across the southern end of the Milky Way. The Serpent also presides over the southern point at which the path of the sun and planets (the ecliptic) crosses the Milky Way, an inherently important location.

Further, Scorpio has an important star in it, the bright red star Antares, located in the approximate position of the head of the creature (Fig. 5.5). The Chickasaw "eye-star" may be a reference to Antares, and the Uktena's jewel may be the same. It is significant that one of the characteristics of the Great Serpent is that it bears upon its head "something red" which becomes an important ritual ingredient in Algonkian life (see Kohl quotation above). If a connection can be made between the Underwater manitou and the celestial figure of the southern sky, then the red object may be seen as cognate with Antares.

There is yet another explanatory dimension of the celestial meaning of the Great Serpent. There is a seasonal aspect to the presence of Scorpio in the sky, as already noted. The Great Serpent (Scorpio) disappears for the winter. This natural phenomenon helps explain the widespread taboo on the telling of myths about the Underwater powers during the summer. The emic explanation that is usually given is that the master of the serpents can overhear any disrespect during those months and will communicate his displeasure to the powers who are close at hand to the erring humans, with dangerous results. A century ago scholars were intrigued by the taboo; they were able to point it out, but were unable to offer an explanation. Chamberlain gathered the data:

> With not a few primitive peoples there exists a taboo of tale-telling in sum-mer. The Ojibwa and certain other Algonkian tribes of the Great Lakes (JAF 4 (1891), p. 195) give as a reason for not telling the "tales of the fathers" in summer, that "frogs and other disagreeable things would enter into the camp" . . . Concerning the Winnebago Indians, Mrs. F. D. Bergen (JAF 9 (1896), 54) observes: — "The old people do not like to tell their stories after the spring opens. The children are told that they would see snakes if they should listen to tales during warm weather." Among the Omaha Indians . . . there is "a superstition which prevents the telling stories in the summer season, as the snakes may hear and do mischief." (Miss Fletcher — JAF 1, p. 120)
>
> Rev. J. Owen Dorsey (JAF 2 (1889):190) tells us: "Myths must not be told during the day, nor in summer, as violation of this rule will cause snakes to come." (Chamberlain 1900)

A century later the taboo still exists among the Ojibwa, and Smith has offered a slightly different explanation, which, however, is not mutually exclu-sive: "Since to speak someone's name was to conjure that person, one had to be very careful not to invite an unwanted presence. While this proscription has been relaxed on Manitoulin, consultants often declined to mention Mishebeshu by name during our summer talks. They most often referred to him as 'that monster,' 'the big snake' " (Smith 1995:52).

Provocative as these notes are, it is evidence from the Pawnee which com-pletes the picture and connects the traditional taboos firmly with the annual appearance of the Great Serpent in the southern sky. For them, also, the Serpent provided an explanation for a widespread taboo on the telling of certain myths during the summer. As Dorsey explained,

> [Coyote] tales are not told during the summer months, for it is supposed that the tutelary god or star of the snake is in direct communication with the star of Coyote, for during these months the Coyote Star is early visible in the eastern horizon, and, not liking to be talked about, directs the Snake-Star to tell the snakes of those who talked about him that they may bite them. (Dorsey 1904a:xxii–xxiii; cf. Weltfish 1977:277–278; Chamberlain 1900; Lankford 1987:49–50)

This ethnographic note from the Pawnee seems to clarify the puzzle. When the Great Serpent ("Snake Star") is in the sky, it is dangerous to run the risk of offending the powers by telling their stories, because the Serpent will send the snakes to punish them. Is it cognate, though? Does this Pawnee belief reflect the same astronomical or mythological complex related to the Great Serpent as has been presented above for the Eastern Woodlands? The Caddoan-speaking Pawnee, especially the Skidi, are generally recognized as the most astronomically oriented people north of Mexico. Their mythology is characterized by clear astronomical references, and their fundamental set of myths and rituals is focused on the conflict and joining of Morning and Evening Star. This sets them apart from the other peoples whose myths of the Great Serpent have been examined thus far. For those groups, their astronomical interests are encoded in their myths in a few obvious ways, with additional subtle references, some of them probably not yet discovered. The Pawnee, however, tend to be blatant in their concern for the celestial world and its relations to the world of humans, although specific identification of stars is far from simple or conclusive.

The most thorough analysis of the ethnographic information about Pawnee ethnoastronomy has been done by Chamberlain, who has ventured an identification of most of the stars and constellations mentioned in the material (Chamberlain 1982). The location of the Serpent is not in question, being universally agreed upon by all informants and interpreters—it is Scorpio. "One of the stars that can be seen to approach her [Evening Star] in this way is Antares, and this star has been identified as the head of the serpent in Skidi constellation lore" (Chamberlain 1982:82). Fletcher had little doubt:

> Fletcher (n.d.) quoted Running Scout and said that "the old man told me to look to the southeast and see a bright star. This is the head of the snake

which is coming up; the snake has many little stars for its body." In her published paper Fletcher (1903:15) added that the body of the Snake lies close to the horizon . . . The Skidi Snake outline probably began with Theta Scorpii at the end of the tail and Antares at the head." (Chamberlain 1982:132)

The location of the Serpent, and therefore Antares, thus seems clear, even though Chamberlain, persuaded by the redness of Antares, also speculated that it was also the red world-quarter star of the southeast (Chamberlain 1982:101). The Pawnee identification, together with their sharing of the seasonal taboo, makes it clear that the celestial appearance of the Great Serpent in the southern sky was a widespread belief. Further, the identification of Scorpio and Antares as the Serpent and his red eye points to a significant ethnoastronomical belief complex which cut across tribal and linguistic lines.

The Great Serpent in Iconography
In the light of this lengthy survey of the lore concerning the figure of the Great Serpent, it is possible to return to the graphic representation of that figure in the Southeastern Ceremonial Complex. Frequently found on pottery (especially at Moundville) as an independent motif, the snake is usually characterized by elaborate or conventionalized wings and horns. The horns, of course, identify the serpent, which often has rattles, as not just a rattlesnake, but the Horned Serpent, and probably the Underwater Serpent in particular.

The wings or feathers attached to the serpent have for decades raised the discussion of Southeastern relationships with Mesoamerica, since the feathered serpent inevitably recalls Quetzalcoatl. In the light of the identification of Scorpio as the celestial form of the Great Serpent, however, it seems reasonable to see those wings/feathers as simply a locative sign, an indication of a specific location in which the Great Serpent is to be encountered—in the sky. When the Underwater Serpent rises from the water world, he does not rise far—just above the southern horizon in the summer, but during that period the Master of the Underwater Powers has enormous power over the earth in general, because he is present in the visible sky. Conceptually, the appearance of the Great Serpent in the sky is of great importance, because it constitutes a change in cosmological levels, from the Beneath World to the Above World. This special mode is iconographically suggested by the wings or feathers, and they give the Great Serpent (Scorpio) with its red jewel or eye (Antares) an iconographic place-indicator, not a change in form. The identification of the wings or feathers as locatives thus

FIGURE 5.6. One of many similar winged serpents found on Moundville, AL, ceramics (Moore 1907:372).

suggests that the subject of the portrayal is not a "feathered serpent," which inevitably points to Mesoamerica, but is the well-known northern Great Serpent in its celestial manifestation. Further, the curiously unnatural curved form of the iconographic snake, especially as seen at Moundville, may be another clue that it is the constellation Scorpio which is the basic image for this serpent, for it resembles the shape of the constellation itself (Fig. 5.6).

These clues open two other archaeoastronomical possibilities which might be considered by archaeologists, for they may be sculptural forms of the Great Serpent. In Ohio, the Adams County Serpent Mound, which has recently been re-dated to late prehistoric times (see Fletcher et al. 1996), appears to be another iconic form of the Great Serpent. Both the curved shape and the peculiar "eye" seem to suggest that identification. Speculations about the strange form at the head have included food being devoured by the serpent and the Cosmic Egg. If the identification of the earthwork is the Great Serpent under discussion, then the oval shape would be readily seen as the red crystal/eye/Antares, and the peculiar globular forms at the base of the head are likely the remnants of some feather locative, which may well have had a more distinctive shape when the sculpture was new (Fig. 5.7).

In Rice County, Kansas, in contrast to the Ohio raised-earth serpent there is an intaglio version (Fig. 5.8). Thought to have been created by the ancestral Wichita, the serpent is cut some ten inches deep into a hilltop; its shape was discernible only by filling the excision with lime. When made visible from above, however, the form seems familiar. The archaeologists who investigated the earthwork were unsure about an interpretation, but in the light of the ar-

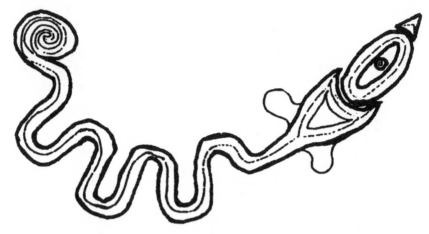

FIGURE 5.7. Map of Serpent Mound, Adams County, OH (adapted from Fletcher et al. 1996).

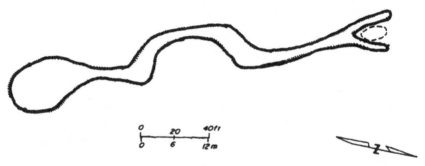

FIGURE 5.8. A serpentine figure carved into a hillside in Rice County, KS (adapted from Mallam n.d.).

gument of this chapter, the widely known Great Serpent seems a fruitful suggestion for exploration (Mallam n.d.).

Conclusion

To the eyes of an outsider, the many references to water panthers, horned water serpents, and feathered snakes appear to point to a multiplicity of imaginative figures. When the evidence is brought together, however, it becomes clear that a single well-known figure is the reference. The fact that people of different ritual organization, different languages, different social and economic structure, all appear to have known the Great Serpent, by whatever name, argues for a widespread religious pattern more powerful than the tendency toward cultural diversity. The evidence suggests further that there was a common ethnoastronomy, at least in regard to the Great Serpent, and a common mythology which referred to that fundamental Power known to everyone in eastern North America until recent times. Such a multicultural reality hints provocatively at more common knowledge which lay behind the façade of cultural diversity united by international trade networks. One likely possibility of a conceptual realm in which that common knowledge became focused is mortuary belief. In Chapter 8, which will explore the symbolism surrounding death, the Great Serpent will reappear as a major figure in the realm of the dead.

6. Identification of a Moth/Butterfly Supernatural in Mississippian Art

Vernon James Knight and Judith A. Franke

Here we shall attempt an iconographic demonstration of the existence of a previously unrecognized supernatural in Mississippian art. The primary natural prototype of this supernatural is, we believe, a moth or butterfly. Further, we will build a case that this curious lepidopteran supernatural has a specifiable relationship to the much more widespread subject in these art systems known as "Birdman" (Strong 1989).

While our point of entry into the corpus is to some degree arbitrary, we choose to begin, and end, our presentation with images from Moundville in west-central Alabama. Midway, we will range to the east and north to discuss images from the Wilbanks and Dallas phases, which skirt the margins of the southern Appalachians. Our strategy of choosing Moundville as our starting point gives us an excuse to make an initial observation that will have some bearing on our thesis later on. As follows: in Moundville art, the figure of Birdman is conspicuously absent, despite its prominence at every other major center of Mississippian figural art, including Spiro, Cahokia, Etowah, and Lake Jackson. For the moment, we must leave that observation hanging and move on to the putative insects.

We begin with the imagery engraved on a paint palette of gray shale from Moundville, currently in the Peabody Museum at Harvard (Fig. 6.1). Although the artifact seems to have no name enshrined in the literature, it surely deserves one, and so we will call it the Willoughby disk in honor of the fact that the original line drawing, published by Clarence Moore (1905:134), was made by Charles C. Willoughby. Stone paint palettes are a reasonably abundant form of elite material culture at Moundville, but this is one of only a handful that carry figural art. Central to the composition is a twisting column decorated with skulls, dividing the remaining surface into two fields. On the right-hand side is some rather familiar subject matter, but the left-hand side, to which we now draw special attention, has generated very little commentary. At first glance, one

FIGURE 6.1. The Willoughby disk, Moundville site, AL. Drawn from a rubbing by Barbara Page (Phillips and Brown 1978:FIGURE 208).

gets the impression of an incomprehensible jumble of elements, which Phillips and Brown (1978:143) have compared to "skillful doodling." But despite this impression they also assume, rightly in our opinion, "that the incomprehensible configuration on the left was just as meaningful to the artist as the rest of the design, possibly essential to an understanding of the whole."

Phillips and Brown call attention to this figure as an exemplar of a category of art they call *phantasmagoria*, a term which they apply to unique, unintelligible, surrealistic designs which nonetheless are executed with assurance. Such a category, which Phillips and Brown refer to as an "intensely personal" impulse of the artist, is, no doubt, appropriate to some of the more bizarre compositions on Spiro shell cups. However, in the case before us, it is our position that this "skillful doodle" is neither unique nor incomprehensible, and is merely a conventionalized version of a design found elsewhere in the Mississippian world.

FIGURE 6.2. Shell gorget from Mound C, Etowah site, GA.

Before proceeding to its homologs, we need to point out that the line drawing before us is incomplete. Surface spalling of the original artifact, the limits of which show clearly in the photograph published by Moore (1905:133), has obliterated a critical portion of the leftmost margin, taking with it the portion of the design next to the concentric circle and dot just below the serrated, fan-like element. Although a careful examination of the original by one of us (VJK) failed to reveal any traces of the missing part of the design, based on what is yet to come we will show in a moment what belongs there.

Departing Moundville, our next exhibit is from Wilbanks phase Etowah, where we cross genres into the medium of engraved shell gorgets (Fig. 6.2). Here is one of several well-known gorgets showing a Birdman in left profile, grasping a chert sword in one hand and a complex form in the other that many have long recognized is at least partly zoomorphic. Regarding the subject being grasped by the Birdman in this and several companion gorgets, Brain and Phillips (1996:45,

48) see it as a "trophy formation" consisting of three elements: first, a rayed circle, which they suggest might be a "morning star emblem of sacrifice"; second, a serpentine zoomorphic figure with a forked tail; and third, a folded bit of decorated fabric. In contrast, it is our contention that all three elements are to be viewed as together comprising a coherent zoomorph, here being seemingly victimized by the Birdman figure. Moreover, despite the difference in style and medium, we think it is the same subject shown on the left-hand register of the Willoughby disk from Moundville.

This identity is best shown by disassociating these forms from their parent compositions and reorienting both to a horizontal axis (Fig. 6.3). By doing so it is easier to envision the figures as zoomorphic, and to note that they have in common a segmented body, differentiated by dorsal and ventral patterning and ending in a forked tail; a head area reduced to a large eye represented by a dotted circle; a short truncated form emanating from the eye area; a rayed spiral anterior to the eye and projected forward and downward; and finally, overlapping, fan-like wings connected to the thorax and decorated with a circle-and-dot border. This comparison allows us also to say with some confidence that the damaged section of the Willoughby disk formerly carried the outline of a second wing, partially hidden behind the complete posterior wing.

In the less abstract version from Etowah we recognize a natural prototype in a butterfly or moth. The rayed spiral is, in our opinion, an exaggerated proboscis. This "feathered" proboscis is, perhaps, visually conflated with the rayed spiral motifs which are particularly common at Moundville, and which, in turn, David Phelps (1970:98) believed were derived in the Mesoamerican manner from a cross-section of a marine shell as a symbol of underworld powers (cf. Brain and Phillips 1996:380). In the upturned, truncated projections from the large eyes, we see antennae; in the fan-like, dotted wings we see an anatomically correct depiction of butterfly wings when folded up, in which the posterior wing overlaps and partially obscures the anterior one. According to a colleague, Illinois State Museum entomologist Everett D. Cashatt, the exaggerated forked abdomen tells us that the insect is a male. A similar Etowah specimen, moreover, appears to have realistic insect legs (Brain and Phillips 1996:45, Ga-Brt-E12). Since it is also our belief that the elite figural art of these two major Mississippian centers, Etowah and Moundville, focuses on the supernatural, otherworldly, and archetypal as opposed to the factual or historical (Knight, Brown, and Lankford 2001), we conclude that this is not an ordinary butterfly or moth but a prominent supernatural.

This trail leads further. It has long been known that the shell gorgets bearing this design are part of a larger series executed in a clearly definable style,

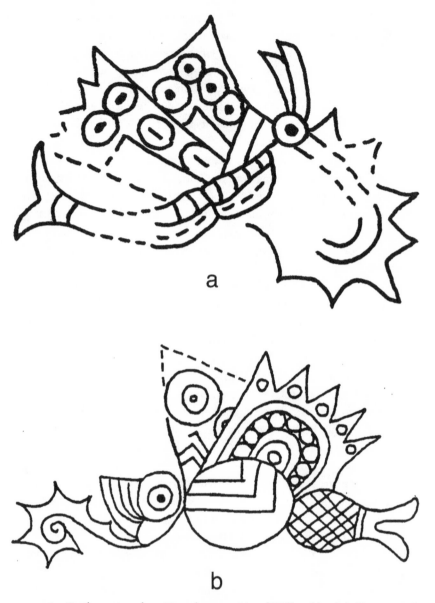

FIGURE 6.3. Configurations from Etowah gorget (a) and Willoughby disk (b) compared.

called Hightower by Jon Muller (1989:20), distributed primarily in Dallas phase and related contexts in the eastern Tennessee River Valley and in Wilbanks phase Etowah, with outliers of the style found in the Central Mississippi and Upper Arkansas River valleys. In their recent compendium Brain and Phillips (1996:44–50) list twenty-eight known examples. Importantly, this style of gorget repeats several conventional themes, or presentations of subject matter, besides that shown in the Etowah gorget already discussed. Armed with a new perspective on what it is that the Etowah Birdman is dispatching with his chert sword, it is possible to venture the opinion that the iconography of the Hightower style, taken as a whole, is intelligible as a series of interrelated vignettes, and that the combative relationship between the Birdman and the butterfly supernatural is a key to that set of iconographic meanings.

Let us briefly consider other Hightower style gorget subjects. First, it is instructive to witness that other kinds of subject matter may substitute for the figure we identify as a butterfly supernatural in a combative relationship with a sword-wielding Birdman. One illustration of this substitution is the gorget from the Hixon site, Tennessee, showing *two* Birdmen locked in symmetrical combat (Fig. 6.4). Our interest in this substitution lies in the fact that, iconographically, it suggests an intriguing *equivalence* at some level between butterfly supernatural and Birdman. Brain and Phillips (1996:45–50) list three other Hightower style gorgets, from Etowah and the Dallas phase Fains Island Mound, showing this particular composition.

What sense can we make of this substitutability between butterfly supernatural and Birdman? A possible answer lies in the iconography of a third series of Hightower style gorgets, illustrated by an example from Etowah (Fig. 6.5). Here, in a seated position, is a Birdman, readily recognizable by his talons substituting for hands, but departing significantly from the former examples in other details. Foremost among these is the nature of the wings. Instead of bird wings shown in the conventional manner as a range of feathers depending from an anterior wing bar, we now have fan-like wings, decorated with dotted circles. Since we have just identified fan-like wings bearing dotted circles as one of the identifying traits of the butterfly supernatural, this leads rather inevitably to the conclusion that we have before us a personage that is a combination of both Birdman *and* butterfly. This conclusion, we believe, is reinforced by the serpentine forms that emit from both wings and which end in scalloped, semicircular elements that bear a web-like design. The serpentine nature of the appendages is strengthened by an example of the same design from Spiro (Brain and Phillips 1996:46) on which the forms are decorated with banded zones of crosshatching. One tentative reading of this composition is that it is depicting yet

FIGURE 6.4. Shell gorget from Hixon site, TN.

another aspect of moth/butterfly, namely, emergence from a cocoon or chrysalis, and in this connection we note that the scalloped form bears a resemblance to some butterfly pupae (Fig. 6.6). Brain and Phillips list ten examples depicting this subject.

All of this depends on our ability to recognize conventionalized natural prototypes in a moderately realistic style, subject, of course, to our own biases. But if any or all of the recognition argument has merit, we have arrived at the point of offering a preliminary model of the meanings conveyed by the entire Hightower style series of shell gorgets. Thus: the gorgets taken together show us a transformation series, in which Birdman in some sense *becomes* butterfly supernatural, or vice versa. They are in complementary opposition; butterfly supernatural is the alter ego of Birdman. And even though the two supernaturals are thus, at one level, the same thing, the complementarity is also depicted as a combat; one form overcomes the other (or itself).

It hardly needs to be said that, to the intended audience, this conflict might have carried a strong metaphorical dimension. To speculate using natural phenomena, for example, a diurnal form replaces a nocturnal form as night gives way to day; alternatively, from the eye of a farmer, a harmful insect is overcome by a helpful bird. But lest we be misjudged in calling up imagery invoking forces of nature in the real world, we still maintain that these elite Mississippian art systems concern *Otherworldly* powers.

Insect imagery has been infrequently recognized in Mississippian figural art. The issue of identification of our subject as a supernatural moth or butterfly leads us to consider more specific natural prototypes among the lepidoptera that might have attracted attention. In that connection, the exaggerated length of the proboscis immediately calls to mind that king of North American moths,

FIGURE 6.5. Shell gorget from Mound C, Etowah site, GA.

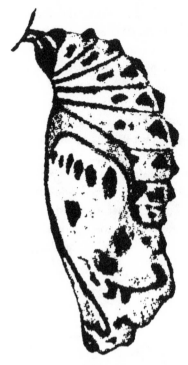

FIGURE 6.6. Pupa of the regal fritillary butterfly. From an illustration by Marjorie B. Statham (Klots 1951:Pl. 6). Copyright © 1951, 1979 by Alexander Klots. Reprinted by permission of Houghton Mifflin. All rights reserved.

the sphinx moth, which, in a surprising convergence, is also known as the "hawk moth" due to its swift, darting habits of flight (Lutz 1948:147). The *Sphingidae* are also known as hummingbird moths, because of their strong resemblance to hummingbirds as they hover over flowers while their enormous proboscides are uncoiled and put to good effect (Holland 1968:11). As is shown here (Fig. 6.7), the sphinx moth is known among entomologists as a premier pollinator of tobacco (Davidson 1965:770–775), a plant of some importance, we must suppose, in Mississippian ritual practice. The fact that the larvae of sphinx moths are the tobacco hornworm and the tomato hornworm certainly adds to the proposed connection. These hornworms feed on the leafy vegetation of plants in the family *Solonaceae* (e.g., potato, tobacco, tomato), and the tobacco hornworm in particular is noted for its ability to ingest, without harm to itself, alkaloids from such narcotic plants such as datura, which are poisonous to other insects. In yet another convergence, our colleague Andrew Fortier (personal communication) has noticed that the white abdominal markings on each segment of the tomato hornworm (Fig. 6.8) faithfully duplicate the "forked eye surround," an SECC motif otherwise commonly associated with the Birdman figure. This caterpillar, in short, with its ability to metamorphose into a winged form and its association with both tobacco and datura, offers itself as a consummate image of shamanic practice.

We are forced to add, however, that the lepidopteran image we have identified in the art is *not* a depiction of a sphinx moth, nor for that matter, any other moth, in any straightforward way. The wings alone tell us that; in profile view they are folded upward rather than spread outward, and this resting position is the distinctive characteristic of butterflies as contrasted to moths. We need not be too concerned; we reiterate our belief that the image is that of a *supernatural*, and most other supernaturals in the art systems in question are manifestly portrayed as composites drawing from a variety of natural prototypes. One of our workshop group, having shown the design to an entomologist, was told that the dotted wing pattern is reminiscent of that of a buckeye butterfly (Fig. 6.9) (Patricia O'Brien, personal communication).

Having come this far, we ask, are there also caterpillar images in the corpus

FIGURE 6.7. Sphinx moth pollinating tobacco at night. Photo courtesy National Geographic Society.

FIGURE 6.8. Tomato hornworm larva (Mitchell and Zim 1987).

FIGURE 6.9. Buckeye butterfly. Photo by Michael Jeffords, courtesy Illinois State Museum.

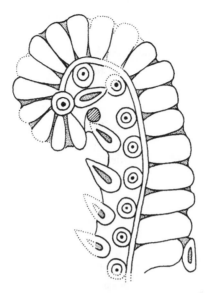

FIGURE 6.10. Engraved plaque of marine shell, Great Mortuary, Craig Mound, Spiro site, OK (Phillips and Brown 1984:Pl. 145).

of Mississippian art? We suspect that the answer is yes, and apropos of this question we offer into evidence one of two similar engraved shell plaques from Spiro (Fig. 6.10) (Phillips and Brown 1984:145). These plaques show what might well be identified as the legs and abdominal respiratory pores of caterpillars; moreover, at least in the orientation shown here, they rear back in that characteristic posture that gives the sphinx moth its name.

As we move on to consider ethnographic analogs that might assist in our search for meaning in these images, we find the Southeast to be rather deficient in moth, butterfly, or caterpillar lore. What does exist, however, is of much interest. Mooney (1898:254–255, 438n) records a Cherokee myth about the origin of tobacco, in which a large red-brown moth, *wasulû*, "which flies about the tobacco flower in the evening," was sent to retrieve tobacco for humanity because it could fly quietly and not be noticed. Other informants substituted a hummingbird in place of the moth, a fact which virtually ensures the identity of *wasulû* as a sphinx moth. One version of the myth, provocatively, has a human conjurer setting out to retrieve the tobacco and transforming himself into the hummingbird character to get past the guardians of tobacco.

For more, we have to go much farther afield, to Iroquoian speakers of the Great Lakes region and to Dhegiha Siouan and Caddoan speakers of the Plains. We admit that any potential relevance of this lore is diminished by geographical and cultural distance, but the payoff lies, perhaps, in sensitizing us to ways in which moths, butterflies, and caterpillars can be imagined as supernaturals in Native American belief. Among the Huron, the Jesuit Fr. LeJeune (Thwaites 1897, vol. 10:195) recorded a belief in 1636 that caterpillars are responsible for drought. In this function caterpillars are opposed by the Thunderers who bring rain. Among the Pawnee, Murie (1989:281–283) records a myth about a young warrior who stumbles onto the lodge of supernatural butterfly men in a hole in the earth. The leader of the butterfly people cures the young man and sends him on his way with war medicine, made partly from yellow butterfly wings. Our interest in this tale is heightened by its obvious parallel to the Thunder Helper myths in the Southeast, in which prowess in war is conferred on a novice by the supernatural Thunderers (Lankford 1987:79–80). Among the Osage, La Flesche (1925:47–50, 1930:665–668) recorded war rites invoking the Great Butterfly, one of several "mystic avengers" of the air who act as all-seeing guardian spirits and dispensers of punishments to initiates who violate their vows. According to Bailey's summary (1995:209), "these avengers are associated with the rain and thunder and travel amidst the winds that rush in advance of the approaching storms. They are spoken of as possessing a power of discernment from which no harmful act can be concealed." If it is permissible for us to generalize from this tiny sample, we thus find a tendency for the insect imagery to be connected, on the one hand, with supernatural thunders, and on the other, with the spiritual attainment of prowess in warfare.

Now let us come full circle again to the imagery from Moundville, where we began with the following puzzle: Why is the Birdman theme absent at Moundville? We now see that one of the most striking ritual images in elite Moundville art, that of the Willoughby disk, prominently depicts a supernatural based on a moth or butterfly. We believe, moreover, that the Willoughby disk is not an import to the site; the style of depiction of skulls, hands, and bi-lobed arrow appears to be compatible with the local corpus. If so, although the Birdman is not to be seen at Moundville, its alter ego, as revealed by the iconography of the Hightower style gorgets, does make an appearance. May we now conclude that the moth/butterfly zoomorph was a major supernatural at Moundville? Not so easily; the composition on the Willoughby disk is absolutely unique.

However, let us now consider the design on a white-on-red painted bottle from one of the final mantle burials in Moundville's Mound C (Fig. 6.11). This is one of three known bottles from the site bearing the same design (the other two are red and black-on-white negative painted). Steponaitis (1983:348) classifies all three as Nashville Negative Painted, with the implication that they are imports. With this assessment we disagree. Technologically identical negative-

FIGURE 6.11. Red-on-white painted bottle, Mound C, Moundville site, AL (Moore 1905:FIGURE 15).

painted vessels are present in the Moundville collections which bear designs that are virtually signature traits of elite Moundville iconography, and the same kind of negative painting occurs on terraced rectangular bowl forms that are certainly local products. The design before us consists of broad, pendant semi-circular elements with dotted decoration and a fringed border. These elements alternate with pendant, rayed spirals. The whole design, we suggest, is a *pars pro toto* representation of the moth supernatural, in which only the two most

FIGURE 6.12. The Douglass gorget, New Madrid County, MO (Phillips and Brown
1978:FIGURE 230).

distinctive traits, the dotted, fan-like wings and the feathered proboscis, were
deemed sufficient to indicate the whole.

Among the numerous whole vessels bearing figural art in the Moundville
corpus, none show our lepidopteran subject. However, a recent study of engraved sherds in this genre (Knight 1995:7) turned up two sherds which appear
to depict portions of the distinctive dotted and rayed wing of our butterfly supernatural, executed in a style reminiscent of the posterior wing of the Willoughby
disk zoomorph.

Our objectives in this chapter are modest ones. We have argued for the existence of a previously unrecognized moth or butterfly supernatural that was
known in Wilbanks and Dallas elite culture, and which seems to have occupied a place of prominence at Moundville. Also, by approaching the imagery

of Hightower style shell gorgets as an iconographically intelligible set, we have concluded that the series taken together transfigures Birdman into its antithesis, the butterfly supernatural. But our brief study also raises new questions which will have to await further analysis. For example, in introducing our model we certainly do not claim to have fully broken the code locked up in the fascinating Hightower gorget set. Doubtless there are additional ethnographically collected myths and beliefs that will shed light on our problem. And finally, as we have hinted by introducing the Spiroan caterpillars, there are probably related images elsewhere in Mississippian elite art that await recognition. We wonder, for example, if the elongated down-curled snout of one of the Classic Etowah style copper Birdman figures from the Lake Jackson site in Florida (Jones 1982:31) and the similar nose on the personage depicted in shell on the Douglass gorget from Missouri (Phillips and Brown 1978:177) are not to be seen as proboscides (Fig. 6.12), and therefore emblematic of lepidopteran elements in these figures. But now we wander too far afield, and thus abandon such possibilities to future pursuits.

7. Ritual, Medicine, and the War Trophy Iconographic Theme in the Mississippian Southeast

David H. Dye

Before they go to War, they have many preparatory
ceremonies of purification and fasting.

—JAMES ADAIR, 1775

Introduction

The symbolic representation of distinctive human trophies plays a prominent role in Mississippian art. As a class of SECC icons they include skulls,
fleshed heads, hands, and forearms, sometimes associated with weapon
forms such as sociotechnic war clubs, typically found on ceramics.

Trophy motifs are most commonly depicted on ceramic vessels from the Central Mississippi Valley and at Moundville. Much of this artistic activity on ceramic media is restricted to the Late Braden style of the fourteenth and perhaps
early fifteenth century, but originates with earlier iconic portrayals of trophy-
taking behavior found engraved on marine shell cups and copper repoussé plates
of the thirteenth century.

Clear archaeological evidence of trophy-taking behavior can be documented
some 5,500 to 6,000 years ago in the Mid-South (Mensforth 2001, 2004; Smith
1997). Actual war trophies, including skulls and forearms, appear in mortuary
and village midden contexts. In addition, actual human trophies and their symbolic counterparts become increasingly associated with elite behavior and the
chiefly cult institution in Mississippian times, serving to further cement elite
political ideology with warfare. The symbolic representation of war trophies
became widespread as Mississippian elites associated success in warfare with a
materialized ideology that places emphasis on mythic narratives of the triumph
of life over death.

Eyewitness accounts of trophy-taking behavior are well documented after
European contact (Axtell and Sturtevant 1980; Bridges, Jacobi, and Powell
2000:36; Owsley and Berryman 1975). Southeastern ethnographic/ethnohis-

toric documentation emphasizes the role of war trophies in revenge, public display, success in warfare, supplication to supernaturals, and perhaps replication of cosmic events, as well as war honors and badges of merit. They were often the necessary requirements for initiation and advancement in warrior societies. Finally, war trophies could be used in mortuary rituals associated with the journey to the afterworld.

War trophy representational art on ceramics appears to have been distinct from iconic three-dimensional arts, functioning as transformational devices for the preparation of sacred medicines. If this hypothesis is true, then it should provide some degree of predictive results. Such testing might include chemical residues of sacred medicines, the correlation of these ceramics with "warrior" burials, and signs that the icons should be read as "severed," including crenellated or serrated heads or hands suggesting stylization of dismemberment representation. While the former two "tests" have yet to be carried out, the latter finds support in the iconography of Braden and Craig imagery from Spiro (Fig. 7.1). For example, severed heads are marked iconographically by serrated human necks (Phillips and Brown 1984:X), and scalloped lines drawn from the nose to the lower ear region perhaps mimic the agnathous human head (Brown and Dye 2007; Brown and Kelly 2000; Phillips and Brown 1978:72).

Mississippian Combat and Ritual Purity

During the early eighteenth century several individuals spent considerable time in residence with the Southeastern Indians. The English trader James Adair, who lived among the Chickasaw, and the Dutch colonist Le Page du Pratz, who owned a plantation in the Natchez polity, both learned Native languages, observed firsthand Southeastern rituals, and understood the dynamics of Native American warfare. Their observations, and the eyewitness accounts of others, provide important insights into the nature of warfare rituals and the iconography of groups who either were, or had recently been, vibrant Mississippian polities.

Undoubtedly, changes took place throughout the intervening centuries between the Middle Mississippian period of the Southeastern Ceremonial Complex and the documentary record of the early Colonial period, but the basic structure, orientation, and objective of war-related rituals may have remained essentially the same as a result of the widespread and commonly shared belief that maintenance of purity and balance was essential for warriors in their quest for spiritual power, supernatural aid, and success in the pursuit of trophies.

The objectives of Southeastern warfare rituals almost certainly centered upon several goals: the reduction of anxiety, the enhancement of group solidarity, the

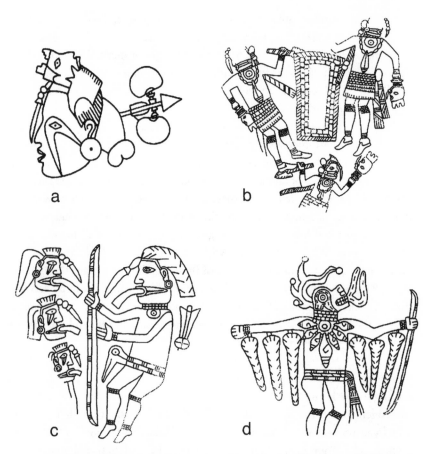

FIGURE 7.1. Imagery from Spiro: (a) warrior with trophy head headdress (Phillips and
Brown 1978:Pl. 17); (b) dancers with trophy heads (Phillips and Brown 1984:Pl. 153);
(c) dancer with trophy heads (Phillips and Brown 1984:Pl. 286.1); (d) dancer with scalps
(Phillips and Brown 1984:Pl. 305).

attainment of purity, the appeal to supernatural powers, the display of supernatural combat, and the re-creation of the cosmos through dramatic ceremonies,
especially those scenes that emphasized or chartered combative and trophy-
taking behavior. According to the Southeastern Native belief system, the desired psychological and emotional states derived from ritual, especially balance,
purity, and harmony, could be achieved only by adherence to socially prescribed
rules and prohibitions (Hudson 1975, 1976), coupled with the consumption and
application of emetic potions or medicines (Williams 1930 [1775]). The necessity for achieving a state of purity and balance may have been so basic to the

achievement of success in warfare that it did not change substantially or fundamentally from the Mississippian through Colonial periods.

As early as the sixteenth century, European observers began documenting the Southeastern "Indians'" concern with achieving ritual purity and balance through the consumption of medicines in preparation for combat. The use of emetic medicines was especially critical when important decisions had to be made, and in rituals preceding and following dangerous or hazardous activities such as warfare.

To ensure success in the uncertain and unpredictable business of combat, the behavior of warriors had to be carefully regulated through the maintenance and control of proper rituals aimed at establishing purity and invoking the assistance of supernatural forces, thus improving or increasing the odds of achieving success in combat. In the case of a war party's failure, the fault or blame typically rested on the warriors' conformity to ritual practice and rules, not with the supernatural forces (Abler and Logan 1988:1; Malinowski 1954). Therefore, the degree and exactness of ritual compliance was imperative for purity, supernatural favor, and, consequently, success in combat.

Two primary warfare-related medicines were consumed in the Southeast: the black drink made from yaupon holly (*Ilex vomitoria*) and the war medicine made from button snakeroot (*Eryngium yuccifolium*). These were prepared and consumed as critical components of rituals whenever hazardous activities, especially warfare, were undertaken. In fact, success in combat was directly related to the strictness with which these rituals were observed (Hudson 1976:244).

Warfare-related rituals which stressed purity, the quest for supernatural aid, and the preparation and use of medicines may have been rooted in the rise of chiefdoms. Emerging chiefly organizations generally are characterized by religious war cults in which the interests of the "war gods" are identified with those of the chief (Reyna 1994:44). Conceptions of purity and pollution appear to have become prominent components of war-related rituals by the twelfth century, if not earlier, in the Midwest and Southeast, based on changes in the nature of warfare and on the predominance of Above World and Beneath World motifs on shell cups and ceramic vessels. Some Mississippian representational motifs associated with combat and death include arrows, maces, human heads, scalplocks, and forearm bones engraved on shell cups and engraved, painted, and incised on ceramic bowls, bottles, plates, and beakers. Nonrepresentational motifs that designate the Above World, Middle World, and Below World include varying combinations of terraces, trilobates, swastikas, rayed circles, crosses in circles, concentric circles, and sun circles, to name a few (Emerson 1997:212–

223; Hilgeman 1985, 2000; Chapter 2 this volume; Pauketat and Emerson 1991; Phillips and Brown 1978, 1984).

The concepts of purity and pollution are as much interdependent and complementary to one another as they are opposed to one another (Churchill 1996:582–584). Both the Above or Celestial World and the watery Below or Beneath Worlds are equally essential sources of sacred power. For example, abominable and anomalous Below World creatures, known variously as Uktenas, Piasas, Underwater Panthers, Horned Underwater Serpents, and the Great Serpent, were dangerous but useful sources of sacred objects, aid, and knowledge. The Above World, likewise, was inhabited by Thunderers and celestial supernaturals, including Morning Star, Red Horn, Storms as He Walks, an Eagle, Old Woman Who Never Dies, a Dog, and Old Man. These supernaturals could confront travelers along the Path of Souls, and oftentimes had to be fought in mortal combat. The resulting violent confrontations often ended with a "war trophy" being taken through the use of sacred weapons or supernatural aid. Both the Above World and the Below World were the locations of powerful forces, inhabited by supernaturals sought after by religious visionaries and warrior priests for much-needed sacred power and aid. Warriors and war priests alike sought supernatural aid and power from the denizens of both worlds, but ran the risk of pollution in the dangerous search. Only those of pure mind and body could survive the quest (see Chapter 8, this volume).

Mississippian Warfare Rituals
Details of Mississippian warfare rituals are sketchy at best, but the broad similarities evident over much of Eastern North America argue for widespread sharing and the probability of considerable time depth. Documentary evidence suggests a basic pattern in the sequence and structure of war rituals, including pre-battle and post-battle ceremonies.

War rituals were also associated with alliance formation or conflict resolution. In negotiations for alliances and resolution of hostilities, diplomatic emissaries smoked, feasted one another, and drank the black drink to remain pure. They danced with raptor-tail fans and sang (Williams 1930:158–169 [1775]; Dye 1995; Swanton 1928d).

The basis for Mississippian warfare rituals in part lies in their apotropaic function: they provided aid in overcoming the repugnance of killing as well as reducing fear, guilt, and anxiety, while reinforcing the solidarity of the warrior group by dramatizing status structure (Kennedy 1971; van der Dennen 1998:175) and supernatural charters and sanctions. In many societies, "Fasting, sexual abstinence, and separation were common, as were ritual responsibilities, such as sacrifices for vows given. Often the returning warrior was considered sacredly polluted and had to undergo additional purification rituals" (van der Dennen 1998:176). Turney-High notes, "There has existed a dread of taking enemy life, a feeling that if the life of a member of the we-group was precious, so was that of a member of the other-group. Fear of death–contamination has demanded expiation or purification among many folk" (1949:225). Warriors, because of their destructive powers, were especially prone to pollution. Immediately before a battle and after returning from battle, Southeastern warriors were separated from the members of their community because of their pollution (Hudson 1976:320–321).

Southeastern pre-battle rituals began with the priestly sanctification of a large, cleared space outside the town. The sacred space symbolically separated the participants from the general populace. Participants included the members of the war expedition: scouts, various warrior grades, war priests, doctors, and the war chief and his assistant(s). The Chickasaw, for example, placed their sacred ark, a portable war shrine or Great Medicine Bundle, in the middle of the clearing and a senior warrior began a lengthy oration, presumably to require oaths of fealty, allegiance, and loyalty and to invoke supernatural powers. During the day a strict fast was observed (Williams 1930 [1775]). The Natchez pre-war ritual involved smoking the war pipe and consuming symbolic foods at a feast. Dog, for example, was eaten to symbolize and encourage a warrior's fidelity, obedience, and attachment to the sacred war chief. The participant's physical actions were also symbolic. While attending the feast, each person walked continuously "to signify that a warrior ought to be always in action and on his guard" (Tregle 1975:372).

After the war feast, the war medicine, prepared from button snakeroot, was consumed and ritual cleansing through vomiting commenced. They then struck the sacred war post, recited their military deeds, and began the war dance in front of the ancestor shrine. This cycle of fasting, feasting, smoking, medicine consumption, vomiting, striking the war post, and dancing continued for three additional days and nights. The war chief's house was ritually cleansed out of fear of pollution by the residing women who were of childbearing (menstruating) age. Accordingly, sexual abstinence was strictly enforced to avoid the polluting effects of women.

Once preparations for combat were finalized, and the prescribed rituals completed, the state of purity achieved in the pre-war rituals was continued throughout the campaign against the enemy. Purity and balance was attained by taking the sacred portable shrine (Great Medicine Bundle) which contained Underwater Panther's horns and bones, cedar sprigs, button snakeroot, live coals from the war fire, a crystal, and consecrated earthen vessels into enemy territory on the back of the sacred war chief or his assistant. Warriors swore loyalty oaths to their leaders, who continued delivering encouraging speeches, and howled like dogs to express their loyalty, fidelity, and obedience to the war chiefs (Hudson 1988). Black drink was sprinkled or sprayed on the warriors. Immediately prior to encountering the enemy they painted themselves red and black to symbolize death and destruction (Hudson 1976:244). At this point they would have been at an elevated emotional and psychological state of purity, but it would have to be carefully maintained to sustain the desired level.

Upon returning from an engagement with the enemy, the war chief's house was ritually cleansed again out of fear of possible pollution and all utensils were removed from the house. The warriors brought into the town any prisoners and war trophies taken during the campaign.

With faces painted red and black, the warriors covered their heads with swan down and affixed tufts of long white feathers to the crown of their heads. Singing their death songs, the warriors walked around the war pole. They continued purifying themselves for three days and nights in a hot house where they applied warm lotions and aspersions of button snakeroot. They drank the war medicine and black drink to avoid the polluting effects of the killings and dismemberments, as well as their associations with enemy prisoners. The warriors were commended by the war leaders for their observance of purity during the raid and were bestowed with war honors, names, titles, and advancement in rank (Hudson 1976:326). At the conclusion of the post-war rituals they bathed and returned to their daily routines.

Warfare rituals changed through time, but the basic ritual structure may have remained essentially the same from late prehistory into the Colonial period. Based on the above description, warfare rituals would have included the creation of sacred space; elite involvement and sponsorship of rituals, especially feasting; use of sacred paraphernalia and props such as horns and feathers of supernaturals, plants, crystals, pipes, paints, and consecrated vessels; emphasis on symbolism in food, behavior, and color; consumption of medicines, including the black drink and the war medicine, for ritual cleansing and purification; acquisition, display, and ritual manipulation of war trophies; and ritual performance, including dancing with raptor tails or wings.

The War Medicine

Adair states, "Before the Indians go to War, they have many preparatory ceremonies of purification and fasting" (Williams 1930 [1775]:158). These ceremonies of purification centered on cleansing through ritual emesis or vomiting.

The most frequently used herbal emetic for warfare in the Southeast was button snakeroot, which has diuretic, expectorant, and diaphoretic properties, and is an emetic when taken in large doses (Hudson 1975:94; Taylor 1940:45–46). Throughout Eastern North America there was a strong belief that success in war was dependent on the potency of the war medicine. Violation of social prohibitions, especially rules of fasting and sexual abstinence, invited disaster for the war party.

The roots of button snakeroot, steeped in warm water prior to consumption and then drunk in large doses, were the most frequently used Southeastern herbal, employed only for religious purposes (Williams 1930:159 [1775]). In addition to drinking the bitter medicine, war leaders applied it to their warriors by sprinkling their bodies in the pre-battle and post-battle rituals and during the campaigns. Adair states that after a fatiguing day's march, and a scanty allowance of water, the warriors were obliged to drink plentiful amounts of water embittered with button snakeroot (Williams 1930:161 [1775]). In the hot houses after a campaign it was applied both as a lotion and as an aspersion.

The Natchez employed the war medicine prior to the war feast. The medicine, prepared from roots, presumably from button snakeroot, was boiled in large kettles. Each warrior drank two pots of the medicine and immediately vomited. After finishing the war feast, the warriors drank the black drink. The Choctaw in the early eighteenth century are said to have fasted as part of the war ritual and to have made "libations of the juice of herbs which the medicine-man gives them, and with which they rub themselves, which has the virtue of giving them strength and courage" (Swanton 1931:162). Cherokee priests rubbed war medicines into cuts made from bone awls to bring the medicine into direct contact with the blood, the better to absorb the medicine. To underscore the supernatural importance of the ritual, they marked off a small space which was consecrated prior to scratching (Hudson 1976:415; Mooney 1891:334). Adair notes that the Southeastern Indians were:

> strict observers of the law of purification, and think it so essential in obtaining health and success at war, as not to allow the best beloved trader that ever lived among them, even to enter the beloved ground, appropriated to the religious duty of being sanctified for war; much less to associate with the camp in the woods, though he went (as I have known it to happen) on the same war design; they oblige him to walk and encamp separate by himself, as an impure animal, till the leader hath purified him, according to their usual time and method, with the consecrated things of the ark. (Williams 1930:159–160 [1775])

The consecrated articles in the ark, or portable shrine, mentioned by Adair included herbs and pottery vessels. As we have seen above, ritual purification, achieved in part through the use of medicines, was an integral component of all phases of rituals related to warfare during the historic period. In order to brew and consume these medicines a variety of cooking, holding, and serving vessels were needed. Adair, in speaking of the sacred ark taken into battle, notes that it "contains several consecrated vessels, made by beloved superannuated women, and of . . . various antiquated forms" (Williams 1930:169 [1775]). The ark, and presumably the objects in it, was considered so sacred and dangerous that no one, including the enemy, dared touch it on any account. Only the war leader as war priest and his attendant were sufficiently purified and sanctified; they alone could handle and transport the sacred ark. The "holy ark" or portable shrine contained not only the necessary consecrated vessels for making the medicine, but also the herbs, including button snakeroot, yaupon holly, and other plants, necessary for brewing the war medicine. These vessels were curated from earlier times and had been made by elder, beloved women. The sacred ark also housed what appear to have been medicine bundles that held various supernatural animal parts that embodied specific powers. It is unknown how the war medicine was brewed during campaigns in the absence of large cooking jars, but because the vessels were carried in the ark they would have been relatively small (about a liter or so) and this may suggest that they were the critical ritual devices for transforming the liquids from profane to sacred, the liquids having been brewed in other containers (Dye 1997).

Chiefly Warfare

Throughout much of the Mississippian world, representations of trophy symbolism abound. The pursuit and acquisition of war trophies through scalping, decapitation, and dismemberment can be traced to the Late Archaic in the Mid-South (Mensforth 2001; Smith 1997). The extent to which Mississippian societies elaborated an already ancient tradition of trophy taking is largely unknown, but based on the incidence of skeletal trauma it had been an important element in intersocietal conflict for some time. In the Mississippian period, physical evidence of war trophies includes scalping, decapitation, and dismemberment of hands, forearms, feet, and legs (Milner 1995).

Trophies played an important role in warfare rituals with their real and figurative display in public forums. For warriors the acquisition of trophies was an important pursuit. On one level they provided positive proof of success in warfare, and on another they allowed opportunities for social mobility. Without demonstrations of success in warfare, Mississippian males would have been at a disadvantage in gaining prestige and status in a competitive social world. War trophies, however, endangered the acquirer by the polluting effects of killing and dismemberment. Through war rituals the warrior was cleansed and protected from this pollution through the acts which lead to purification.

The SECC iconographic corpus may reflect a deep concern with the acquisition of trophies and perhaps the resulting purification and cleansing required as a result of the polluting effects of their acquisition and the intimate association with the dead person's spirit which would remain with the trophy.

The War Trophy Theme

Representational motifs of human trophies collectively may be termed *war trophy symbols*. The depiction of war trophy motifs on shell cups and ceramic bottles, while not common, is found along a wide band of the Southeast stretching from eastern Oklahoma across the Mississippi Valley to western Georgia. This iconographic theme of war trophies is an important component of the SECC and serves to underline the significant role ceramic vessels and shell cups played in Southeastern rituals associated with combat and death and the central focus of the trophies themselves for supernatural appeals for gifts, knowledge, and power.

The SECC trophy theme is outlined in the work of Knight (1995), Lacefield (1995:42–43), and Gillies (1998:56–62), based on their work with Moundville engraved ceramics. They identify eleven specific themes in Moundville engraved ceramic art in the Hemphill style (Figs. 7.2–7.6). Of these, the trophy theme is the second most prevalent theme, judging from their sample of motifs (Lacefield 1995:37).

The components of the trophy theme include the scalplock on a hoop, human skull, forearm bones, and hand-and-eye motifs, occurring in various combinations. Serrated or dismembered human heads and heads and tails also belong to the trophy theme (Gillies 1998:34, 96; Knight 1995:5). The vessel form at Moundville that exhibits this theme is the subglobular bottle using the body register for the area of decoration (Gillies 1998:74).

Knight (1995:5) notes that:

The validity of the trophy theme is not readily apparent until one examines vessels as compositions, particularly those vessels showing the hand, forearm bone, skull, and scalp motifs. One finds on certain vessels a pairing of hands and forearm bones, on others, hands and skulls, and on still others,

FIGURE 7.2. Moundville vessel—bottle with hands.

hands and scalps, and so on. In other words these associations together
allow the definition of a cluster of motifs, which appear to have in common
a potential reference to trophies of combat.

In the Central Mississippi Valley ceramic vessels, primarily bottles, are mod-
eled as body parts, especially heads, feet, and legs, and painted, engraved, incised, and appliquéd with representational motifs depicting scalplocks, human
heads, skulls, forearm bones, and hands and eyes similar to those found at
Moundville, with some variations in design, combination sets, and execution
(Fundaburk and Foreman 1957, Hathcock 1983, 1988; Holmes 1903; Morse and
Morse 1998; Phillips 1939; Phillips, Ford, and Griffin 1951; Westbrook 1982)
(Figs. 7.7–7.13). These motifs were shared by, and had mutually understood con-
ventional meanings among, a number of polities in the Central Mississippi Val-

FIGURE 7.3. Moundville bowl with hands and forearms on rim—Hemphill engraved.

FIGURE 7.4. Moundville bowl with hands and forearms—Hemphill engraved.

FIGURE 7.5. Moundville bottle with heads and forearm bones—Hemphill engraved.

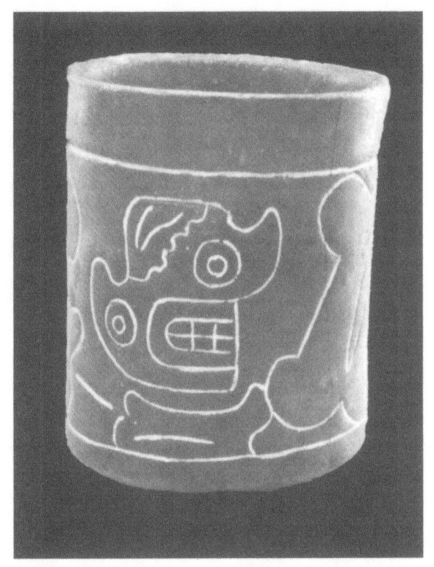

FIGURE 7.6. Moundville beaker with heads and forearms—Hemphill engraved.

ley. Unlike the case at Moundville, maces, scrolls, terraces, and arrowsnakes are often found in combination with the trophy theme in the Central Mississippi Valley (Dye 1998; Morse and Morse 1983, 1998; O'Brien 1994). Also unlike Moundville, trophy motifs sometimes occur on vessel necks and bases.

A third area which exhibits the war trophy theme is Spiro. Here motifs are expressed on shell cups (Duffield 1964; Phillips and Brown 1978, 1984) and share

FIGURE 7.7. Bottle with hands, heads, and forearms. De Soto Co., MS (CMVI).

some features with the Central Mississippi Valley and Moundville, including human heads, skulls, hands and eyes, forearm bones, dismembered birds, and scalplocks.

The general similarity between Walls and Moundville engraved motifs on ceramics of similar form argues for some equivalence of temporal overlap during the period between about A.D. 1300 and 1450. However, the Spiro shell cups predate the ceramic vessels by at least a century or more (Brown 1996) and the motifs appear ultimately to have been derived from the Mississippi Valley in the Cahokia area (Brown and Kelly 2000).

Discussion

Mississippian politics were in large measure driven by a combination of division caused by internal factionalism and cohesion engendered by external warfare. Internal factionalism combined with external warfare provided one of several avenues for leaders to gain and exercise control over a following; warfare rituals were important political mechanisms for elites. The need for leaders to maintain

FIGURE 7.8. Bottle with hands and forearms. Bradley site, Crittenden Co., AR (CMV2).

FIGURE 7.9. Bottle with human heads and broken maces. Young site, Crittenden Co., AR (CMV3).

FIGURE 7.10. Drawing from bottle with human heads and broken maces. Young site, Crittenden Co., AR (CMV3b) (Phillips and Brown 1978:FIGURE 263, redrawn from Roberts 1969).

FIGURE 7.11. Bottle with long bones. Mississippi County, AR (CMV4).

FIGURE 7.12. Bottle with human faces. Belle Meade site, Crittenden Co., AR (CMV5).

some degree of control over their access to finances and wealth aided them in keeping and maintaining their pool of faithful supporters, and was enhanced by opportunities provided through warfare rituals. Likewise, the need to establish and maintain sovereignty in the face of external threats also created opportunities for control.

While kinship played an important role in an individual's status, this status was subject to negotiation throughout the individual's life within the political contexts of particular events. Warfare provides the occasion for those events through the pursuit of clear, but temporary, military status distinctions. This hierarchical structure was based in part on the successful acquisition and public

FIGURE 7.13. Bottle with hand on neck. Twist site, Cross Co., AR (CMV6).

display of war trophies. Warfare rituals, as elite-sponsored and -supplied events, created or reinforced horizontal as well as vertical social and political relationships among warrior elites and the various warrior grades. They also helped generate loyalties and consensus among individuals. At public events involving feasting, purification, and fasting, a dynamic political arena was created (Dietler 1996; Hayden 1996; VanDerwarker 1999). Southeastern warriors competed and negotiated for social standing based on their record of success in trophy taking in the context of such feasts. The acquisition, display, and manipulation of war trophies, therefore, was an important means for social and political survival.

Although feasting provided opportunities for individuals to advance their social status, it was warfare and its attendant rituals that provided one of the most important occasions for ritual feasting. Warfare, perhaps more than any other ritual, enabled male participants to negotiate their political and social status based on rewards and honors in part resulting from trophy taking. Perhaps for this reason, rituals associated with warfare may have been perpetuated from prehistory well into the eighteenth century as warfare among Native groups and with European powers embroiled virtually all polities throughout Eastern North America.

Central to this social and political process was the use of ceramics encoded with representational motifs to transform war medicines from profane to sacred. As portable icons of public display manipulated in ritual contexts, sacred ceramic vessels were ideal signifiers of individual social position, ritual authority, and warrior rank, effectively carrying the message beyond death when placed in mortuary contexts. The strong evidence of vessel wear in the form of extensive basal abrasion and lip chippage confirms that these vessels were extensively used in the preparation, transformation, and consumption of war medicines in ritual contexts.

Ceramic vessels displaying trophy motifs exhibit coded information that could be communicated directly to a large audience. Some vessels contain trophy motifs on the base, which could be seen only during the act of pouring or drinking. These ceramic vessels effectively materialize the social position of the owner at low production cost, yet their ownership and use could be carefully restricted, protected, and guarded through elite enforced sumptuary rules. Such objects would facilitate symbolic communication among individuals within social segments or between polities, and readily provide information about group membership and social position. Socially restricted, ceramic vessels bearing war trophy motifs could be deliberately controlled through strategic production and distribution among the ranks of elites. At the Upper Nodena site in eastern Arkansas, for example, six of seven recovered bottles bearing skull motifs were found in mortuary mound contexts, and all seven examples represent individuals who were ranked higher than the average person in the Nodena population. Several burials within the mound also contained what appear to be trophy skulls, suggesting they were individuals who possessed war honors and military rank (Fisher-Carroll 1997).

As an additional layer of meaning, the motifs of the war trophy theme certainly allude to the mythic Land of the Dead or the Path of Souls where mortal combat by the living, the deceased, and the supernaturals was played out. Native traditions throughout much of the eastern Plains and Woodlands describe combat in the Above World by visionary priests and the dead, and between mythical heroes and supernatural beings (Knight, Brown, and Lankford 2001; Chapter 8, this volume). The journey along the path of souls was fraught with dangerous deities and perilous adventures involving combat with sacred or magical weapons. Decapitation and dismemberment are regular motifs in these adventures of mortals and supernaturals. Mythic events portraying the exploits of supernatural warrior-heroes and preternatural spirit-beings may have been an important component of war rituals as the ritual re-creation of the cosmos and the reenactment of mortal combat generally chartered trophy-taking behavior among Eastern North American cultures. The consumption of sacred medicines would have imbued warriors, both in life and in death, with the purity necessary for supernatural aid and power in combat in This World and the Other World.

Summary
In summary, the war trophy iconographic theme in the Southeast embodies combat-related images engraved, painted, and appliquéd on ceramic vessels and shell cups: scalplocks, fleshed heads, forearm bones, and severed hands. Given motif context and possible association with warfare, the Mississippian war trophy theme, and the vessels upon which the motifs occur, appear to have served as a critical metaphorical and visual component of warfare rituals that focused on the preparation, transformation, and consumption of war medicines for achieving purity and seeking supernatural aid and protection through the transformative powers of Above and Below World motifs. The vessels would have acted as transformational devices in the creation of specific sacred medicines prepared from profane mixtures and transformed into sacred medicines based on design motifs encoded on the vessel. The coded motifs may have signaled the type of medicine to be manufactured in order to perform a specific action. The interment of the war trophy vessels, which had seen extensive use in the mortal world, may indicate that the production and consumption of sacred medicines in the After World was critical for the deceased elite.

Mississippian war rituals may have allowed elites to legitimize their position of authority over their subjects, to expedite their call to arms, to promote their ability to create military alliances, and to facilitate governance through various degrees of authority over specific social segments through shared symbolic communication based in part on the war trophy theme. Rituals and portable ritual paraphernalia symbolize social relations, provide a venue for elite authority, and create opportunities for ideology to be expressed in material form. Ideologies associated with specific social segments, such as ruling elites, must be materialized in order to become strategic sources of power. Thus, the shared, common experience of rituals and the resulting uniform ideology seen in special sets of ritual paraphernalia permit opportunities for elite governance through ritual. Participation in ritual events, in turn, reinforces shared ideology and the logic and meaning in key iconographic motifs, and therefore communicates a standardized message to participant and viewer alike.

Large-scale ritual events, such as those described in the eighteenth century for the Natchez and Chickasaw, provided the means of control by restricting ritual involvement to specific sets of individuals, by establishing the form and sequence of the ritual, and by requiring leadership for coordinating and mobilizing resource flows from nearby centers for financing. Through ritual, leaders could demonstrate their capacity to garner food, orchestrate their followers, and acculturate individuals through dramatic performances, especially war ceremonies, with their emphasis on altered states of consciousness, purification, torture, sacrifice, and reallocation of captives. Ownership of symbolic objects likewise provides a means of authority by regulating the public display of icons and the information they encode, thus signifying who will and who will not hold political or ritual offices and social positions. Ceramics, coded with explicit expressions of celestial mortal combat, can communicate symbolically to participants in ceremonial dramas, a standardized political, religious, and social message. Access to symbolically coded ceramic vessels may be restricted by controlling their production or distribution. Although portable symbolic objects can be traded, stolen, counterfeited, or seized, their use can be carefully controlled through established sumptuary rules that dictate ownership and use. Ceramic vessels associated with war trophy symbolism were central to rituals that involved the preparation of purifying medicines and served to charter combative and trophy-taking behavior.

Trophy imagery served as an ideological archetype associated with combat both in this world as powerful symbols of war prowess and as a trope for the renewal or regeneration of human life. In the latter case, trophy taking likely served as an inspiration for the practice of warfare and raiding in a conscious emulation of heroic combat for cosmological renewal, rather than as pictorial documentation (Brown and Dye 2007).

8. The "Path of Souls": Some Death Imagery in the Southeastern Ceremonial Complex

George E. Lankford

The multiple-mound site at Moundville, Alabama, has produced a large collection of whole ceramic vessels, many of which bear engraved designs which are part of the iconography of the Southeastern Ceremonial Complex. The Moundville appearances of the interregional distribution of SECC images are useful for analysis because they are part of a large local collection which has been well studied and can thus be quantified (Steponaitis 1983). An examination of the Moundville SECC imagery reveals five images that seem to be closely related—hand-and-eye, skull, bone, winged serpent, and raptor (Fig. 8.1).

Of the five motifs, the winged serpent and the hand-and-eye appear most frequently. In Steponaitis's catalog they are listed thirty-three and thirty-one times, respectively. The hand-and-eye motif appears to be the connector for the cluster, appearing in connection with all of the other motifs. On twenty vessels it is found alone; on seven it appears with bones; and on two it has a skull with it. The hand-and-eye motif also appears once with a raptor head and once with a winged serpent, but the raptor is alone in its other eleven showings, and the winged serpent stands alone on its other thirty-two bottles. Finally, the skull and bone appear together on three vessels. Neither the skull nor the bone ever appears alone on the ceramics at Moundville, according to Steponaitis's listing (Steponaitis 1983).

This cluster of five motifs thus is distinctive in the Moundville iconographic corpus, for it has no other associations. Each of the motifs stands alone or in association with one of the other four. They appear together, but they do not appear randomly in conjunction with the many other images of the SECC. That pattern suggests that the five images are related—hand-and-eye, skull, bones, raptor, and winged serpent belong together in a single iconographic complex.

This discrete grouping of five SECC images is the focus of this chapter. Although the evidence is complicated, the argument is simple: the artistic clus-

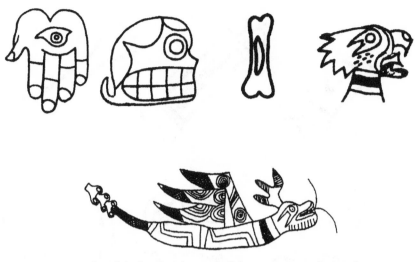

FIGURE 8.1. Examples of the hand-and-eye, skull, bone, raptor, and winged serpent as found on Moundville ceramics (Moore 1905:175, 226, 229, and Moore 1907:350).

ter illustrates a complex of beliefs regarding the death of human beings. The mortuary belief complex in question manifests variation in ethnographic details from one tribal group to another, as might be expected, but there is a unifying metaphor which argues for a common core of belief across the Eastern Woodlands and Plains, and probably far beyond that area. That unifying notion is an understanding of the Milky Way as the path on which the souls of the deceased must walk.

Demonstrating this interpretation of the iconographic cluster is a complicated problem, for it involves analyzing ethnographic notes and myth texts from a large geographical area, coupled with ethnoastronomical considerations, to produce a synthetic model of the Path of Souls belief complex. That model must then be matched with the iconographic cluster to offer plausible meanings for the images as they were used in the art of Moundville and other SECC sites. What will be offered here is a generalized model of the Path of Souls complex, with examples of the SECC iconographic images from Moundville as they might have fit into the overall mortuary belief pattern.

The Path of Souls Model

At a crucial point in the dying process, the "free-soul," the one that is self-aware and has an identifiable personality in relation to the deceased, separates from the body, leaving behind the life-soul, a mindless force which can be dangerous to the living, trapped in or near the physical remains. The free-soul remains

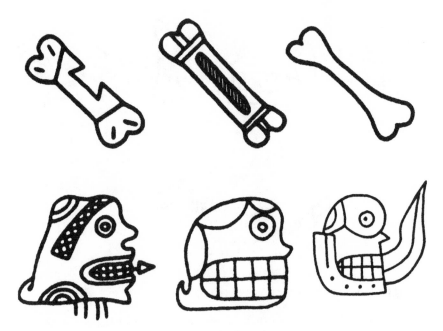

FIGURE 8.2. The dead person in iconography (Phillips and Brown 1978, and Moore 1905).

present in the vicinity for a brief time, then gathers the spirit version of various tools given to it by the living and sets off toward the west on its final journey (Fig. 8.2).

The path leads toward the west, the place of the setting sun, the end of the east-west cosmic passage, the point of the transition from day to night. The journey of the free-soul takes days, four or more. If at any time along the route the free-soul gains the power or will to return to earthly life, then it may retrace its steps and reenter its body. This happens not infrequently to the ill and the powerful who deliberately make spirit journeys—just as they are given up for dead, they awaken. During this period, the living take special care of the body, on the chance that death may not have arrived for the perhaps-deceased. If, however, the free-soul does not wish—or is not able—to return, then the soul reaches the edge of the earth-disk, the land mass which floats upon the water or upon the backs of water creatures.

There may be a camping place for the free-soul on the shore, for there may be a wait until conditions are right to continue the journey. What the free-soul must do to continue the journey to the realm of the dead is to make a terrifying leap. The realm of the dead is far to the south, and it can only be reached by

walking the Path of Souls, the Milky Way, across the night sky. To get to the
Path, however, one must leave the earth-disk and enter the celestial realm. The
portal that is appointed for the free-soul at death is to be seen on the edge of
the Path of Souls. It is a constellation in the shape of a hand, and the portal is
in its palm (Fig. 8.3).

The portal in the Hand must be entered by a leap at the optimum time, which
is a ten-minute window which occurs once each night from November 29, when
the Hand vanishes into the water in the West just at dawn, to April 25, when
the Hand sinks at dusk not to be seen again for six months. During that winter
period the portal is on the horizon for a breathless few minutes each night, and
the free-souls must enter at that time or be lost. Free-souls who do not make
the transition remain in the west and can eventually become unhappy threats
to the realm of the living.

When the free-soul has entered the celestial realm, the Path of Souls stretches
out before it. By most accounts it is a realm much like the earthly one left behind, but some describe it as a river of light with free-souls camped alongside.
The free-soul must journey down the Path to the realm of the dead in the far
south. The western entrance into the portal and the destination in the south are
not inconsistent, because the Path in the west swings to the north, thus causing
a serious directional shift. The physical change from east-west to north-south
that the Path makes clearly has symbolic value, and it may be that a shift from

FIGURE 8.3. The Hand Constellation portal in iconography (Moore 1905:134).

FIGURE 8.4. The raptor in Moundville iconography (Moore 1907:390).

east-west to north-south marks a change from a life orientation to a death orientation, and the free-soul thus makes an important psychological shift at the same time.

The journey itself is characterized by some encounters with important beings who live on the Path. While there is disagreement on the number and nature of the encounters and the beings, there is widespread agreement on two features: a bridge and a dog. The free-soul comes to a stream which cannot be forded or swum, because ghosts cannot cross water (see Hall 1976). It must be crossed over, and there is a log bridge (some say it is really a serpent) which can be induced to fall across the chasm. This task must be accomplished by the free-soul, and the bridge traversed in safety. (Some peoples think the bridge is really a way of talking about the portal and place it at that point in their account of the journey). Then, either before or after the bridge, there is a ferocious dog which must be dealt with. If the free-soul does so successfully, then the path lies open. Other beings sometimes encountered include an old man, an old woman, serpents, or a raptor (Fig. 8.4).

The goal of the journey is the Realm of the Dead, which lies at the southern end of the Path. It is protected by the Great Serpent with the red jewel in its forehead (Fig. 8.5)(Scorpio; see Chapter 5, this volume).

The Serpent can only be seen from the northern hemisphere during the summer months, but the soul on the Path can encounter it at any time. If the free-soul knows how to deal with the Serpent and is permitted to pass, then it enters the Realm of the Dead, envisioned as a perfected version of this world, where village life is always pleasant and happy. Some think that the free-souls who have made a successful journey and are happy in their new home are then available to their living descendants for counsel and power; others think the successful free-soul is then ready for rebirth, possibly *as* one of its descendants.

This is the generalized model of the understanding of the death process in eastern North America. SECC images which are thought to be illustrations of key elements in the process have been inserted in the narrative in order to make clear the argument of this chapter. As has been indicated, the support for this model is lengthy, and so only a brief summary will be offered here.

Who Used the Path of Souls?

In the scientific worldview, the galaxy within which the earth is located can be seen only by looking from our position close to the edge toward the center, and it appears as a streak of intense starlight across the night sky. From a more traditional descriptive view, that galaxy is simply the "Milky Way," a white path across the dark sky. In the worldview of many (perhaps all) of the Native Americans of North America, that distinctive feature of the night sky is identified as the "Path of Souls," and had to do with death.

That identification is virtually universal in the early ethnographic literature of North America. It is recorded from the Ojibwa, Fox, Sauk, Menomini, Miami, Delaware, Shawnee, Powhatan, Cheyenne, Huron, Iroquois, Oglala, Osage, Omaha, Quapaw, Saponi, Caddo, Pawnee, Chickasaw, and Creek, and

FIGURE 8.5. The Great Serpent (Scorpio) in the southern sky.

the designation extends at least as far south as the Andes (Sullivan 1996:58–75), as far north as Siberia (Eliade 1974:188, 248–251, 295, 466), and as far west as California (see Krupp 1995). It seems certain that this aggregation of peoples, which cuts across geographic and linguistic boundaries, is only a partial listing of Native Americans who considered the Milky Way to be the Path of Souls. The universality of this identification is not news, of course, for it has been a standard bit of ethnographic information for centuries. What may be surprising, however, is the notion advanced in this chapter—that the Path of Souls is not a poetic metaphor, but a literal understanding of the relation of humans to the sky.

The ethnographic information about the process of transformation of a living person into a dead one, sketchy though it often appears in a particular tribal collection, seems remarkably similar from one tribal group to another. When all the information is gathered together, in fact, despite the inevitable ethnic variation, there is a general agreement upon the nature of the death process across the Eastern Woodlands and Plains.

Basic to the vision of death is the concept of souls. Ake Hultkrantz did the classic study of the beliefs in souls among Native Americans (Hultkrantz 1953). He found that while some people (especially Siouan-speakers) believed in as many as four souls, two was the basic number for most of North America. Even where there was testimony in belief in four souls, he determined that the functions were still basically twofold:

> ... a person has two opposed souls, or two opposed soul systems, one representing the forces that keep the body vital and active, another representing the person himself in his extracorporeal form, as he experiences himself in dreams or as others experience him in their dreams. The former soul, the "body soul," keeps the body alive while the "free-soul" or "dream soul" makes its dream wanderings. (Hultkrantz 1992:32)

This statement neatly summarizes the native understanding: the free-soul is able to leave the body before death, as in dreams, illness, coma, insanity, or spirit travel, while the life-soul is so closely linked to the body that its absence causes death. This dual soul concept has the virtue of explaining human states, such as drunkenness or sleep, in which the mind is absent or less able to function than normally. It also provides an explanation for the recovery of people who had been ill, demented, or in a death-like coma—the free-soul had been away for some reason. Moreover, "soul loss" serves as an explanation for disease and supplies the framework for understanding the tasks and skills of the healers. The location of the two souls in the body apparently differs from group to group, but all seem united in the belief in the dual nature of the human spirit.

Mortuary ritual must therefore include at least two different tasks, taking care of the two different souls. Their fates are not considered to be the same. Referring to Jones's data on the Ojibwa, Landes observed that one soul leaves the dead body and goes to the realm of dead spirits, while the other remains with the body. The life-soul comes and goes from the grave for a time, but the key question is whether the free-soul will return. If it does not, then death has occurred. Thus the "dead" are almost never buried immediately, and most people have a ritually specified time of waiting. Jones spoke of the Ojibwa "habit of keeping the dead four days, in the hope that the soul of the spirit world would return and the person come back to life" (Landes 1968:190–191n; see Hultkrantz 1953:480).

There is an additional complexity with some peoples, in that not everyone was treated the same way after death—that is to say, their fates were not conceived to be the same. The Central Algonkian give some signs that it was true for them. Hultkrantz noted that the Ojibwa on Parry Island "are able to decide the fates of the various souls after death according to the age and occupation of the deceased and the manner in which he met his death. The ego-soul of the wicked sorcerer succumbs on its way to the realm of the dead, but his shadow-soul—the ghost, the wraith—goes on. The unburied and the too early deceased do not reach the realm of the dead, but their ego-soul, like the shadow-soul, becomes a spook-ghost on earth" (Hultkrantz 1953:478). Moreover, some peoples believe that particular individuals will be born into new bodies, thus bypassing the final realm of the dead and the Path of Souls. For every group of people, then, the question of which types of people are conceived to walk the Path of Souls and enter the realm of the dead is an important one, for there are many conceptual possibilities of how to organize the world of the dead.

Among the Central Algonkian there are three types of references to the journey of the free-soul at death. One speaks of walking the Path of Souls, which is widely understood to refer to the Milky Way, and a second indicates that souls must go to the realm of the dead in the south. The most widespread reference is a third—that the souls walk to the west, where they will meet with the first person to die, Wolf, the brother of Nanabush. The one characteristic on which all informants are agreed is that the soul takes a journey, and the journey is described in many variants within a basically uniform structure. Barnouw collected a short version of the mythic form:

Wenebojo buried his brother for four days, but forgot to come back for
him, and he died. "I will make a road for the people to travel along when
this thing [death] happens to them . . . I am leaving you our dish, and this
is what the people will do when this thing happens to them." . . . He went
toward the sunset.

As he went along, he made four signs of places. He put four manidog
along the way . . . [Otter on right-hand side, owl on left, hills (snakes) on
both sides, river with snake/log.] When it's referred to, it's spoken of as
a log, but the Indians know it's a snake. The water is swift there. The log
bobs up and down all the time. [Then the road forks: a short path, which is
bad and forever, and one which continues on] behind the sky, behind the
sunset. (Barnouw 1977:17–19)

This mythic description provides the way in which the path was originally
created, but it becomes more elaborate when it is described as a set of guide-
lines for the dead soul from the perspective of the Medicine Lodge. Information
from Ontario's Manitou Indians establishes a sequence of events: (1) a dark tunnel and (2) a race across land to (3) Our Grandmother, who directs the soul to
(4) four "Grandfathers," who warn about (5) a log bridge over a river; the soul
deals with (6) a log which blocks the path, then (7) shoots arrows toward the
realm of the dead and follows them in, where it meets (8) Shell Woman or Man
(Landes 1968:196–197).

The first step is an important one, because it defines the location of the Path,
and, unfortunately, this "tunnel" is not helpful, because it is a unique variant
and simply obscures the issue. The Fox indicated their basic agreement on the
initial movement of the soul. "Mortals go beyond the setting sun when they
die. They stay about the earthly home 4 days, and then go west along a deep,
narrow path until they come to a river which flows along with great rapidity"
(Jones 1939:16). The westward movement and the river are clear, but Jones was
not certain of the connection with the celestial path of souls. He pointed out
the importance of the Milky Way in their scheme. The "White River" is a river
of stars along which are the dwellings of the manitous, former human beings
who were spirit travelers in life and have now become manitous in the sky. That
connection seems to bring the soul's journey to the west together with the celestial path of souls. The Sauk version is similar: the soul "follows the Milky Way
(Wabise'pu, the White River), until it arrives at the river which all Sauk must
cross before entering the Afterworld, which is controlled by Ya'pata, brother of
Wi'saka" (Skinner 1923a:36).

This excursion in Central Algonkian cosmology is frustratingly imprecise, a situation that is probably caused by a combination of ethnographers' lack of gathering information and secretiveness on the part of the Medicine Lodge, a powerful religious force in the life of all of these peoples for centuries. The importance of the latter in the death process is indicated by several comments. It is the Medicine Society that makes the journey possible for the dead, for Landes spoke of the soul's "dangerous path to its final haven, one beset by evils insurmountable *without midé aid*" (Landes 1968:189–190). Hoffman, too, suggested a crucial role: "There is another body among the Ojibwa termed the Ghost society . . . [which initiates a substitute into the Midewiwin, then celebrates] a feast of the dead, designed to release his 'shadow' and to permit it to depart to the land of mysteries, or the place of the setting sun" (Hoffman 1896:67–68). There seems to be a general belief that the soul is provided with a guide (Smith 1995:58), and the Medicine Lodge is probably the source of that guidance. The Lodge's major role in this process suggests that there are reasons for the general lack of knowledge about the details of the route and the spiritual methods of making the journey successful.

These clues, sparse though they may be, at least permit the conclusion that the Central Algonkian saw the process of dying as including a journey of the soul from the body to the west, where the soul waits until the proper time for departure from the Middle World to the Milky Way, a journey along that path (among manitous) to a river which must be crossed to pass into the realm of the dead. The neighboring Miamis believed in a Path of Souls which included the log bridge and a dog, while the Shawnee understanding included the four-day wait, a rising and falling sky which could crush the unwary, the Milky Way path, a fork in the path, the log bridge across the river, and four dogs which attack souls on the bridge (Kinietz 1938:52–53; Schutz 1975:95–97).

Thus the Path of Souls journey seems to be a general understanding among the various groups of the Central Algonkian. An interesting check on this material is the ethnographic information from the Delaware, or the Lenape, who were originally from the Atlantic Coast. Their importance is suggested by the fact that other Algonkian-speaking peoples considered them the oldest tribe of them all. The ethnographic data from the Lenape generally support the model and suggest that the traditional image of the Path of Souls is ancient, rather than just a recent development among the Central Algonkian peoples. As has been seen to be the case among other Algonkian, there are also two different explanations of the outcome of the journey: "Sun and everything else goes toward the west, even the dead when they die, [and] the Land of the Spirits lies in the

Southwest, in the country of good hunting." But "once the [free soul] had departed from the body, it traveled along the Milky Way and eventually joined the Creator in the twelfth heaven" (Kraft 1986:189, 192). Even though the "twelfth heaven" is a new specification, the journey is apparently much the same, for there are several references to the bridge and the dogs which guard it, and even a mention of the fork in the Path.

On the northeastern side of the Central Algonkian cluster, the Iroquois Six Nations and the Huron appear to fit into the same Path of Souls pattern. Since their cosmogonic myths have different beginnings, in that the Iroquoians tell of the Woman Who Fell through the Hole in the Sky to the water world, where her daughter gave birth to the Twins who then created the earth by means of the Earth-Diver and various creative exploits, the Iroquoian group might be expected to have a different view of the fate of the dead, but it seems remarkably close to the Algonkian understanding. Accounts from 1610 on make it clear that the Huron believed in the Milky Way as the Path of Souls, despite the journey to the west, and their vision of the path was characterized by the standard Algonkian motifs of the Brain-Taker, the river, the log bridge, and the dog (Thwaites 1896–1901:vol. 1, 263, 287, 289; vol. 10, 147). It seems clear that the Huron, who are otherwise different from their neighbors, both Algonkian and Iroquoian, in their emphasis on the Feast of the Dead (Tooker 1964:134n), participated in the standard Path of Souls model.

The Iroquois nations, proper, apparently believed much the same. A nineteenth-century report indicated the basic model, which included a gulf and a "great dog" which had to be crossed on a "small pole" (Beauchamp 1976 [1922]:158–159). Tooker confirms that this image of the Path is celestial, both for the Huron and the Iroquois, pointing out that the Iroquois believe both that the journey to the village of the dead is to the west and that "the souls travel along the Milky Way to the land of the dead" (Tooker 1964:140).

The cosmological ideas of the Siouan-speaking peoples do not contradict Algonkian cosmology, and the myths and a few of the stated beliefs suggest that the Siouans are aware of the traditions of the Algonkian and that they share them in different degrees from group to group. Despite some differences between Algonkian and Siouan cosmological visions, the Oglala understanding of the journey of the soul is similar to that of the Algonkian peoples. Black Elk explained that the souls of "bad people" wander about on earth, but that others ascend to Wakan Tanka (Brown 1953:11). The ritual symbol of this journey is a tripod, which indicates that the above world and the south are the destination of the soul (Brown 1953:17n). Other details confirm the similarity to the general model:

It is held by the Sioux that the released soul travels southward along the "Spirit Path" (the Milky Way) until it comes to a place where the way divides. Here an old woman, called *Maya owichapaha*, sits; "She who pushes them over the bank," who judges the souls; the worthy ones she allows to travel on the path which goes to the right, but the unworthy she "pushes over the bank," to the left. Those who go to the right attain union with Wakan-Tanka, but the ones who go to the left must remain in a conditional state until they become sufficiently purified. (Brown 1953:29n)

The Lakota data thus show basic agreement with the general understanding of the Path of Souls—the Path is on the Milky Way, they go from north to south, where they will pass beneath the earth-disk, and they encounter an Old Woman who makes the judgment whether they are permitted to pass (Powers 1975:52–53, 93, 191–192).

The Omaha and Osage also participated in the general model. According to the standard ethnographic information for the Omaha,

The Milky Way was regarded as a path made by the spirits of men as they passed to the realm of the dead . . .

It was said that at the forks of the path of the dead (the Milky Way) there sat an old man wrapped in a buffalo robe, and when the spirits of the dead passed along he turned the steps of the good and peaceable people toward the short path which led directly to the abode of their relatives, but allowed the contumacious to take the long path, over which they wearily traveled. It is probable that the difference in the treatment believed to be accorded the good and the bad indicates white influence as does also the story that there is a log across a chasm over which the dead must pass; the good experience no difficulty, but the bad in crossing find the log so unstable that they sometimes fall off and are lost. The simple and ancient belief seems to have been that the Milky Way is the path of the dead. (Fletcher and La Flesche 1911:588, 590)

The Omaha were reported as identifying the four winds as psychopomps, coming to escort the soul on its journey (Hultkrantz 1953:184). The Omaha believed that communication can be achieved with the departed souls, who are thus "able to come near their kindred on the earth and to lend their assistance." Moreover, they believed in levels of the sky: "It was said that there are seven spirit worlds, each higher than the one next preceding, and that after people have lived for a time in one world they die to that world and pass on to the one next above." They did not, however, believe in reincarnation, and they denied multiple souls (Fletcher and La Flesche 1911:588–589). The Osage defined "wa-çí-da u-zhon-ge" as both "harvest path" and the Milky Way (La Flesche 1932:186). Their closely related neighbors, the Quapaw, have left only the record of their belief that "the Milky Way is called the Road of the Ghosts" (Dorsey 1895:130).

The Siouan-speaking peoples apparently experienced a major prehistoric separation, because a significant group of them were found living on the Atlantic coast at the time of contact (Swanton 1946:23–24, 30). That separation, presumably over centuries, could well have led to significant deviation in belief systems. It is therefore of great interest to find indications of the same model of beliefs about the dead existing among the eastern Siouans. William Byrd reported that an "orator" at a Saponi mortuary ritual told him of their beliefs about the journey of the soul which included the same basic elements: the Path to the south, where a power reigns over the South, the fork in the road, an Old Man who makes the judgment, the Old Woman who receives the malefactors, and ultimate reincarnation (Swanton 1946:750, 752).

The Winnebago, from their unusual position as Chiwere Siouan speakers living in the midst of the Central Algonkian peoples, might be expected to share in elements of the journey of the dead from both Algonkian and Siouans, and so it appears to be. Radin reported that the Winnebago testified to a fairly abstract theology centered around Earthmaker and focused on life in this world as lived by souls reincarnated many times. The recycling process is so strong that Radin noted, "In the myth of the journey of the soul to spirit land the ghost is not entirely a spirit until the old woman whom he meets brains him, thus, by destroying the seat of consciousness, depriving him of all corporeality and carnal desires. The ghost then becomes a spirit, in some cases of the same type as the true spirits" (Radin 1923:266–268).

Other than to note that the Plains Siouans formed a special group in their common belief in four souls, Hultkrantz was fairly dismissive of the Siouan deviation from the two-soul model, on the grounds that the Siouan four souls were functionally equivalent (Hultkrantz 1953:116–118). The evidence from the Mandan and Hidatsa is confusing, for there was disagreement on the fate of the soul. The dispute was over the question of a celestial location of the realm of the dead. As Bushnell noted, "Some of the inhabitants of the Mandan Villages are said not to believe all these particulars, and suppose that after death they will live in the sun or in a certain star" (Bushnell 1920:70).

Among the Hidatsa the disagreement was even more focused, because one whole village was said to believe in a celestial model different from that of their neighbors: "Awatixa village, however, thought they came from the sky (not emergence, like the other Hidatsa). 'Sometimes a person would say that he came from above when he was born and that, when he died, he would return to the land above. Then the people would say that he talked just like an Awatixa'" (Bowers 1963:127). They believed that "on death they returned to the sky," and at least some people believed in a special treatment or fate of the soul of a religious specialist: "[W]hen a prominent medicine man died, his spirit father would come to meet him and escort him to the village of his spirit people" (Bowers 1963:174). Further, in this apparent amalgamation of two different understandings of the fate of souls is a clue of a special adaptation of the Path of Souls model. According to Bowers, both the Mandan and the Hidatsa believed that the souls of children lived under hills until they were born again, when they had to take a miniature version of the journey:

Each hill was believed to be an earth lodge in which the babies lived and were cared for by an old man . . . According to native beliefs, children desiring to leave the hill and be born, must crawl across a ditch within this earth lodge on an ash pole. If they succeeded in reaching the opposite side without falling into the ditch, they would be born into the tribe soon afterward. (Bowers 1963:126)

A few final clues support the hypothesis of a special adaptation of the model. In the mythology of the Mandan and Hidatsa, there appears to be a double origin myth, an emergence/migration legend and the Sacred Arrows myth in which there were thirteen lodges in the sky. In the Grandson myth, the boy came from the sky and returned there at the end of his story, accompanied by six clans which became constellations. There thus appears to be a complicated special development in the belief system of the Village Siouans.

The Caddoan-speaking Pawnee, especially the Skidi, are generally recognized as the most astronomically oriented people north of Mexico. Their mythology is characterized by clear astronomical references, and their fundamental set of myths and rituals is focused on the conflict and joining of Morning and Evening Star. This sets them apart from the other peoples whose deathlore has been examined thus far. For those groups, their astronomical interests are encoded in their myths in a few obvious ways, with many more subtle references. The Pawnee tend to be blatant in their concern for the celestial world and its relations to the world of humans, although specific identification of stars is far from simple or conclusive.

The most thorough analysis of the ethnographic information about the Pawnee ethnoastronomy has been done by Von Del Chamberlain, who has ventured an identification of most of the stars and constellations mentioned in the material (Chamberlain 1982). Because of the extensive elaboration of astronomical lore in the Pawnee data, the question of their participation in the Path of Souls model is as complicated as it is important. The basic interpretive choice is whether to see the Pawnee ethnoastronomy as a completely different system from the general understanding in the eastern Woodlands, or whether it is a special development which embodies that general ethnoastronomy. Because there are clues which suggest the Path of Souls model, the position taken here is the latter—that the eastern Path of Souls was known to the Pawnee and was incorporated in their more elaborate astronomical vision.

As seems to be so frequently the case, there are two understandings of the Milky Way, and probably the progress of the soul after death, as well.

> The Milky Way is called by the Pawnees "The Pathway of Departed Spirits," because after death the spirit passes on this pathway to the Southern Star, the abiding place of the dead. A star that stands in the north first receives the spirit and sends it onward to the Southern Star. This is the sacred belief, known to the priests, but the common people say that the Milky Way is the dust of the Buffalo (the Spirit-Buffalo). The Southern Star is not always seen. At a certain time in the summer, just at dusk, it rises like fire for a moment, and then disappears. When the star rises thus, it means that a great man will die. (Chamberlain 1982:21n)

Priestly lore thus affirmed that the Milky Way was the path of souls, that the entrance is a star in the north, and that the soul goes to a specific star in the south, which is seen in the summer. Moreover, embedded in the myth of the conflict between the Evening and Morning Stars is the information that Evening Star's major supporters were the four direction powers (Bear, Panther, Wildcat, and Wolf), and that "there was also a great serpent group of stars" (Murie 1914 and 1981, quoted in Chamberlain 1982:58). These astronomical details sound very much like the Path of Souls model and suggest closer examination. There are hints in the Pawnee mortuary lore that there were different outcomes of the death process for different people. Dorsey and Murie left this note:

> At death, the soul goes off the way a cloud comes up and disappears, or the way a wind blows up and dies down. The souls of people who have been seen by the Star of Disease and who have as a result died of illness are taken by the South Star to his home in the south. The disposition of all other souls is determined by the Morning Star, who decides whether they

shall be restored to life, taken with him to the east, or sent to the south. And it is the Morning Star's importance in this matter that caused the Skidi to bury their dead with the head toward the east. (Dorsey and Murie 1940:102, in Chamberlain 1982:91)

This additional bit of information adds Morning Star as a power who makes determinations of the direction each soul should take, a role similar to that of the Old Man or Old Woman in other versions of the Path of Souls. All those who died of illness went to the south, and others were directed there by Morning Star. Thus the Milky Way was a major path for a significant group of Pawnee souls; there was a portal toward the northern end which provided access to the souls, and a South Star was found at the southern end of the Path. This general layout was confirmed by Fletcher when she was examining the role of the winds in the death process: According to her, the wind of the spirits "takes the spirits of the dead from the north, from some star in the north to which the dead immediately pass from the earth, and blows or drives the ghosts along the way, to the star at the southern end of the path . . . The Milky Way is the path taken by the spirits as they pass along, driven by the wind which starts at the north, to the star in the south, at the end of the way" (Fletcher 1903:13). The winds here have a special role in regard to the souls, but some Dhegiha Siouans regarded the Four Winds as psychopomps, so this reference may be simply the Pawnee version of that same belief. Fletcher spoke of this passage of souls down the Path in such a general way that it appears she thought of this as the major way in which souls were treated in the Pawnee afterlife. She also added the fact that the Pawnee recognize the fork in the Path, as did Murie: "There are two paths in the Milky Way. One of these is for warriors killed in battle, the other for those who die of disease or in bed" (Murie 1981:42). Their destination was "the star in the south where the spirits of the dead dwell."

It seems reasonable to conclude that the Pawnee, despite extensive elaboration of their ethnoastronomy and the accompanying mythology, participated in the general Path of Souls model for their understanding of the fate of souls. The Milky Way was the path that the souls took, either led or driven by the winds, to the guardian star in the south.

For other Caddoan speakers there is sparse information. For the Caddo, there is at least a suggestive note from the eighteenth century. Espinosa wrote in 1746:

They say that as soon as the spirits leave the bodies, they journey at once to a place in the west, then ascend into the air, and pass near by the place of the Great Chief, whom they call Caddi Ayo. From here they go to stop at a house, situated in the south, which, they say, is the house of Death. (Bolton 1987:146)

Even though there is no explicit mention of the Milky Way, it is an appropriate description of the Path of Souls. It mentions the journey to the west, the ascent into the celestial sphere, the continuation of the journey past the dwelling of the Great Spirit, and arrival at the realm of the dead, which is located in the south. Further, the burial ritual for important persons, such as the grand *xinesi*, included a speech to the dead man instructing him to "go peacefully to 'that other house' to join the other dead, and take up their life." At the grave, volleys of arrows were shot into the air to "arouse the keeper of the house 'on the other side' " (Newcomb 1961:301–302). It thus appears that at least some of the Caddoan peoples—the Skidi Pawnee and the Caddo, for certain—participated in the Path of Souls model, despite the fact that all of them were believers in the emergence myth, a theoretical stance that separates them from almost all other Eastern Woodlands peoples and would appear to be in opposition to a celestial worldview concerning death.

In the Southeast the unusual mixture of peoples, their many languages (even though Muskhogean was the primary family, there were many linguistic isolates and isolated representatives of other families) and the early date at which they began reacting to European influences have left the cultural traditions difficult to interpret. The Cherokee, as might be expected of the Southeastern representatives of the Iroquoian peoples, were participants in the Path of Souls mythology. Hagar identified two "dog stars," Sirius and Antares, as guards of the two "opposite points of the sky, where the Milky Way touches the horizon." The souls cross a torrent on a narrow pole, and some fall off. The souls go east, then west, following the Milky Way trail to a fork at which a dog must be fed. If they are successful at passing that dog, then they follow the trail to a second dog, which must also be fed. If a soul does not have enough food to feed both of the dogs, then it is trapped between them, a clear warning to the living to make sure they provide ample burial offerings of food for the journey (Hagar 1906:354–356).

Among the Muskhogean-speaking peoples there are only a few hints of participation in the Path of Souls model. The Creek name for the Milky Way was *poya fik-tcalk innini*, "the spirits' road" (Swanton 1928a:479). Swanton's summaries of the Creek view of the journey are brief:

All accounts agree that after the soul had been induced to leave the neighborhood of his living relatives he traveled westward, passed under the sky and proceeded upward upon it to the land of The One Above or the Breath Holder. The name "spirits' road" given to the milky way shows that this was regarded as the trail upon which souls ascended. (Swanton 1928a:256)

Swanton later added to this spare account, noting that some spirits did not make the transition to the sky and remained in the west as malevolent ghosts, and that unavenged spirits haunted the family members until they did their duty (Swanton 1946:776). The Milky Way as the Path of Souls seems clear, but there is little of the detail of the general model. The dog is also found in Southeastern lore, but in an unusual way. The Natchez and the Cherokee both tell a myth of the origin of the Milky Way in which a dog spilled maize flour across the sky, creating the path (Swanton 1928a:479; Mooney 1900:259). Although the texts were not collected, the linguistic clues (Milky Way = "white dog's road") suggest that the Choctaw, Chickasaw, and Yuchi also knew the myth (Byington 1915; Munro and Willmond 1994; Speck 1909). This story, which seems to be almost at the level of a tale for children, does enshrine a dog in connection with the Path, but whether the connection to the model is real or illusory is impossible to judge.

Of the river, the log bridge, the fork, the Old Woman, and the snake there is no mention. If the Southeastern peoples participated fully in the Path of Souls model at some time in the past, it has left little imprint on the ethnographic record. That is disappointing, since the SECC images from Moundville which are the focus of this chapter were almost certainly created by some Muskhogean group. Nonetheless, the clues indicate Southeastern belief in some form of the Path of Souls model, and it is not too great a leap to use that general model to interpret the icons.

Icons of the Soul

A survey of the SECC imagery reveals two icons in particular that suggest the dead—the skull and bone. Some of the skulls are characterized by a "tongue" or an arrow which protrudes from the mouth, and that same tongue appears a few times in Spiro images as emanating from the center of a broken bone. The importance of the mortuary complex in Native American culture makes it a reasonable leap from the dead bones to the identity of the tongue and arrow as icons of the soul (Fig. 8.6).

It seems likely that the tongue shape at Spiro represents soul-stuff, because it is believed by some of the Eastern Woodlands peoples that the life-soul, and perhaps the free-soul in some cases, resides in bones. Thus the taboos surrounding hunters' treatment of the slain bodies of the quarry—if the bones are bro-

FIGURE 8.6. A skull and two bones, with "tongues," from Spiro (adapted from Phillips and Brown 1978:Pl. 57).

ken, the animals cannot be resuscitated or reborn. If the tongue shape represents soul-stuff in the broken-bone image, then it may be assumed to mean the same when it emerges from the mouth of the skull, and the arrow point appears to be an allomorph of the same thing. Myths of various peoples speak of heroic figures who are able to fly through the air or up to the sky by transforming themselves into feathers or arrows (motif Magic Arrow Flight:D1092, D1526.1 [Thompson 1956:Note 145a]). With the soul-stuff emanating from a skull or bone, the specification would be the soul of a deceased human, rather than the free soul of a religious specialist on an out-of-body journey. In these images the basic meaning is probably the obvious one: the soul is released from the physical body. Within that general field of mortuary symbolism, the precise meaning in the iconography is not clear: the skull and bone may be simply indicators of death (the cultural mortuary context), or signs of the Realm of the Dead or the Path to it (place indicators). Either would work well in this context. The skull has long been interpreted as a death sign, of course, even leading the Southeastern Ceremonial Complex to be called a "Death Cult" many years ago (Howard 1968:7; Muller 1989:11). This interpretation based on the Path of Souls model differs only in that it is more specific—the reference is to the journey of the soul or the end of it, and the skull and bone are part of the larger conceptual model of the Path of Souls.

How Does the Soul Get on the Path?

While the evidence just summarized makes it clear that most peoples of eastern North America believed that the free soul walked the celestial Path of Souls, it does not answer the problem of how the journey to the West, an almost equally prevalent belief, correlates with the Path. Where and how does the soul make the transition from the western land path to the Milky Way? There are various clues which suggest a solution to the problem.

Just off the edge of the Milky Way there is a readily identifiable constellation within which is the portal into the sky world. That constellation, part of what is known in the celestial system derived from Greek mythology as Orion, is the Hand. Inside that constellation lies a galaxy (Messier 42) visible as a fuzzy star that is understood to be a hole in the sky, a portal. Unlike some of the other Native American constellations, such as the Path of Souls and the Great Serpent, there is a restricted quality to the Hand identification. The major focus appears to be Siouan, and not even all of the Siouan peoples. It is found clearly among the Lakota, Mandan, Hidatsa, and Crow, with suggestive references from the Kansas and Arapaho. A brief survey of the material will clarify the nature of this shared constellation (Fig. 8.7).

In the Mandan version of the "Lodge-boy and Thrown-away" myth, there is a mythological charter for the Hand constellation. Spring-boy was captured by the chief of the sky village, Long Arm, but his brother Lodge-boy rescued him in the form of a spider. As they fled to the hole in the sky through which they would escape to earth,

> Long Arm went and placed his hand over the hole by which they passed through so as to catch them. Spring-boy made a motion with the hatchet as if to cut it off at the wrist and said, "This second time your hand has committed a crime, and it shall be a sign to the people on earth." So it is today that we see the hand in the heavens. The white people call it Orion. The belt is where they cut across the wrist, the thumb and fingers also show; they are hanging down like a hand. "The hand star" it is called.
>
> The boys went back to the place where they had left the arrows sticking in the ground, pulled out the arrows and went home to their mother. She told them that the people in the sky were like birds, they could fly about as they pleased. Since the opening was made in the heavens they may come down to earth. If a person lives well on earth his spirit takes flight to the skies and is able to come back again and be reborn, but if he does evil he will wander about on earth and never leave it for the skies. A baby born

with a slit in the ear at the place where earrings are hung is such a reborn child from the people in the skies. (Beckwith 1930:41f)

This myth is connected to the Mandan *okipa,* a ceremony with similarities to the Sun Dance of other Plains tribes, and in that ritual the Hand is present in trophy form.

> The chief celebrant at these ceremonies has usually killed an enemy. He cuts off the hand, brings it home, skins it, removing the bones, and fills it with sand. After it dries he empties out the sand and wears it at the back of the neck, where it flaps up and down as he dances. It represents Long Arm's hand. (Beckwith 1930:43)

In this practice, the hand has several layers of meaning, including punishment for evil intentions, but the one of significance for this inquiry is the identification of the hand with the attempt to use it to close the portal into the sky and the labeling of that portal as a specific constellation. A Hidatsa note on the Sun Dance provides another link between the rituals and belief complexes: "The sacred objects needed for the dance included a buffalo skull, *an enemy's left hand,* a scalp, and one whole rabbitskin to be used for a crown" (Lowie 1919:421; emphasis added).

The Hidatsa also knew both the Hand constellation and the Long Arm mythic episode, as might be expected from their historic proximity to the Mandan. It is of greater significance, perhaps, that the Crow, who split off from the Hidatsa several centuries ago and adopted a quite different lifestyle, also know the myth and its constellation. As "Ben," one of Goodman's informants, explained,

> A constellation that is prominent in the stars is the Hand Star. It is usually in the east. The Crows used to look at that constellation. It is most prominent in the evening or early morning, so they looked at that star and when the hand was tilted to the left then they say that the birds will be coming soon. But in the evening the hand is straight up. Then, they will say that the birds will be leaving. So that's what they used the Hand Star for.
>
> The Hand Star is the lower half of Orion. To the Greeks, Orion looked like a man. But when the Crows saw it, it was actually a left hand with all the fingers stretched out. So that's what it looked like to the Crows and that's what they called it, they called it Ihkawaleische [Hand Star]. (McCleary 1997:21; see also text on 22)

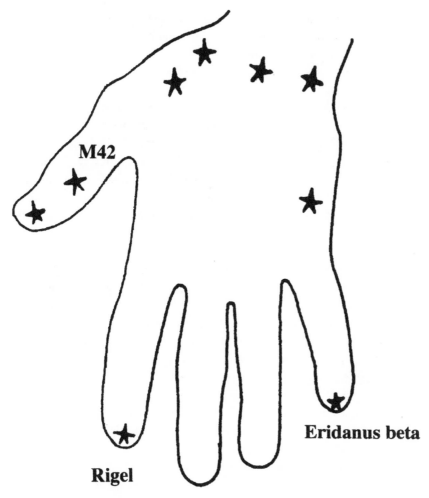

FIGURE 8.7. The Hand as it appears in the sky adjacent to the Milky Way. After Goodman 1992.

The Crow mythological explanation for the Hand is curious, in that there are alternate versions of the event. Here are three summaries. "In the first version, as told by Peter, an elder from Pryor, there is a close resemblance to the story as told by the Hidatsa" (McCleary 1997:51). The second is a bit altered:

He thought about it and he figured that it must have been Baaáalichke [One with a Long Arm] who took [his brother]. He looked to the sky and saw a hole. He then shot his arrows and where his arrows went he went. When he got to the sky, he found a camp and life there . . . Baaáalichke dropped the twin. Thrown Behind The Tipi Lining helped his twin up and put him on his shoulder and took him to the opening in the sky. He threw his arrows, which took them back to earth.

Thrown Behind The Tipi Lining put his brother down on the ground. Then Baaáalichke reached down from the sky and tried to pick up Thrown Into The Spring, but Thrown Into The Spring cut the hand off at the wrist and it hit the ground. Then Thrown Into The Spring threw the hand back to the sky where it became the Hand Star. Thrown Into The Spring said, "You will no longer eat or destroy others. Your hand in the sky will be a symbol for all time of your cruelty." And that is how the Hand Star came to be. (McCleary 1997:56–57)

A third version features Red Woman as the malefactor. The twins chased her, cutting off parts of her with a sharp beaver's tail and leaving the hand in the sky (McCleary 1997:61).

Despite the existence of variants, the basic similarity of the Crow and Hidatsa accounts indicates the importance of the mythic incident, which explains the constellation in which both tribes believe. It is of interest that the Lakota also know the constellation and the myth, even though they locate the incident in another mythological context, that of the Star Boy myth. Goodman has provided a precise identification of the Lakota understanding of this constellation's makeup, ensuring that it is the same Hand as the Plains Village constellation:

The Hand constellation (nape), which was identified for me by William Red Bird of the Rosebud Sioux Reservation in 1986, occurs in Orion, and represents the hand that the Chief lost when he lost his arm. The belt of Orion is the wrist. The Sword of Orion is the thumb. Rigel makes the index finger. The star for the little finger is the northernmost star in Eridanus, Eridanus beta. (Goodman 1992:219)

Goodman's informants connected the Hand constellation with the myth of the recovery of a chief's arm which was ripped off by the Thunderers, which is interpreted as dealing with the necessity for blood sacrifice in order to restore fertility to the world.

[T]he Lakota regard the disappearance from the night sky of The Hand constellation as a divine signal of impending loss of fertility . . . The reappearance in the night sky of the *nape* constellation occurred in autumn. It then approached the meridian shortly before winter solstice. Thus, at one time, the *nape* announced the imminent onset of the two great divisions of the year: the summer and winter solstices. (Goodman 1992:219–220)

This observation of the function of the Hand as a seasonal marker parallels that of the Crow informants, who said that it "indicated the beginning and end of winter" (McCleary 1997:21).

The incident of the cutting off of the chief's hand is curious for several reasons. First, it is clearly a free-floating myth, independent of its contemporary mythic context. This is demonstrated by the fact that it appears in both the Twins (Lodge-boy and Thrown-away) myth and the Star Boy myth (the sequel to the Star-Husband myth). (See Thompson 1956:126–130 for notes on the distribution of the Star-Husband). Moreover, the Hand myth does *not* appear in the majority of the texts of either of those famous myth cycles. It is, in other words, an incident of limited distribution that is found in different contexts in the small group which knows the myth of the Hand constellation. In light of this situation, it is not surprising that its interpretation varies even within the small group. Whereas the Mandan/Hidatsa/Crow emphasis seems to be on the calendrical significance of the Hand, rooted in the creative activity of the hero, the Lakota focus is on the theme of sacrifice for the good of the people, a view appropriate for the Sun Dance connection. That same sacrificial view, however, appears in a suggestive note from the Siouan-speaking Kansas, whose mourning ceremony includes a "song of sacrifice to the deities." On the ritual mnemonic chart, the sign indicating this song was "a hand of which four fingers are seen" (Dorsey 1885:676–677). This brief note is only a step away from an indication that the Kansas also knew the constellation and the sacrificial interpretation of the myth.

As if to confirm the point of the diversity in the mythic charter for the Hand constellation, the Arapaho have provided evidence of their belief. A description of their unique ritual object, the Sacred Wheel, provides a list of celestial phenomena symbolized upon it:

After the Wheel was nicely shaped, this man in the usual method, painted it, and placed the Four-Old-Men at the four cardinal points. Not only were these Old-Men being located on the Wheel, but also the morning star (cross); a collection of stars sitting together, perhaps the Pleiades; the evening star (Lone-Star); chain of stars, seven buffalo bulls; *five stars called a hand*, and a chain of stars, which is the lance; a circular group of seven stars

overhead, called the "old-camp"; the sun, moon, and Milky Way. (Dorsey
1903:205; italics added)

The Arapaho explanation of the hand is a brief reference to a heroic myth:
"That small group of stars early at night, with a row of stars along the side represents the hand of Little-Star with his lance" (Dorsey 1903:228).

The Hand constellation thus appears to have been known to at least a small
group of tribes in the Plains—Mandan, Hidatsa, Crow, Kansas, Arapaho, Lakota.
Connected to the constellation was a myth explaining its origin, basically a
heroic cutting off of the hand of a sky power who blocked a portal in the sky,
but the mythic incident has found its home in different locations in the tribal
mythologies. Although this ethnographic information now seems restricted to
this small Plains group, it is possible that the Hand belief complex was more
widely known in Mississippian times, or that, even without the mythic charter, the image of the hand-and-eye as constellation and sky portal was widely
known to people who later lost the information. Such a possibility seems more
reasonable if the Hand complex was associated with a widespread ritual which
has become extinct in the Southeast. That link may be provided by an indication
of a connection with the Plains ritual of the Sun Dance/*okipa*.

At the beginning of the twentieth century there was a concerted effort to
record the ethnographic details of the Sun Dance as practiced by various tribes.
The project culminated in Spier's attempt to do a comparative study of them
all. He assessed the wide diversity of purpose, organization, ritual details, and
beliefs involved in the Sun Dance, and he concluded that a lowest-common-
denominator definition is a simple one: "[T]he essential performance is simply
erecting a pole within an encircling structure, before which the votaries dance"
(Spier 1921:491). He quoted Brackenridge's 1811 observation of a Siouan Sun
Dance as a good summary: "a space, about twenty feet in diameter, enclosed
with poles, with a post in the middle, painted red, and at the same distance, a
buffalo head raised upon a little mound of earth" (Spier 1921:493). Additional
details make it clear that this pole and circle are cosmological in nature, not
just a utilitarian dance ground. The center pole is forked on top, it is painted
(red or red-and-white striped), it has a Thunderbird "nest" placed at the fork,
along with buffalo hide or skull, and it is raised in a ritual manner by magic or a
mythical bird (Spier 1921:468–470; see Dorsey 1905:87 for a Ponca description).
Although Spier did not discuss the details, since he was doing trait-list comparison, it is not difficult to recognize in the building of the Sun Dance lodge the
reenactment of the cosmogony. That surmise is supported by statements of purpose such as this from the Cheyenne: the Sun Dance is to "reanimate the earth

and its life," an elegant description of the nature of ritual repetition of archetypes (Spier 1921:503). To assert this interpretation is to take a leap, of course, for even in recent years a researcher could comment that "very little is known of the ceremony's symbolism and its interpretation by religious specialists within each tribe: no adequate studies of these things have ever been made" (Liberty 1980:164).

Spier was eager to arrive at some acceptable hypothesis about the origin and diffusion of the Sun Dance. He was aware that the ritual was not restricted just to those who identified it as the Sun Dance, for he pointed to the similarities between it and the Omaha *hedewatci*, the Mandan *okipa*, the Pawnee four-pole ceremony, and the Osage mourning ceremony (all tribes without a Sun Dance, strictly defined). After comparing and analyzing the various traits as they were distributed across the Plains, he concluded that the tradition probably began with the Village Tribes (Hidatsa and Arikara), Cheyenne, and Arapaho, and then spread to the Oglala, after which it diffused to the rest of the Plains tribes (Spier 1921:480). His conclusions are not the last word on the subject, of course, for some of his assumptions bear reexamination, but it is provocative to note the overlap between Spier's core Sun Dance group and the group which has preserved memory of the Hand constellation.

The Pawnee also believed in a portal into the sky to gain access to the Milky Way, but its identity is not certain. Fletcher's comments, quoted above, shed no light on the nature of the portal. Chamberlain, however, suggested that Polaris was meant in the references:

Fletcher (1903:13), Murie (1981:42), and Dorsey (1904a:57) all referred to a star at the north end of the Milky Way which guarded the pathway, received the spirits of the dead, and started them on their journey toward the south . . . The literature on the star at the north end of the Milky Way is somewhat confused, with statements which seem to suggest that the North Star (Polaris) is the one that received the spirits of the dead. Actually, this is a good possibility; Polaris is not too far away from the Milky Way, and Skidi mythology portrays the North Star as the son of the South Star, who received the spirits at the end of their journey. It seems quite logical to conceive of the son (the chief of all stars) as receiving the spirits, and then sending them on to his own father. (Chamberlain 1982:113)

Chamberlain's view may well be the correct identification of the northern portal, but the ambiguity of the materials makes that conclusion only a hypothesis. Evidence for the Orion location of the portal is missing, for there is no allusion to a Hand constellation in Pawnee lore, and Chamberlain offers another identification for Orion, the three "Deer" stars in a row. That constellation could just as well be the Hyades, however—an identification which would leave Orion completely without identity in the Pawnee lore, and thus available for reassignment to an unmentioned "Hand." Polaris may be what was intended by the Pawnee, as Chamberlain suggests, but the Hand portal cannot be ruled out on the present evidence.

All this leads to a grand hypothesis which can only be stated here, since to follow it would take this exploration too far afield. An ancient prehistoric tradition involved a cosmogonic ritual which incorporated the creation of the axis mundi, whether solar or stellar, and the recognition of movement between cosmic levels (see Chapter 2, this volume, for a survey of the cosmic structure). This crystallized by Mississippian times into a ritual occurring outside of the normal architectural structures—the building of the microcosm was an essential part of the ritual, so old architecture would not serve. Such structures would look like circles of posts surrounding a center post, similar to the so-called "Woodhenge" at Cahokia. Such structures could not be torn down after use, logically, for that would be an act destructive of the cosmos, nor could they be recycled, so they would be left to the protection of the cosmic powers—precisely the treatment which is accorded to the Sun Dance lodges to the present day. This ritual/belief complex moved into the Plains by migration and by trade/communication, finding a core group in the Village tribes and their neighbors (see Schlesier 1994 for a summary of the close relationships of these peoples over the last millennium). Time, diffusion, and adaptation took their toll, and the result is the wide diversity in Sun Dance and related rituals, including the myths and celestial knowledge. Time also took its toll in the extinction of the lore surrounding the cosmogonic traditions, so that only a small group remembered the Hand constellation and its role. One of the major losses appears to be the awareness that the Hand also contains a portal, one that could be available to Sun Dancers at any time, but which would be available to all during part of the year—when the Hand touches the western horizon.

If this grand hypothesis has any merit, it would point to the existence of a regional oicotype, a particular type of cosmogonic ritual tied to a particular area. That argument has a corollary, in that the dynamics of mythological transformations suggest a prior "raw material" from which the Hand complex might be derived. From this viewpoint, it is instructive to note that the Hand is not completely unknown elsewhere. There are only two clues, but they suggest ancient Algonkian knowledge of the celestial meaning for the Hand. In her study of Ojibwa artistic designs, Coleman found the hand design used both in a cosmo-

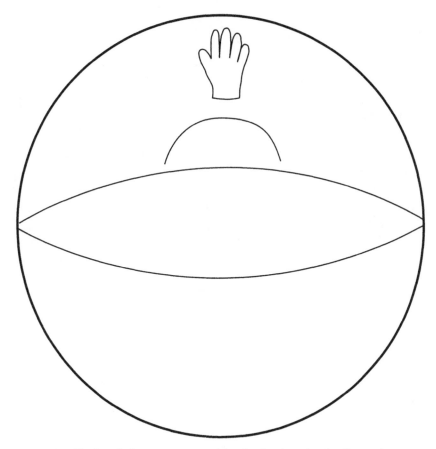

FIGURE 8.8. The Hand of Kijé manito stands in the sky above his dwelling. After Coleman 1947.

logical pattern and by itself on peace pipes. Although one informant interpreted it as representing the hand of the gambler, it is likely that she had derived her understanding from its appearance on the side of a drum used in the gambling game, and there are cosmic uses and meanings of the drum which might indicate a more profound early meaning of the sign. "Other informants referred to the design as the hand of Kijé manito, representing universal power. It was also used on legal documents signifying the honor of the tribe. The hand strengthened an agreement or treaty, and consequently was used on the peace pipe" (Fig. 8.8) (Coleman 1947:12–13; cf. 86).

This Central Algonkian hand of the Great Spirit probably should be considered the same as the hand of the Creator, who, according to the Delaware,

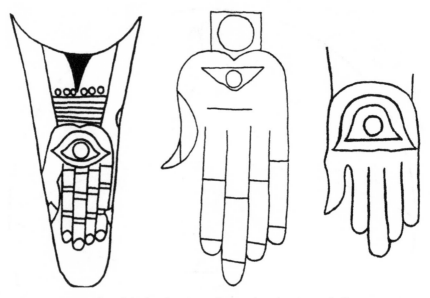

FIGURE 8.9. Examples of the hand-and-eye designs found on Moundville copper, ceramics, and stone (Moore 1905:134, 149, and Moore 1907:400).

sits in the twelfth level of sky and rests his hand upon the central post (Müller 1968:168). The reference is almost certainly to the Big House ceremony, and the central post is surely the world axis. The Hand may thus have become a metaphor for a particular location in the celestial realm, whether or not it was originally understood to be a portal. It seems clear that the Delaware image is cognate to the Hand pictured in Fig. 8.8, which is presented as a known iconographic object in the Ojibwa world; both are connected with the Great Spirit, who lives on the Milky Way. The hand is thus a celestial sign, and all that is missing is an indication that it is in fact a visible phenomenon in the sky. It is not a great leap to see this Eastern Woodlands Hand as an ancestor of the Hand which distilled out into the Mississippian Hand constellation, became known as a portal, and was eventually enshrined as the hand-and-eye design of the SECC. In a further elaboration, Robert Hall has pointed out the hand/portal connection in regard to face-painting and other manifestations (Fig. 8.9) (Hall 1997:126–127).

The hand-and-eye refers to the major portal for the passage of the dead from the earth to the Path of Souls. Iconographically, the hole in the sky is indicated as a slit being pulled apart, and the fact that it is celestial is frequently elaborated by the inclusion of a star circle or dot. The resulting double sign thus gives the appearance of being an eye, but the interpretation offered here argues that it is a coincidental similarity. The "eye" is but a portal with a star in its center. The hand-and-eye combination thus indicates the beginning of the spirit journey, the entry of the soul onto the Milky Way at Orion.

With the portal in the sky identified, it is possible to clarify the details of the journey. The dead soul travels from its physical body in a western direction until it reaches the edge of the earth-disk. There it must wait until the Hand constellation descends to its proper place confronting the soul waiting on the bank. That place is precisely on the western horizon, and the Hand is visible at night, and therefore available for use, during the winter months. When the Hand reaches the level of the earth, the soul must make a leap for the portal during the few minutes before it continues beneath the water, with the Milky Way, like a wall, falling into the water behind the Hand.

Is there any evidence to support such a scenario? Two of the major mythic vehicles for perpetuating the knowledge of the journey of the soul after death are the "Orpheus" myth (Motif F81.1) and the "Journey to the Sky" (Motifs F0 and F15), both of which offer descriptions of the journey to the realm of the dead and/or the celestial realm (see Thompson 1956:337, 330ff). Both are widely known in North America. Two major studies of the "Orpheus" myth in North America have been made, and extensive bibliographies will be found in both (Gayton 1935; Hultkrantz 1956). At least some of the information which has been used in the present study has probably been derived from Orpheus texts, but, as Gayton pointed out, it is frequently impossible to tell whether ethnographic data about life after death was derived from a tribal belief system independent of the myth or whether it was actually rooted in the myth itself. The "Journey to the Sky," the other widespread myth which tells of the passage to the realm of the dead, is very close to the Orpheus texts. In fact, both Gayton and Hultkrantz spoke of their difficulties in separating the two myths, particularly when both forms were recorded from the same ethnic group. In many cases the only difference between the two is the motivation in "Orpheus" of seeking to recover the dead person, with the motif of the broken taboo. In other words, the Journey to the Sky and Orpheus are in many cases virtually the same myth, the distinction depending solely upon the soul-recovery episode.

It should be noted that attempting to use these two myths as sources of Mississippian-era details about the Path of Souls is difficult, because the Orpheus myth was used in historic times as the charter myth of the late nineteenth century Ghost Dance, which accounts for its distribution with minimal variation as far as the Pacific coast. Despite differences in their approaches, however, the three major scholars who have studied the North American Orpheus tradition all wrestled with the connection of the myth with the Ghost Dance and the evidence of its antiquity. Brumbaugh was the scholar who best articulated their conclusion, that the Orpheus myth as used in historic times was not a new creation, but an example of reuse of an old tradition (Gayton 1935, Hultkrantz 1957, and Brumbaugh 1995). Combined with the older dating argued in the Path of Souls hypothesis, Brumbaugh's thesis of the historic role of the myth as the "core text" of the revitalization movement provides both an impressive history of the myth and an explanation for the appearance of unusual similarity in the preserved form of the Orpheus myth—it had been refreshed in historic times, possibly suppressing differences or even oicotypes. The reuse of Orpheus in recent history thus explains the wide distribution and Gayton's "uniformity of plot," but it does not impeach the story as an ancient myth embodying a mortuary complex of beliefs in the Eastern Woodlands.

In many of the texts of both the myths is found a curious motif, referred to as "The Rising and Falling Sky" (Motif F791). It tells of the death of one or more of the travelers caused by the rising and falling sky. In one case, that of the Chitimacha text, more than twenty travelers set out on the journey, but all of them except six were killed in trying to pass through the dangerous conjunction of the earth and the sky (Swanton 1911:358). It is an important motif for consideration from the viewpoint of the Path of Souls, because it is the focus of a problem at hand. The motif of the rising and falling sky, found from the Plains Siouans to the Alabamas in "The Journey to the Sky," appears to be the mythic way of talking about this crucial point on the journey of the soul. From December to April, the Milky Way can be seen nightly to drop below the western horizon. As it falls, it assumes a basically horizontal position, and it thus could be described as a "falling sky." Native recognition of that phenomenon would square the simplistic metaphor with their astronomical knowledge that the celestial world does not end at the western edge of the world but continues down below it. The soul on its journey must gain access to the Milky Way by leaping through the portal in the western sky, but the window of opportunity each night is only a few minutes. If the soul leaps at the wrong moment, the result will be to miss the portal and to fall into the Beneath World or be condemned to remain in the west as a soul which did not make it onto the Path of Souls for the rest of the journey. The known distribution of this myth is spotty, but it seems certain that the coverage was more thorough than myth collection would indicate: Kaska, Tahltan, Ponca, Fox, Seneca, Navaho, Chitimacha, Alabama, Koasati, Yuchi, Cherokee, Choctaw, and Shawnee (Fig. 8.10) (see Dorsey 1904a; Swanton 1929; Thompson 1956:275–276).

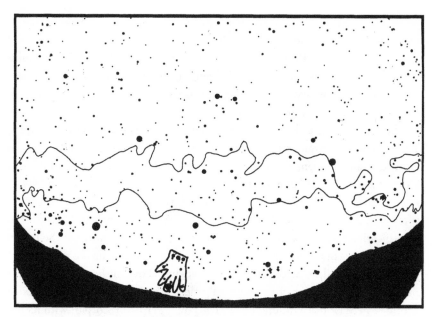

FIGURE 8.10. Falling sky. The Milky Way sinks into the west. Left of center is the Hand portal (Orion) just before it is available for the leap of souls through it onto the Path.

Where Does the Soul Go on the Path?

At the end of the Path, far to the south, lies the realm of the dead, which is related both to Wolf and to the Great Serpent. In Central Algonkian cosmology, as has been seen, the Wolf is usually located in the west, which is the direction of the soul's first leg of the journey, but there are also many references to the south as the preferred direction. How can the apparently conflicting testimony about the west and the south as the directions of the realm of the dead be explained? The answer lies in the apparent behavior of the Milky Way. The portion of the Milky Way that contains the portal in the west—the Hand—swings toward the north in the sky, so that the leg of the journey actually *on* the Path is no longer oriented east and west, but north and south (Fig. 8.11).

This direction change is noted in the ceremonial procedures of the Central Algonkian. When the Midé Society shifted to the Ghost Society for mortuary rites, the members physically changed location from an east-west long lodge to one constructed with a north-south axis. "The earth 'lodge' or Sky 'nest' became oriented north and south instead of the Life's east and west" (Landes 1968:189–190). The peculiar movement of the Milky Way is a neat explanation of this ritual directional shift, and it clarifies the otherwise confusing references to the realm of the dead in the *south*. That direction is an important clue to the other major figure of the Path, the serpent. The Great Serpent lying across the Milky Way in the south has been discussed at length, with the evidence for the celestial role of that divinity, in Chapter 5 in this volume, so the presentation here will be only a brief summary.

The argument is a clear one, even if the evidence is mainly circumstantial. There are ample ethnographic references to the Underwater Panther and the Horned Water Serpent throughout the Eastern Woodlands and the Plains to indicate a widespread belief in this important "master" of the Beneath World, referred to here as the "Great Serpent" for clarity. That serpent is also to be identified with the constellation Scorpio, as the Pawnees made explicit. That celestial identification means that the Great Serpent, although the master of the Below World, appears in the Above World for part of the year, for during the summer months Scorpio "flies" across the southern sky just above the horizon. The Great Serpent, though master of the Below World, is thus sometimes in the Above World, where he has a different role. The Great Serpent (Scorpio) with its red jewel or eye (Antares) is the guardian and master of the realm of the dead at the southern end of the Path of Souls. The curious unnatural curved form of the iconographic snake, especially as seen at Moundville, may be another clue that it is the constellation Scorpio which is the basic image for this serpent, for it resembles the shape of the constellation itself (Fig. 8.12).

The Great Serpent, able to live in two worlds, has a dual role. As master of the Beneath World and the other Powers which inhabit that world, the Great

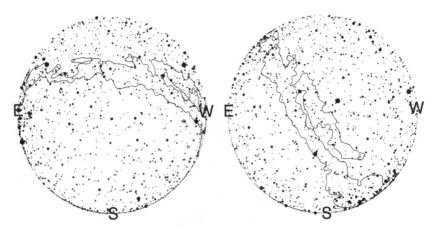

FIGURE 8.11. Two views of the Milky Way: east/west and north/south.

FIGURE 8.12. The Great Serpent in celestial mode on Moundville ceramics (Moore 1905:229).

Serpent is known as a major source of power, both for healers and for sorcerers. As the figure who rises from the water in the summer into the southern sky, the Great Serpent becomes the ruler of the realm of the dead, guardian of the southern end of the Path of Souls. This dual role may be connected to a prominent Mesoamerican belief that celestial figures have dual identities, one when they are seen in the Above World and another when they are below the horizon, in the Beneath World; some scholars believe that this belief was prevalent north of Mesoamerica as well (see, for example, Hall 1997:133–137). Iconographically the shift to the mortuary aspect of the Great Serpent is accomplished by the simple addition of a wing or feathers to the serpent's image. At Moundville, the prevalence of the winged serpent on the ceramics fits well with the circumscribed set of mortuary symbols which is the focus of this chapter.

What Adventures Occur on the Path?

There are other figures who are envisioned as having a role in the soul's journey on the Path. As befits the heroic style of myths which tell of men who dare to attempt to travel to the realm of the dead (especially Orpheus and Journey to the Sky), there are adventures and tests which the travelers must face, presumably reflecting the beliefs regarding the tasks of the soul on its journey. Many of them have been mentioned in the survey of the literature on the Path of Souls. Such figures as the Serpent/log, the Dog or dogs, the four manitous, the Old Woman, and the Old Man have been encountered several times in the survey.

Unfortunately, there is no standard set of figures. It seems a safe conclusion that the adventures on the Path will tend to be regionalized or even tribe-specific, since those adventures will need to fit the larger mythic corpus and the other Powers who are believed locally to play a role in the cosmic structure. The list of figures to be found along the Path is therefore one which contains more figures than are to be found in any single tribe's lore. What may be anticipated is

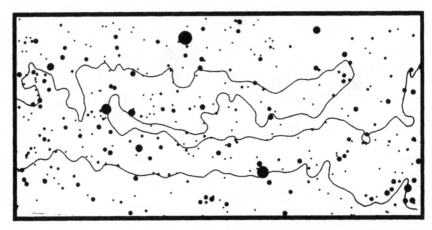

FIGURE 8.13. The Fork in the Path. Deneb in Cygnus is the bright star right at the split.

that the figures can be grouped into oicotypes or regional clusters which reflect diffusion within a coherent geographical or cultural set.

The conceptual focus is the decision about the soul which is made at some point along the path. It is possible that some of the souls will not be permitted to complete the journey to the realm of the dead. One way in which this idea is symbolized is the image of a fork in the Path of Souls. At that point a choice must be made, one path or the other, and the two are not quite the same. According to Barnouw's Algonkian informants, one path is short, and it does not go to the realm of the dead. It is a bad path, and it is a permanent diversion. The other continues on "behind the sky, behind the sunset" (Barnouw 1977:18). The identification of a bad path, or one which can be considered a punishment for some souls, sounds like Christian influence, and it seems impossible to determine whether this ethical interpretation of the fork is pre-contact or later. The fact of the fork, however, seems undeniable—the Milky Way does split, and there is one path which leads to an open gap before the main path can be rejoined. The other path simply continues on without hiatus. There is even a bright star—Deneb—that is placed right at the fork in the path and thus could serve as a marker for the decision point or a figure who does the deciding (Fig. 8.13).

It may be Deneb which is interpreted by a frightening image fairly widespread in Eastern Woodlands mythology. In considering the possibility of memory loss for the dead souls, Hultkrantz discussed "a guard on the road to the realm of the dead [who] deprives the recently deceased person who passes by of his brain by taking it out or smashing it." He noted that this idea occurs among the Penobscot, Huron, Iroquois, Ojibwa, Menomini, Sauk, and Fox and the Siouan-speaking Winnebago. "The Sauk and perhaps the Fox believed that 'the brain-smasher' must be avoided by the dead, since with his measure he deprives them of their existence altogether" (Hultkrantz 1953:215). Among the Sauk this figure is located at the point at which the soul approaches the log over the chasm; if the soul can avoid a watchdog and the "Brain Taker," it can cross the log into the abode of the dead (Skinner 1923a:36).

In this account the river/chasm, the bridge, the dog, and the guardian all become part of the same event on the journey of the soul, and the fork in the Path of Souls appears to be the location for this expanded version of the event. Thus the site for the log bridge becomes situated at a reasonable point on the Milky Way—the gap (or "river") which blocks the path on one of the forks.

Iconographically, there are images that may be expressions of the various figures to be found at the fork on the Path, such as statues of kneeling men and women, dog effigies, quadripartite effigy ceramics, and so on. Such possible correspondences with figures on the Path should be explored, but this chapter is not the place for that extended examination. Since the focus of this current study is on the cluster of images from Moundville ceramics, however, it seems reasonable to explore one such regionalized figure. The image in question is the remaining one of the five originally identified—the Raptor (Fig. 8.14).

What is peculiar about the Moundville Raptor is its participation in this collection of mortuary iconography. The Raptor, whether modeled after an eagle or a hawk, does not seem to have the same associations at other sites, such as Etowah, where a chief was even buried in raptorial regalia. At Moundville, how-

FIGURE 8.14. A special example of the raptor as seen on Moundville pottery (Moore 1905:206).

FIGURE 8.15. The raptor in conjunction with the Hand and Eye on Moundville ceramics (Moore 1907:351).

ever, the Raptor seems to be part of the Path of Souls group: it is found on the same type of pottery, it is located in graves with other Path engraved images, and it appears in a single instance on the same Moundville Engraved variety Hemphill bottle with the hand-and-eye (Fig. 8.15). In another example, the Raptor's head is attached to the same wing which, in the case of the Great Serpent, has been identified as a locative element indicating the celestial realm (Fig. 8.14) (see Chapter 5, this volume).

The Moundville usage of the Raptor seems to place it in the Path of Souls complex, and the most likely role for it would be as one of the adventures on the Path, since there is no other available slot in the literature surveyed. Astoundingly, there is a reference to an eagle in the role of the antagonist against the soul. It comes only from the Alabamas and the Seminoles, two groups who are major candidates for descendants of the prehistoric inhabitants of Moundville. The Alabamas specified that an eagle was encountered by the soul on the Path: "[A] knife is said to have been put into the hand of an Alabama Indian with which to fight an eagle supposed to beset the spirit trail" (Swanton 1946:724). The same custom and belief was recorded for the Seminoles (MacCauley 1887:522; Judith Knight, personal communication, 1996; Mary Johns, personal communication, 1997). That satisfying correspondence between the ethnographic data and the iconographic situation suggested by the Path of Souls model makes it likely that the Raptor on the Path is an oicotype of the Southeastern Moundville people, a regionalized image which is peculiar to them, but fills the slot known to other peoples as the location of the other figures already mentioned. That the Moundvillians made such a peculiar local adaptation of a widely known symbol suggests a fixation on the Path of Souls, which in turn serves to reinforce the argument of Knight and Steponaitis (1998:19–20) that after 1300 A.D. the Moundville site lost a great portion of its population and became transformed into a mortuary center. The use during that time period of a ceramic array of more than sixty vessels with mortuary iconography (counting Great Serpent, raptor, and the hand-and-eye groups) may be a reflection of that new cultural role for Moundville.

A further support for the identification is suggested by the nature of the constellation of Cygnus. The cross shape of the constellation, with Deneb as its alpha star, has led in Greek astronomy to the identification of it with a bird. It is a satisfying coincidental possibility that the people of Moundville saw it the same way, but with the identity of an eagle rather than a swan.

Summary

With that brief look at one of the possible adventures on the Path, together with its artistic representation, this interpretation of the five mortuary symbols in the Moundville cluster comes to its conclusion. It has been argued here that the Path of Souls astronomical vision was linked with a set of beliefs about the nature of death and the outcome of the transformation of the soul to the realm of the dead. Further, this survey, while not exhaustive, offers substantial evidence that the Path of Souls model was widely known in eastern North America. That model suggests that there was in the Eastern Woodlands and Plains a set of beliefs which interpreted some celestial phenomena of the night sky as the geography of the journey of the dead to their new home. Given the presumed antiquity of the belief complex, as suggested by the wide geographic area in which the complex can still be traced, the development of the details of the beliefs into oicotypal groups is an outcome to be expected.

One such group, the Moundville mortuary cluster, was identified by its statistical importance and its isolation from other iconographic images. Local meanings for the five symbols — skull, bone, hand-and-eye, winged serpent, and Raptor — have been offered on the basis of the Path of Souls model: hand-and-eye = celestial portal in Orion, skull = body with free-soul, bone = life-soul, winged serpent = Great Serpent in celestial mode (Scorpio), Raptor = the eagle adversary on the Path (Cygnus). Together they mark important points on the soul's journey on the Path of Souls — the release of the soul from the body, the leap to the Above World and entrance through a portal, the confrontation with the adversary/judge on the Path, and the reception to the Realm of the Dead by the Master of the Beneath World.

These conclusions do not necessitate a universality of those meanings, of course, because one of the discoveries in the process is the use of the Raptor image at Moundville in a way which appears unique, and that fact argues for caution in the interpretation of universal symbols used in regional contexts. Nor does this mortuary complex hypothesis suggest that all of the secc imagery is to be interpreted within this framework, even at Moundville. It is enough to conclude that some of these images—perhaps only these five—were part of the understanding of death in some places in the prehistoric Southeast.

While it is beyond the purpose of this chapter to indicate a time depth for the Path of Souls, it is surely significant that Krupp has surveyed the quite similar understanding of the Milky Way among Siberian groups and various tribes in California (Krupp 1995). That distribution, when added to the eastern occurrences discussed in this chapter, suggests an impressive time-depth. Furthermore, archaeological examination of various Eastern Woodland sites has revealed a long-term focus on death, a cultural concern which can be traced back at least as far as the Archaic. If the Path of Souls belief complex is part of the ideology which belongs with the physical remains of the ancient mortuary patterns, then the native peoples of North America have been familiar with a culturally important part of the skyscape—the Path of Souls—for millennia.

9. Sequencing the Braden Style within Mississippian Period Art and Iconography

James Brown

The history of iconographic analysis of Southeastern Ceremonial Complex subject matter can rightly be said to have started with Phil Phillips's long-term study of the amazing collection of more than 1,000 engraved shell cups, gorgets, and unassignable fragments from the Craig Mound at Spiro. The size and scope of the collection lent themselves well to iconographic analysis, but equally important to the success of the project was Phillips's resolve to study the way in which theme and motif were expressed in the cup and gorget media. He realized that before one could tackle iconographic issues one had to come to grips with the matter of style. The analysis was complicated because the collection was composed of two readily distinguishable styles (to say nothing of a few gorgets representing additional styles that were obviously exogenous to the site and the area). In the case of what he called the Craig School, a sequence revealed a developmental history in a direction away from the forms of expression common in the other, Braden, school. Phillips held firm, however, to the unity of what he called the Braden and Craig schools of a single site-based "Spiro style," mainly because there existed no rival collection on which to base disparate craft shop origins (Phillips and Brown 1978:208, Brain and Phillips 1996). However, the profound preferences in representation of each revealed a more fundamental stylistic schism than was implied by the association of two styles at a single site. In contrast to the "Spiro-unity" line of thought, it had always seemed to me that a site as small as Spiro and one located at the western edge of the floodplain economies sustaining Mississippian Period complexity was an unlikely place for supporting two schools as different as these two, to say nothing of any other two styles.

As I began to cast around for clues as to which was resident, it was evident that the Craig style was the one that had the regional connections, whereas the Braden style did not. At Spiro, Craig outnumbered Braden two to one, and all examples of shell cup recycling were from Braden cups into Craig gorgets.

These facts are consistent with Craig as the home style and Braden as the exotic. Furthermore, the Braden style had congeners with engraved pottery found at Cahokia that possessed pastes from the American Bottom (Brown 1989). By linking, thereby, engraved pottery style with engraved marine shell style, it was possible to construct an argument about locations for the styles of both. Ever since the Cottonlandia Conference in 1984 where this argument was initially advanced, evidence has been accumulating that adds to our knowledge of the likely locations of styles used in the sense employed here (Brown 1989). Jon Muller (1997a, 1999) has contributed to these understandings by confirming and adding to this picture with his density maps for specific styles. All of these clues point to Cahokia and its environs as the source for the Classic Braden figural style. Nonfigural images are present in many more contexts and ones that are far less exclusive.

A word here is necessary about the subject of style. This is a notoriously slippery concept that has been used to cover an extraordinary range of products and performances. But some basic characteristics have received wide acceptance in anthropology and art history, and thus provide a basis for productive common ground on which useful research can proceed. A basic element to style is the distinctive patterning accruing from deeply ingrained procedures that humans recognize in products and performances (Davis 1990). These sequences can be long or short, embedded in production or consciously incorporated within, and they can even be patterned interactions at many different levels of production. All examples of style have orderedness brought about by prior conditions and sustained and enhanced by production itself. Since any single step in production is partially conditioned by preceding steps, any product is stylistically conditioned before the process has physically begun, even at the attitudinal and perceptual level. Hence we can conclude that all human acts tending toward the rote through repetition are very much a part of style. It is little wonder that style can be recognized all around us, particularly when so much of what we do is done unconsciously or out of habit and without reflection. (For extended discussion on these and related issues, see Conkey and Hastorf 1990 and Dobres and Hoffman 1994.)

With his study of engraved shell gorgets, Jon Muller (1966, 1979) introduced a notion of style in conformity with such principles into SECC studies. He was able to demonstrate that distinctive style patternings were the products of specific patterns of linked, clearly sequential steps in production that can be represented by generative rules. He proceeded to delineate three superficially similar stylistic renderings of a rattlesnake image in common—the Lick Creek, Citico, and Saltville styles. The first of these was essentially a precursor to the second, with certain structural and morphological changes (Muller 1999:156). The third represents a copy or adaptation of the first in appearance only, without the requisite incorporation of the actual steps required to create the first image. The result was a distinctly different style, although the rattlesnake subject matter was the same.

A compatible perspective was advanced by Phil Phillips (Phillips and Brown 1989:xi) in his systematic study of a corpus of 274 engraved shell cups, 560 cup fragments, 50 gorgets, 105 gorget fragments, and 31 other artifacts—both whole and fragmentary. In Phillips's study of Spiro shell engraving (Phillips and Brown 1978), he clearly distinguished thematic imagery from styles of representation. This led to the recognition of a number of distinct styles in which the same thematic materials were reiterated. In the spirit of the Spiro shell engraving project, I have tried to follow suit, although I realize that my sketches should really be thought of as a study in progress rather than a thoroughgoing structural analysis.

Other perspectives have dominated the study of style in SECC studies. When Waring and Holder (1945:21) discussed style, albeit briefly, they had in mind what might better be called thematic types. These types were nominalized into traits that became identified by their subject matter (e.g., "eagle dancer"). This trait-based approach has remained commonplace in archaeological practice. In the exhaustive study titled *Shell Gorgets: Styles of the Late Prehistoric and Proto-historic Southeast* (Brain and Phillips 1996), a classification was advanced that relied upon small-scale groupings of stylistic features and themes, with thematic considerations clearly dominating the classification. Major patterns of representation receive only a single page of comments, without enlarging significantly on observations already provided by Muller (1966, 1989). The organization of procedure and execution of elements are downplayed to the level of commentary (Muller 1997b). In Muller's (1997b) terms the shell gorget "styles" are cultural historical types with varying degrees of commonality of design and compositional grammar. The important distinction that Phil Phillips made between subject matter and manner of representation in the Spiro study was put aside for a typological approach to design that was informed to one degree or another by stylistic and grammatical considerations.

This chapter will focus on one of the major styles—and that is one I will call, for convenience, the Braden style. Before defining what is signified by this term, allow me to elaborate some of the advantages of a stylistic analysis with particular reference to the SECC. First of all, this perspective allows specific kinds of imagery to be understood as a pattern of visual representation that is implicitly rule-based. Phil Phillips recognized such patterning in the form of two distinct styles in the Spiro collection, each with its own course of development. This perspective carries with it an acknowledgment that style exists in a tension between the particularity of time, place, ethnicity, and class on the one hand and its communicative function through widespread and time-honored understandings on the other. This means that one would expect to find only a single style among the relatively small-scale societies of the ancient Southeast. Not surprisingly, in every case where SECC imagery is found on locally made pottery (e.g., Cahokia, Moundville), only one style is represented. On the other hand, the sources for display goods and preciosities are diverse, commonly dominated by exotics as in the case of Spiro. But both local and exotic images can be expected to conform to a system with a common visual vocabulary.

Now that we have settled upon a firm basis for connecting specific societies with particular styles (or style variants), we enable ourselves to recognize that the histories of imagery on display goods of varying value and ritual importance can be charted in time and space just as can the histories of more humble material culture, such as domestic pottery. Although the SECC imagery customarily has been credited to the place where it was found irrespective of the degree of diversity in style, it is difficult to believe that crafts people approached their projects with styles so individual that one person's style bore little relation to another—although they supposedly lived in the same face-to-face community. A simple division along lines of inexpensive versus relatively expensive raw materials achieves the requisite clarification. Once we approach the SECC material with this understanding, other benefits become available. For instance, through chronological change in the Braden style sequence we can address the SECC in terms of history; through geographic focus we can better match ethnicity and myth; and through all of these we can address the subject of meaning. Meaning is possible only once style is controlled as a historical entity having a particular geographical fix. Before a study of the SECC can be conducted, the matter of style has to be controlled; it becomes a precondition to further analysis.

What does the style approach accomplish for us that the trait-centered and typological approaches do not?

1. Style is a culturally shaped vehicle through which subject matter is expressed.
2. Temporal change is implicit in a style.
3. Style has a specific geographical locus.
4. Style has a close connection with the history of specific culturally connected groups.

What is the Braden Figural Style?

But first, it is necessary to offer some definitions that will be useful in the following remarks. Here I am conscious of the volume and breadth of information that a full formal definition of what, say, the Classic Braden figural style requires. Needless to say, much more subject material would be desirable, indeed even necessary to confirm the claims that follow. My analysis is merely intended to organize a specific range of representations by focusing on the human figure and leaving aside the "abstract" nonfigural ones. Nor do I consider, say, what the boundary conditions of Braden style might be.

In this chapter I propose to group under *Classic Braden* images that are encompassed by Braden A shell cup engraving, Muller's (1989) Eddyville shell gorget engraving[1] and Phillips's Etowah Copper style. I also include in this category certain imagery incorporated in engraved ceramics (Brown and Kelly 2000), pictographs (e.g., Rattlesnake Bluff [Diaz-Granados and Duncan 2000:115]), and three-dimensional sculpture (Birger and Sponemann pipestone sculptures from the American Bottom [Emerson et al. 2003], amphisbaena rim effigy bowl from Moundville [Brown 1991, Fig. 431; Moore 1905:237–240, Figs. 167–170]). Material post-dating Classic Braden that can be thought of as possessing important Braden features I will call *Late Braden* to acknowledge its stylistic antecedents in Classic Braden. Posed complimentarily to these developmentally related categories is what I am calling *Generalized Braden*, which probably includes some of Phillips's Braden C and quite a bit of "Bradenish" imagery engraved on pottery.[2] All of these are encompassed within the umbrella category of the *Braden* style (Table 9.1).

A definition for Classic Braden proceeds from Phil Phillips's (Phillips and Brown 1978) study, supplemented by Jon Muller's (1966, 1979) important analyses. These criteria have proven to have been remarkably robust. Leaving aside the criteria that are specific to shell cups and gorgets and focusing only on the presentation of the human figure in the Classic Braden style, it can be concluded that the human figure and its parts are relatively "naturalistic." Figures are drawn close to their natural proportions. All parts of the body receive equal attention, and all are well realized, especially mouths, hands, and feet. The head has an almond-shaped profile in which the forehead and the lower jawline are placed on the upper and lower parts of the same curve. The neck and throat are set off from the body by chokers, necklaces, and the like; the neck is not cut off from the body by a shoulder line drawn straight across the body. Dress, footwear, jewelry, weapons, and regalia are individually distinguished with little conflation. The individuality of the figures is clearly important, and this is ac-

Table 9.1. Divisions of the Braden Style

Canonical versions	LATE BRADEN: embracing Braden B shell engraving, and similar work in other media CLASSIC BRADEN: embracing Braden A shell engraving, Eddyville shell gorget style, Etowah copper style, and similar work in other media
Non-canonical versions	GENERALIZED BRADEN: embracing Braden C shell engraving, and similar work in other media

complished through variations in dress, hair adornments, headdress, and decoration of the body and face. Often figures are shown in postures of vigorous
running and dancing. The "tiptoe" position of the feet is common (Phillips and
Brown 1975b:x).

Certain attributes have been singled out as important in distinguishing Classic Braden from Late Braden. The latter possesses "lips [that are] heavy, angu-
lar, protruding often competing with the nose" (Phillips and Brown 1975c:x),
the "snarling mouth" imparted by an upturned upper lip joined to a horizontal lower lip, and the distinctive mouth surround, designated as the "Wulfing
mouth," having the appearance of three fingers across the mouth. The ear detail
present in Classic Braden is absent in Late Braden. Further details can be found
in Phillips and Brown (1975a:39–102; 1975b:ix–xi; 1975c:viii–xvi; 1982:xi–xv).
A discussion of the degrees of similarity can be found in Phillips and Brown
(1978:186–189). Brown (1989, 1996) and Sampson and Esarey (1993) have additional remarks.[3]

Just as important as the recognition of what constitutes the Braden style is a
complementary acknowledgment of what is definitely excluded. First and foremost is the Craig style belonging to the Caddoan Area (Brown 1989, Phillips
and Brown 1978, 1984). A considerable corpus of engraved shell cups and gorgets has provided us with an in-depth knowledge of this style. Some copper
plates, engraved pottery, and carved wood extend this corpus (Brown 1989,
1996:Figs. 2-77a, 2-140, Brown and Rogers 1989, Sievert 1992:142–143). Another is the Hightower style of shell gorgets from Etowah and eastern Tennessee
(Muller 1989). This style probably encompasses the "Stack" style of copperwork,
known from many examples included in a specific pile of plates once placed in
the early fifteenth-century Great Mortuary of Spiro (Hamilton, Hamilton, and
Chapman 1974). A third shell style is the spaghetti (Brain and Phillips 1996) or
Williams Island style (Muller 1989) that is found predominantly in the medium
of shell gorgets, although one repoussé copper is known (Hamilton, Hamilton,
and Chapman 1974:Pls. 16, 17).

Braden Style Geography

Accumulated evidence points strongly to an Eastern Prairies homeland and to the American Bottom and the great town of Cahokia in particular. Brown and Kelly (2000) have reviewed the evidence for the presence of this major representational style at Cahokia. Its indigenous connection is documented by the appearance of the style on pottery and stone materials of local American Bottom origin. The sheer density of Braden representations reaching back into Late Woodland times leaves little room for doubt. Even the spatial distribution of Eddyville style gorgets argues for a northern, not a southern, origin, although Muller (1999) has argued recently that the Ohio-Mississippi confluence region has to be included as well.

Confirmation of this geographical assignment is even more persuasively demonstrated by features of figural representation discovered in rock shelter art of the Eastern Prairies. The first of these discoveries was the instance of a human figure from the Gottschall Shelter in southeastern Wisconsin that places this site close to the northern margins of the Eastern Prairies. The figure is painted in a distinctively lined pattern with a "spud-like" element that recalls to an amazing degree the famous Akron shell cup belonging to the Braden style (Fig. 9.2, Salzer 1987:454–455). But this Gottschall site figure's resemblance in certain details to a figure engraved on a shell cup in the Braden style from Spiro provides the most convincing tie. These details consist of the general handling of the figure, the stance of the upper torso and arms, and the pattern of linear body decoration (Phillips and Brown 1978:Pl. 6, also Pl. 20). This Stovall Cup (Spiro cup 6) is one of the core documents of the Braden style in the Spiro corpus (Fig. 9.1).

Nearer to the American Bottom lie caves and rockshelters with pictographs bearing striking Braden stylistic attributes (Diaz-Granados and Duncan 2000:115). The Rattlesnake Bluff site is important in this respect. It has a solidly painted human figure that duplicates remarkably the "dancing" stance of Braden shell figural art. At the Picture Cave site there are line drawings of figures remarkably similar to those to the north at the Gottschall site in Wisconsin. One in particular is noteworthy for the long-nosed god mask painted in white on the side of a red-colored human face. Several figures at Picture Cave are like Gottschall in being rendered with closely spaced red lines portraying either body painting or tattooing. From these widely separated occurrences of rock art in a generalized Braden style within the Eastern Prairies we can conclude that the locus of this style lies in the upper Mississippi valley. Since the Eastern Prairies were dominated likewise by a common ceramic decorative vocabulary (Hall 1991), we can conclude, in addition, that the cultures of the area as a whole were participants in the Braden style.

FIGURE 9.1. Classic Braden "Multiple Figures in Action," Spiro Cup 6 (Phillips and Brown 1975:Pl. 6).

Outside of the Midwest, Classic Braden style is exemplified only by transportable display goods and preciosities in a number of sites scattered over the Southeast (Brown 1989). Although by far the greatest number come from Spiro, there is no compelling reason to believe that this site is the location of production. Quite contrary to the opinion expressed in the *Pre-Columbian Shell Engravings* work (Phillips and Brown 1978), only one style is at home. The more numerous and better-preserved Craig style of shell engraving is the indigenous style to Spiro (Brown 1989). The presence of Braden, albeit in significant numbers, has a quite different importance. Images in the Braden style are clearly exotic to the site and the region. The same conclusion must be reached about the great number of copper repoussé plates in Classic Braden style that have been found in the graves of Mound C at Etowah. At both Spiro and Etowah there is no carryover of the Classic Braden style from display goods to ceramics, stone sculpture, or rock art (Brown 1989).

In contrast to the geographic specificity of the Classic Braden style is the absence of such a regional fixity for Late Braden. As will be indicated below, the geographic ties are more complex and involve much more than the Eastern Prairies. Indeed, this region probably did not figure importantly at all when the Late Braden style flourished in the fourteenth century.

Age of Braden Style Sequence

The age of the classical form of the Braden style is controversial (Muller 1997b), with some advocating the fifteenth or sixteenth century (Brain and Phillips 1996, Larson 1993). The combined weight of archaeological associations and radiocarbon dates places this style in the thirteenth century, however, if not earlier (Brown and Kelly 2000, Brown and Rogers 1999).

Braden style drafting has a long history at the Cahokia site (Brown and Kelly 2000). Starting as early as late in the Lohmann Phase, a sherd with significant Braden attributes shows up at the BBB Motor site (Emerson 1989:Fig. 10, 1995).[4] Thereafter, many more examples of Classic Braden rendering appear on different media, particularly on pottery (Brown 1989, Brown and Kelly 1997, Emerson 1989:78–80, Phillips and Brown 1978:172). Brown and Kelly (1997, 2000) have argued that the highly formalized Classic Braden style probably came into being as the canonical form out of a Generalized Braden background sometime around 1200. Prior to that date the refinement epitomized by Classic Braden cups had yet to appear, although a wide range of thematic material was already in existence.

The details represented in these Stirling and Moorehead phase examples are significant. Of prime importance is the appearance of the "Akron Grid," which is a pattern of closely spaced parallel lines with distinctive terminations in either a "T" or a triangle. Three instances are revealed in the archaeological record at Cahokia. A duck head effigy adorno from an Early Stirling context has been decorated with this pattern. The ceramic instance is from a locally produced bowl found in an impeccable context at a housing tract. This and the tattooed duck head effigy adorno confirm the tie that this diagnostic Braden signature trait has with Stirling and Moorehead phase Cahokia.

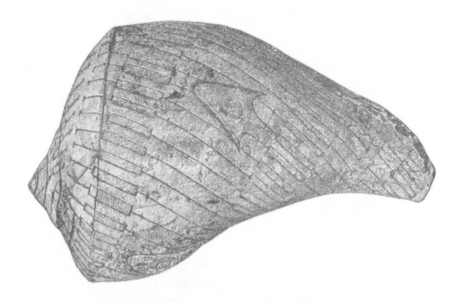

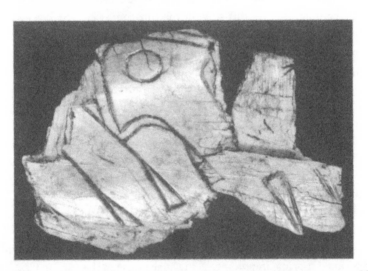

FIGURE 9.2. The Akron Grid. Classic Braden cup from Akron, AR, superimposed by engraved shell cup fragments with the same motif from Cahokia Mound 34. Akron cup from Thomas 1894:FIGURE 133; photograph of cup fragments from Cahokia reproduced by permission of the Museum of Anthropology, University of Michigan (UMMA 54483).

Table 9.2. Radiocarbon Dates (according to OxCal v 2:18 conversions)

Site/Provenience	Assay Age	1s	2s
Cahokia Mound 34‡	670± 200 BP (M-635)	1030–1480 (1.00)	800–present
Etowah Mound B "Orange Layer" average	av. 635± 35 BP	1300–1320 (.22) 1340–1395 (.78)	1290–1400 (1.00)
Etowah Mound C average*	av. 688± 100 BP	1200–1400 (1.00)	1160–1450 (1.00)
Material Service Quarry	815± 95 BP.(GX-833)	1050–1090 (.15) 1120–1280 (.85)	1010–1310 (.98) 1350–1390 (.02)
Spiro A6a (Spiro IV)	430± 65 BP (Beta-31101)	1410–1520 (.91) 1600–1620 (.09)	1400–1640
Spiro B122 (Spiro III)	850± 65 BP (Beta-31103)	1050–1090 (.17) 1120–1260 (.83)	1030–1270
Yokum Mound C	760± 110 BP (M-1976)	1060–1080 (.04) 1120–1310 (.83) 1350–1390 (.11)	1030–1400 (1.00)

‡ not reported in Fig. A
* excluding the sample taken on shell beads (M-543)
Sources of ^{14}C assays: Etowah (King 2003); Spiro (Brown 1996); Material Service Quarry (Bareis 1965); Yokum (Perino 1971).

The third is a fragment of an engraved shell cup from Mound 34 (Phillips and Brown 1978:171, Pl. 15). The fragment was comprised of two pieces of engraved shell from different parts of the same "ritual" trench context (Fig. 9.2). An old carbon black radiocarbon date from a fire basin within the mound is 670±250 BP (M-635). Although the mean age is acceptable as it stands, the assay is not precise enough to match the level of refinement required by the local ceramic chronology, nor does it allow for useful inter-date comparisons (Table 9.2).

The discovery of shell cup fragments from Cahokia Mound 34 provides our best information as to the age of Classic Braden (Phillips and Brown 1978). The details of design bear an even closer approximation to engraved shell cups, par-ticularly the Akron cup from a site near Akron, Arkansas. These fragments be-long to a Moorehead phase context that spans the period between 1200 and 1275 (Brown and Kelly 2000). Although Brain and Phillips (1996:264–265) have tried to argue for a significantly later dating for these fragments, both the radiocar-bon date and artifacts from the mound point solely to a Moorehead Phase age. All artifacts from the inception of mound building to its completion belong to this phase. Nor has anything been found there or in the immediate vicinity of the mound that is clearly of a later period (Kelly et al. n.d.).

If one were inclined to question the import of these three pieces, one need only refer to the famous Gottschall tattooed stone sculptured head to confirm

FIGURE 9.3. Classic Braden "Ceramic Designs." *Left:* Design from Spiro Cup 46. *Right:* Ceramic beaker (shell tempered) from Cahokia (Phillips and Brown 1975:FIGURE 224).

the very early, midwestern provenience of this Braden attribute. Other important linking motifs are the blocked line scroll or spiral ("Spiro Spiral") and Davis Rectangle motifs (Brown and Kelly 1997). Of these, Classic Braden shell cup designs from Spiro (Cup #46) have connections with ceramic designs that belong to the thirteenth century (Fig. 9.3).

From further afield the important site of Cahokia has produced other testimonials as to the age of the Classic Braden style. A copper plate from Spiro of the so-called "Classic Etowah Copper" style has a relevant radiocarbon date (Phillips and Brown 1978). This copper repoussé plate bears a typical profiled warrior image of the supposed "decapitated" type that came from a redeposited gravelot, B122, in the Craig Mound (Brown 1976:549–550, Pl. 2-108a; Phillips and Brown 1978:190). Plant fiber cordage and hide preserved next to this copper plate have an AMS date of 850±65 BP (Beta-31103) (Brown 1996:154, Brown and Rogers 1999). The calibrated probability distribution with the highest likelihood falls within a period equivalent to the Late Stirling and Moorehead phases at Cahokia.

The head on this same Spiro plate bore a long-nosed god maskette as an ear ornament, thereby providing a connection between the Classic Braden repoussé and this time-sensitive ear adornment (Fig. 9.4a). Spiro cup #17 provides another Classic Braden example of the long-nosed god maskette. This cup, exemplifying the Classic Braden style, is decorated with multiple severed warrior heads (Fig. 9.4b, Phillips and Brown 1978:190, Pl. 17).

The age of the long-nosed god ear ornaments provides another chronological fix (Kelly 1991, Williams and Goggin 1956). Mound 3 at the Yokum site (Pike Co., Illinois), north of Cahokia in the Mississippi River valley, is thought to be the site where four shell long-nosed god maskettes were found (Bareis and Gardner 1968, Perino 1971:149, 177–178). Although the mound was badly damaged by looting, a radiocarbon date was run on remaining in-situ charcoal that came in at 760±110 BP (M-1976) (Perino 1971:182). Calibration provides a probability distribution that is essentially identical to that of the copper plate B-122 cited above. The thirteenth-century age of these dated objects fits well with the age usually assigned on the basis of cultural associations (Anderson 1975, Hall 1991, Harn 1975).

In the Caddoan Area the Harlan burial mound, located in eastern Oklahoma, has yielded pertinent chronological information (Bell 1972). A pair of copper maskettes was found next to the skull of Burial 37 in Unit 1B that Bell (1972:43) placed in the middle level of this tri-lobed saddle-shaped accretional mound. No radiocarbon tests were run on Unit 1 material, but dates from the other contemporary lobes of the same mound were no later than the thirteenth century. Ceramic and other artifacts support a thirteenth-century age for Burial 37. These and other reasons have led to the conclusion that the Harlan burial mound was abandoned around 1250 and that later graves were located at the nearby Norman site (Brown 1996). Hence, the discovery of copper long-nosed god maskettes

FIGURE 9.4. The long-nosed god motif. *Left:* Design from a repoussé copper plate of the Classic Braden style from a Spiro III gravelot (B122). *Right:* Design detail from an engraved shell cup (#17) of the Classic Braden style from Spiro (Phillips and Brown 1975:FIGURE 247).

and some embossed copper ornaments convincingly documents these artifacts in a pre-1250 period (Bell 1972). In short, Classic Braden cup fragments have a dated context at Cahokia Mound 34 that matches both that of a copper plate in the same style from Spiro and dated examples of the long-nosed god maskette objects in other locations.

At both the Etowah and Spiro sites, the major examples of the Classic Braden style appear to be the product of wide-scale exchange. Shell gorgets of this style known in Muller's terms as the "Eddyville style" and as the Eddyville, McAdams, and possibly Russell "style theme" types of Brain and Phillips (1996). They were widely exchanged throughout the Southeast (Muller 1997a, 1999), and some of the best examples of these engraved shell artifacts entered the archaeological record in distant locations (Brain and Phillips 1996, Muller 1999). At the Spiro site in eastern Oklahoma, Classic Braden expressions are clearly much later than at their probable place of origin. The Great Mortuary provenience of the Craig Mound at the Spiro site (Phillips and Brown 1978) had an average ^{14}C date of A.D. 1405 (Brown 1996:154, Brown and Rogers 1999).

In sum, an important precedence is created for Cahokia. The Stirling phase date for the associations of engraved pottery and the Moorehead phase contexts for marine shell cups at Mound 34 place the Classic Braden style back to a time around one hundred years earlier than similar engraved work and related copperwork at other SECC sites. Considering the importance of this dated find, we will have to consider a much longer tradition of artwork in the Greater Braden style than that envisioned by Brain and Phillips (1996),[5] and furthermore, we will have to consider the prospect that many of the examples of Braden style shellwork and copperwork found at the classic SECC sites are well separated from their sources of fabrication.

The Problem with the Rogan Plates

Copper plates executed in Classic Braden style are, of course, well known from the Wilbanks Phase graves at Etowah Mound C. The famous Rogan Plates stand for many as the archetype of SECC forms of representation. But they are by no means alone. Most of the copper repoussé work recovered from Mound B probably belongs to this style. So much has been recovered by John Rogan, Warren K. Moorehead, and Lewis Larson in three separate field projects that the assemblages of copper and marine shell artifacts from this famous site have become synonymous with the SECC.

The Classic Braden presence at Etowah is reinforced by the appearance of light engraving on both sides of the fans or lobes of the copper bi-lobe arrow hair ornament from Moorehead's Burial 1 (Brain and Phillips 1996:136, Byers

1962:Fig. 5). The engraved warrior heads were shown by Brain and Phillips to correspond closely in form and line to Classic Braden cup and Eddyville (*sensu* Muller) gorget delineation of human heads (Fig. 9.5). The problem with the Mound C provenience is that it is clearly later than others we have dealt with (Table 9.1).

All of the SECC material comes from graves placed in Mound C that can be attributed to what was formerly undifferentiated as simply the "Wilbanks Phase" (Larson 1989, 1993).[6] King (2003) recognizes this period to be divided into Early Wilbanks (1250–1325) and Late Wilbanks (1325–1375) phases. King was able to distinguish the latter by the appearance of exotic ceramics, such as Rudder Comb Incised,[7] a Pisgah-like complicated stamped, and distinctive rim modes associated with Pisgah Complicated Stamped. Prior to the constructional episodes of the Early and Late Wilbanks phases the Etowah site was unoccupied. At the close of Wilbanks time, around 1375, the site was abandoned in time to miss the early Lamar period pottery developments in the Southern Appalachians marked by the Duvall Phase (Williams and Shapiro 1990b:34). When Etowah was reoccupied in the Brewster Phase, the Lamar ceramic horizon was already well developed. In sum, a regional perspective has revealed that Etowah was occupied episodically during the Mississippian Period with periods of intense occupation alternating with abandonment (Williams and Shapiro 1990a). This pattern was discovered to have been commonplace in the Southern Appalachian region.

Brain and Phillips (1996:164–169) have argued that broad similarities in grave goods point to the graves located on the summit as being a complement to the outer ring of burials at the toe slope of the Mound's "Final Mantle" (see the plan in Brain and Phillips 1996:144). In his synthesis of Mound C, Adam King (1996, 2003) argues for these summit burials as belonging instead to the first three of seven mound constructional episodes. The final 3 meters of massive fill overlying these burials belongs to the fourth to seventh phases, during which time, according to King, interment appears to be confined to the outer ring of burials at the toe slope and to projections at the mound's north end. These are assigned to Late Wilbanks and the first three belong to Early Wilbanks.

Larson (1993) has argued for a sixteenth-century age for the Late Wilbanks Phase based on stylistic connections between a tortoiseshell pin from a "Final Mantle" toe slope grave (#109) with similar pins of Spanish gold from post-contact sites in Florida (Brain and Phillips 1996:161). These stylistic arguments, however, pay little attention to the effect that differences in details have on the pin as a time-sensitive marker. Little can be said as to how long this type of bird-headed pin persisted when we have only two examples from which to judge. Adam King (1996, 2003), on the other hand, has run radiocarbon dates

Upper Bluff Lake

Etowah

Upper Bluff Lake

Etowah

Spiro

Castalian Springs

FIGURE 9.5. Classic Braden style human heads engraved on a bi-lobed arrow headdress from Moorehead's excavations in Mound C at Etowah, compared with heads from an engraved cup from Spiro, an engraved shell gorget from Castalian Springs, and an embossed copper plate from Upper Bluff Lake site (from Brain and Phillips 1996:135).

on samples from Mounds B and C from good Wilbanks contexts (Table 9.1). Averaging samples from both proveniences has demonstrated that both Wilbanks phases belong primarily to the fourteenth century and do not prolong into the following century. In light of these dates the aforementioned stylistic argument for contemporaneity of bird-head pins has to yield authority to radiocarbon dating. The proper focus for advancing such a stylistic argument should identify the time-sensitive details of the imagery rather than the image as a recognizable theme.

The Contradiction of the Rogan Plates

The presence of anachronistic objects in the Early Wilbanks burials of Etowah Mound C contradicts the portrayal of these gravelot assemblages by Brain and Phillips (1996) as synchronous and contemporaneous. We can start with the two Rogan Birdman plates since they are considered archetypal of the copper plate assemblage. John P. Rogan recovered these plates from a stone box grave (his grave "a") located beneath the summit of Mound C (Thomas 1894:302) from a zone King assigns to the first three constructional episodes. In 1925, Warren K. Moorehead excavated a third copper Birdman from a nearby grave during his first season at the site (Moorehead 1932:39, Fig. 12). Both discoveries are from grave pits located in the same summit zone as Moorehead's (1932:Fig. 41) cross-sections disclose (see also Brain and Phillips 1996). Moorehead (1932:39) recorded grave 19 as lying eleven feet below the surface. Likewise, he determined that Rogan's excavation pit did not probe lower than ten feet, far short of other more deeply located graves that Moorehead found (Moorehead 1932:77–79). Adam King (1996, 2003) identified the densely packed clay overlying these graves with the fourth to seventh constructional stages. King places this context entirely within the Early Wilbanks Phase. From the same depositional context came an oblong pendant of sheet copper. This sheet copper comes from Moorehead Burial 76 at Etowah Mound C that was deposited in a stone box grave lying nine feet beneath the surface of the summit (Moorehead 1932:Fig. 23). According to King (1996, 2003), the archaeological context appears to be Early Wilbanks and roughly the same as that of the graves that yielded the Rogan and Moorehead Birdman plates (Moorehead 1932:45).

The Rogan Birdman plates bear heart-shaped aprons on each of the figures (Figs. 4.1c, d, this volume). This article of costume, which is actually the scalp of a slain supernatural, conforms rather graphically to a large scalp complete with a rectangular frontlet headdress, shell beads, and long hair (Brown n.d.). A good series of images is available to show that over time the rectangular frontlet is replaced by a round one (roundel) and that the hair becomes conventionalized into a V-shaped symmetrical border (Brown n.d.; Phillips and Brown 1978:98–101). Hence this image is time-sensitive, being an object transformed over time into an oblong device, known as the "oblong pendant," with one or more roundels within the border. I might add that the essential "V" shape is preserved in the instance of the Etowah example from Burial 76 by the simple expedient of reducing the size of the roundels toward the narrow end. Hence, the unusual number of roundels in this specimen is no occasion for concluding that it does not conform to the standard scalp device with the single circular head plate. With a near-contemporary interment of an early and late form of the same device, it is obvious that the representation of scalps found on the Rogan plates represents anachronous forms.

The Moorehead copper Birdman plate, which bears a heart-shaped apron like the two Rogan plates (Fig. 4.2b, this volume), instructs us about stylistic diversity with the gravelots of the two Wilbanks phases at Etowah. In contrast to the absence of coverts on the Rogan hawk wings, the Moorehead plate has the inverted V-shaped coverts that are present on the Edwards, Malden, and Spiro A6a hawk plates. The Moorehead plate is not alone. A hawk plate found by Rogan (Thomas 1894:Pl. 18) aligns itself with the Peoria plate on the wing covert detail (Sampson and Esarey 1993). From these details we can conclude that the copper plates found at Etowah Mound C are hardly uniform and speak to two or more source areas, hardly an argument that the site is the major source for the same plates.

Another instance of contemporary deposition of objects of clearly different age occurs in the case of the many stone statues found at Etowah (Brown 2001). One was buried in a stone box grave at or very near the end of the last mound increment, pointing to the presence of a triggering event that stimulated the deposition of so much anachronistic art. The pair of stone statues was similarly interred at the close of the mound. These stylistically diverse pieces point to distinct origins, much like the Rogan plates (Brown 2001). In short, coppers interred contemporaneously at Etowah Mound C included both relatively recently made pieces and clearly older ones. Sources of origin were likewise diverse. In the case of both copper and stone sculpture, there can be no single source to account for this diversity (Brown 2001).

In the end, we return to the point stated at the beginning, that key assemblages from benchmark SECC sites embrace too much stylistic diversity. Collections from these sites require partitioning into more homogeneous style sets for the purpose of style definition. In both cases, preciosities from distant or unknown sources comprise the SECC assemblages, not imagery placed on locally made ceramics (or ceramics traceable to source area) (Brown 1989). In the two cases, Cahokia and Moundville, where SECC imagery comes primarily or predominantly from pottery, a much more secure basis for stylistic attribution is ensured. Ironically, one of the two sites, Cahokia, is customarily excluded from prominence in matters having to do with the SECC (Brown and Kelly 2000, Emerson et al. 2003). At Moundville a substantial number of preciosities similar to Wilbanks-phase Etowah are likewise from diverse sources. In view of these observations, it is evident that craft locations have to be determined from independent kinds of information.

The Late Braden Style

Over time we should expect Classic Braden style to have undergone transformation into another kind of Braden. But what evidence is there for such a transformation? The best document is the "Wilbanks Ax"—a monolithic ax with engraved imagery on the right side of the upper haft (Fig. 9.6a). Here we have two human heads in profile that compare well with the Braden head profiles on the Rogan plates. Are the differences a measure of time? The answer comes from the scalp motif just below the two heads. Instead of the "heart-shaped apron" device, the scalp on the Wilbanks Ax incorporates a circular head plate and approaches in overall form the oblong pendants known from Moundville. This kind of head plate marks off the later forms of the scalp device from the earlier ones so archetypically represented by the rectangular head plate on the Rogan coppers. The provenience of the ax, unfortunately, can only be placed in the vicinity of the Wilbanks site (Waring 1968). Nonetheless it is significant that this is the type site for the phase of that name, although earlier components are found as well (Sears 1958). There are good reasons for assigning this hypertrophic weapon form to the Wilbanks phases. For one, monolithic axes can only be attributed to this timeline; the later age of the Spiro Great Mortuary context is much too late (Brown 1996:480–481). For another, the imagery is consistent with the presence of circular head plates on the oblong pendant cited above from an Early Wilbanks grave at Etowah Mound C.

The human images on the Wilbanks Ax possess the "snarling mouths" that Phil Phillips regarded as diagnostic of Late Braden. Important examples of this diagnostic can be found on the copper plates of the Old Okahumpka type (Fig. 9.6b). Plates of this type from two different sites bear human heads that compare well with the those on the Wilbanks Ax head.[8] These plates delineate the important "dancer" stance found on Classic Braden copper plates. The feet of the figures are of the Classic Braden prancing form. Note that horizontal arrowheads are arranged along the back of the head, roughly in the same position as the bi-lobed arrow on the Rogan plates.[9] If we accept the arrows as a shorthand

FIGURE 9.6. Late Braden style human head imagery. *Left:* Wilbanks ax in stone. *Right:* Repoussé copper plate from the "Stack" set, Spiro Great Mortuary (Phillips and Brown 1975:FIGURE 253, redrawn from Waring 1968:Figs. 16 and 17).

expression for the bi-lobed arrow, then we have another point of continuity with the Classic Braden Rogan plates.

Late Braden, of course, is well expressed on engraved shell cups from the Spiro Great Mortuary. The early fifteenth-century date for this massive feature does not help us because it was an "after-the-fact" creation from scavenged gravelots of earlier times (Brown 1996). At least twelve engraved cups bear human heads, all except two bearing the diagnostic "snarling mouth" (Phillips and Brown 1978:Pls. 53–63).

Although we know of Late Braden cups from the Spiro engraved shell study, identification of contemporary engraved shell gorgets in this style variant is another matter. However, two style types in the Brain and Phillips system fit the criteria for membership in Late Braden. The first of these is a fenestrated gorget of the Cartersville type (Fig. 9.7a). The head is delimited from the body by a well-drafted beaded necklace. An attribute of considerable importance as a multimedia link is the consistent use of a scalloped line drawn from the nose to the lower ear region, thereby setting off the jaw from the upper face. This peculiar convention is found on the two Walls Engraved pots from the Memphis area mentioned below. It is also present on a Braden A shell cup fragment (Phillips and Brown 1978:Pl. 5), which could just as easily be classified as Braden B, considering the casualness with which the arrowhead was drafted.

A Late Braden position of Spiro cup 5 is signaled by an organizational feature not found in Classic Braden. The legs of the figural pair are arranged in an unnatural manner, something not seen in Classic Braden, but found on a Late Braden cup, specifically in the pseudo-amphisbaena snake drafting on Spiro cup 69, in which the heads are symmetrically paired, but at 90 degrees from where they would emerge naturally from their bodies. On a well-preserved Cartersville gorget from a site near Saundersville, Sumner County, Tennessee (Brain and Phillips 1996:51), the legs are pulled away from the body axis to form the base of a triangular configuration with two raised arms forming the apex. Each "angle" is composed of an arm and a leg from each figure, not the same one. In this carefully arranged composition the triangular arrangement of leg and arm pairs is integrated with the cruciform or saltire arrangement of heads and bodies, much like the St. Andrews cross on the flag of the United Kingdom (Fig. 9.7a). This kind of subordination of imagery to an underlying geometry is one that seems to be specific to Late Braden and is not found in any other style (see Brain and Phillips 1996:50).

In noting the Braden connections of this gorget type, citing Plates 1 through 6 in Phillips and Brown (1978), Brain and Phillips made a connection to Classic Braden in the fine horizontal line decoration of the human bodies and in figures "fussily elaborated with ornaments, headdresses, and body markings" (Brain and Phillips 1996:50). Note that comparison with other examples of engraving is compromised by the influence that the edge of the fenestration has on the figural outline. Furthermore, the treatment of the human figure is not particularly close to that of the Eddyville style that is in so many respects far closer to Classic Braden design vocabulary.

The gravelot association of the Cartersville type of gorget at Etowah Mound C is significant in a chronological placement of Late Braden manifestations (Brain and Phillips 1996:50–51). Brain and Phillips (1996:165) assigned

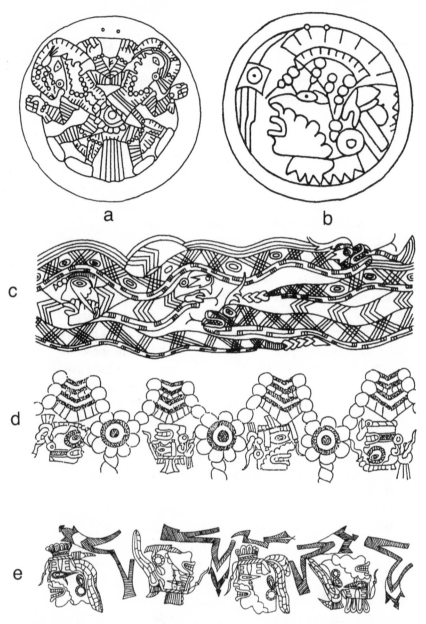

FIGURE 9.7. Late Braden style imagery. (a) Cartersville type shell gorget (Brain and Phillips 1996:51, FIGURE Sr S1, redrawn from a photo by Jon Griffin); (b) shell gorget, Moundville (Phillips and Brown 1975:FIGURE 256); (c) ceramic vessel, Hollywood site (Phillips and Brown 1975:FIGURE 254, redrawn from Thomas 1894:FIGURE 201 and Holmes 1903:Pl. 119); (d) Walls engraved ceramic vessel, Memphis area (Childs 1993:FIGURE 5a); (e) Walls engraved ceramic vessel, Memphis area (Phillips and Brown 1975:FIGURE 263).

both to Final Mantle graves. One was discovered by Rogan at the summit in grave "f" (Thomas 1894:303–304); a second was discovered in the Final Mantle grave at the foot of the mound Burial 19 (Brain and Phillips 1996:151–152). King (2003) would assign the former to the Late Wilbanks phase and the latter to late in Early Wilbanks.

The second candidate for a Late Braden shell gorget is an unfenestrated human head gorget from Moundville that was found with Burial 98 located south of Mound D (Fig. 9.7b, Brain and Phillips 1996:300). Brain and Phillips (1996:68) do not provide an assignment since it is of its own genre, but by Phillips's criteria it has an acceptable "snarling mouth" lip treatment that places it in Late Braden (Phillips and Brown 1975c:x). Of greater, telltale significance, however, is the scalloped line running diagonally from the nose down to a position beneath the ear that we have noticed on the Cartersville gorgets. Parenthetically, this line treatment suggests an attempt to mimic the agnathous (jawless) head, if we suppose that the jaw area was colored suitably dark in contrast to the face proper.[10]

Late Braden is rich in stylistic diversity as indicated by engraved pots, particularly from the Memphis area of the Lower Mississippi Valley. One of these is the "Roberts" engraved pot from St. Francis County, Arkansas (Fig. 9.7e, Phillips and Brown 1978:201, Fig. 263; Roberts 1969). The vessel, which unfortunately lacks any provenience, is a short-necked slipped and polished jar (or a bottle with a shortened neck) nominally falling within the ceramic type, Walls Engraved, *var. Belle Meade* (Childs 1993:143). The panel of severed warrior heads has been placed in the Late Braden phase by Phil Phillips (Phillips and Brown 1978:201). Splintered, half-snapped clubs of good Classic Braden affiliation occupy an upper panel. A second engraved pot, assigned to the same variety, is stylistically close to the Roberts pot. The vessel comes from the Young site (Fig. 9.7d, Childs 1993:Fig. 5a). Hair and headdress treatment on both pots has a distinctive bunched appearance. Of importance in affirming a Late Braden style group is the appearance on faces from both vessels of the scalloped-line facial treatment cited above in the context of shell cups and gorgets. The "rubbery lips" on a mouth full of clenched teeth suggest, however, a distinct variant. These pots testify to an extension of the primary locus of Braden style engraving to the Memphis area by the time of the Late Braden phase, although the sample of two appears to be a slender basis on which to make much of an assessment.[11]

A third example of engraving is important for its linkage with the snakes that are so common iconographically during the later fourteenth and early fifteenth centuries. This late, ostensibly post–Classic Braden style application is represented by an engraved panel on the "Hollywood" beaker from a site on the

Savannah River of that name (Fig. 9.7c, Phillips and Brown 1978:Fig. 254). As it has been clarified by Phil Phillips, the image is a complex interweaving of three snakes, each with its own distinctive body marking. The middle band is occupied by what appears to be an amphisbaena snake with warrior heads at each end, depending upon how one resolves the separated ends of a creature with the same chevron body marking. Above and below are simple horned rattlesnakes. Phillips and Brown (1978:194) saw parallels with the Late Braden cup 68 from Spiro in its three linearly arranged winged snakes with back-curved antlers. The human heads are Late Braden, and one clearly bears the scalloped facial line observed on other Late Braden human heads. This beaker was associated with poorly preserved repoussé copper plates with "Mexican figures in relief" (Thomas 1894:324) that Anderson (1994:352) interprets as falcon warrior plates. The period for the lower burials from which these gravegoods were recovered is coeval with the Wilbanks phases.[12]

The winged serpent imagery provides support for the chronological position of Late Braden. A sequence of winged serpents was arranged by Kevin Schatte (1997) from engraved pottery that can be tied to grave periods and mound-building episodes at that site. The earliest phase is characterized by none other than serpents with back-curved antlers and wing tip rendering. This phase is anchored to the Moundville II period because a sherd was found beneath Mound Q. Subsequent phases depart from this antler-and-wing configuration.

Schatte (1997:8) added to what Phillips and Brown (1978) have observed by ticking off several points of similarity between Moundville winged serpents and Late Braden serpents. For instance, Spiro cup 80 has the highly recurvate antlers and basal tine that are present on what Schatte identifies as early serpents on Moundville vessel SD836. The body decoration on this Spiro serpent is the same as that on Moundville vessel ND"B." The step element on Spiro cup 82 is replicated on Moundville vessel NR17. He adds that the "three fingers" motif operated as an independent device on Spiro cup 78 as well as on the bodies of serpents from Moundville vessels SD87/M7 and SD33/M7.[13] Both of these Spiro cups are assigned to Late Braden (Phillips and Brown 1978).

All told, these serpentine connections are important for placing both Late Braden and early Moundville imagery on the same time line. However, we should not leap to the conclusion that the Late Braden serpents are part of a unified sequence that necessarily leads to Moundville, although this remains a possibility. In detailed respects the winged serpents from the respective locations are sufficiently different as to raise major questions as to whether they are part of a single stylistic series. Nonetheless, the similarities can be regarded minimally as chronological horizon markers.

With the Cartersville style type of gorgets, the Moundville severed human head shell gorget, the Wilbanks Ax, the Hollywood beaker, two Walls Engraved pots, and the Old Okahumpka plates as supportable late, post–Classic Braden period documents, we can substantiate Phil Phillips's conceptualization of Late Braden as a stylistic development from Classic Braden. We have continuity, as well, in two forms of craftworking: that of copper repoussé work and engraving on pottery, stone, shell cups, and shell gorgets.

Braden Hawk Plates

To finish off this review of credible Late Braden imagery, we need to deal, albeit superficially, with a type of copperwork known as the hawk plate. Phillips and Brown (1978) have drawn attention to the well-drafted Late Braden head on one of the plates found near Malden, Missouri (Fowke 1910:Pl. 15–19, Sampson and Esarey 1993, Watson 1950). The mouth has a distinctive "handprint" circumoral marking that may be related to the "three finger" marking found on at least a few Late Braden cups from Spiro (Phillips and Brown 1978:Pls. 55–58). But the Malden connection with the Late Braden cup engraving opens the question of what relationship other anthropomorphized hawk/falcons have to the Late Braden style.

The earliest example, known as the "Edwards" plate, comes from a grave at the Material Service Quarry site of the Langford tradition in the Upper Illinois Valley. A ^{14}C date run from a different grave of the same component gave a mean age of 815±95 B.P. (GX-833) (Bareis 1965). The calibrated age falls basically in the thirteenth century (Table 9.1). In contexts dating approximately a century later are falcon plates from three separate gravelots at Etowah, dating to Late Wilbanks time. They are Rogan grave "c" (Brain and Phillips 1996:135, Thomas 1894:303) and Moorehead's Burials 6 and 51 (Brain and Phillips 1996:138, 142). An additional two come from graves in Lake Jackson Mound 3 (Jones 1982). In significantly later contexts is one radiocarbon-dated set of six copper hawk plates from Spiro (A6a) that has an AMS date of 430±65 BP (Beta-31101) from organics adhering to the plates (Brown and Rogers 1999) (Table 9.1). The associated probabilities at both one and two standard deviations are no earlier than 1410 and 1400 respectively. A range in time is demonstrated that is distinctly later than either the B122 Spiro sample, the Edward plate, or the averaged samples from Etowah Mounds B and C. Barring prolonged curation of these hawk plates, the differences in dates offer the possibility for a developmental history within this genre.

The range in age of these hawk plates opens the possibility that temporal differences are expressed in this Braden thematic type in addition to ones of re-

gional significance. Chronological benchmarks are provided by the hawk plates
from the site near Peoria and from Rogan's grave "c" excavations (Thomas 1894)
into the summit of Etowah Mound C. These plates constitute what Sampson
and Esarey (1993:466) call an "Etowah" pattern that one can argue belongs
to an avian congener of the Classic Braden figural style.[14] Wing coverts are
oval or "shingle" shaped and the legs are bent outward at right angles to each
other. A chronologically relevant observation was made by Sampson and Esarey
(1993:468) that the Peoria hawk plate has a length-to-width ratio and flared
wing tips identical to those of the Rogan plates. They pointed out an essential similarity between the Peoria hawk plate and the hawk wings of the Rogan
plates. Although the hawk wings of the Rogan plates lack wing coverts[15] of any
kind, the strong reference of these plates to the Classic Braden style of the thirteenth century provides a Classic Braden tie-in to the hawk genre.

Differences between the Rogan and Late Braden plates open up the interesting possibility that changes in wing covert shape signal temporal change.
Note that the famous anthropomorphized hawk plate from Malden bears inverted V-shaped coverts, meaning a pattern of vertically lined coverts within
an inverted V-shaped zone described by the "arm" of the wings. Plates of this
"Malden style"—to borrow a phrase of Sampson and Esarey's (1993:468) for
this style phase—seem to belong to a late thirteenth-century date, judging
from the chronological position of the site producing the Edwards hawk plate
in the local Upper Illinois Valley sequence. A relatively homogeneous group of
four plates of the seven from Spiro gravelot A6a have relatively simply drafted
human heads compared to the elegant and elaborate head from the Malden cache
(Brown 1996:538, 548). To further complicate this comparison, the Moorehead Birdman from the second mantle context in Etowah Mound C displays
"Malden" type wing covert drafting that is otherwise found much later than the
fourteenth century. Although a prolonged holdover of the Spiro examples could
account for the 400-radiocarbon-year spread among dated examples, systematic
differences between Peoria and Rogan hawk plate features and those associated
with the Malden or Spiro A6a caches may point to changes in the Braden style
sequence over time.

Other details present on the Rogan plates argue for a relatively early provenience for Classic Braden. It could be argued on the basis of continuity in
the details of falcon wings that the falcon plates without human detail replaced
plates in which humans possess falcon detail. Over time it is possible to conceive
of human images on hawk plates as exhibiting increasingly avian characteristics. Lest one conclude that Birdman imagery was replaced by anthropomorphic
hawks and eventual simple hawk images, there is ample evidence that hawks and

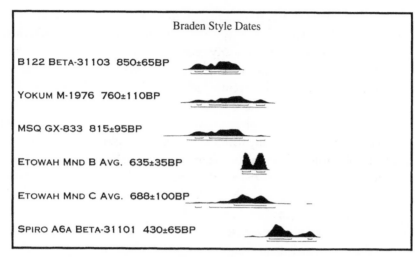

FIGURE 9.8. Radiocarbon date distributions. M. Stuiver and R. S. Kra, eds. 1986. *Radiocarbon* 28(2B):805–1030: OxCal v2.18 cub R:4 SD:12 Prob (chron).

Birdmen coexisted during both Classic and Late Braden style phases. Diversity in the former is documented by the Edwards, Peoria, and Rogan plates; similar diversity is to be found in Late Braden (cf. Hamilton, Hamilton, and Chapman 1974:Figs. 60a, 67, 69).

Style Chronology

At this point it is necessary to review the import of the various radiocarbon dates cited above that have been run on relevant artifacts and their contexts (Table 9.1). As a group the calibrated dates reinforce the chronology portrayed above (Fig. 9.8). The distribution of probabilities divides into three different periods. Classic Braden alone appears in the first subset of dates with high thirteenth-century calibrated date probabilities. It is set off from another subset of fourteenth-century dates that are equally distinct. These date the Wilbanks phases at Etowah and by association some Late Braden images on the Cartersville style of gorget. The third subset provided by the Spiro A6a cache of coppers belongs to the fifteenth century. The probability curves of each of the dates fall neatly into three different centuries, in which the earlier and later sets of dates bracket the Late Wilbanks set, falling mainly within the fourteenth century. Late Wilbanks dates much later than the early- to mid-thirteenth century of Classic Braden at Cahokia and the Spiro III grave period as well.

The first point that can be made is that the three contexts cannot be subsumed within each other. While there may be nuances of age concealed within these centuries-long spans, the dates clearly speak, as they stand, to a multicentury span in the use and archaeological deposition of Greater Braden material. Although the span of time of three centuries seems to be indicated, the period over which this material was fabricated is likely to be much shorter.

Second, the B122 copper plate bearing a human head with a long-nosed god maskette is placed roughly within the same century as the long-nosed god maskettes of marine shell from the Yokum Mound. Thus we have a conjunction, or near conjunction, of form and age that goes far to demonstrating the coexistence of Classic Braden style with the "long-nosed god horizon" advocated by Williams and Goggin (1956) and Sears (1964). From this one can conclude that for practical reasons this horizon is simply an early Classic Braden manifestation within the Braden style sequence.

Third, the Edwards hawk plate from the Material Service Quarry site, together with the appearance in the thirteenth century of Classic Braden human imagery on the Spiro B122 plate, clearly demonstrates the development of Classic Braden copperwork well before the multitude of examples make their appearance in the fourteenth-century graves of the Wilbanks phases at Etowah Mound C. This temporal disparity sheds new light on the significance of the old distinction between the long-nosed god horizon of Williams and Goggin (1956) and the horizon of the so-called true SECC. Both as an image and as an artifact the long-nosed god maskette does identify an earlier phase in the development of the Braden style. But the period of the "true" Southern Cult identifies a period of relatively intense deposition of objects that includes both Classic Braden and Late Braden images. Obviously, a taphonomic issue is involved here that has gone unappreciated. Contemporary Late Braden artwork does not receive the attention it is due, mainly because it is overshadowed by the more visually appealing Classic Braden work.

The division between Classic and Late Braden advanced in this chapter is likely to be arbitrary and grossly conceived, and it certainly will undergo modification and refinement with subsequent analysis, particularly with the addition of new material. For instance, the Rogan plates following Phil Phillips's conception belong to Classic Braden. However, it can be argued that the mouth of the better-preserved piece has a "snarling" configuration that Phil credits to a subsequent phase. This is not a constraint imposed by copperwork technology because the classical mouth is well expressed on the head plate, B-122, from Spiro. Hence, the two Rogan plates may be more intermediate than hitherto recognized between the Classic Braden type facial treatment and the Late Braden treatment seen in the Old Okahumpka plates. The point to this discussion is not to reopen the classification of these plates as much as it is to point up the un-addressed discrepancies in the present classification that future reanalysis can focus fruitfully upon.

The fourth point is the obvious variety that is present in the Late Braden style group that is not present in the preceding Classic Braden. The point-by-point similarity among human images in various media of Classic Braden is not present to the same degree in the Late Braden. The presence of both a toothy mouth surrounded by "rubbery lips" and a toothless "snarling mouth" in the latter makes this reasonable. Although a much larger body of material for the later period may produce a greater coherence to this style phase, it must be recognized for the time being that this variation may be a signature of Late Braden.

Style Geography and Language Groups

While three of the four points implicit in the subject of style have been elaborated upon in the course of this chapter, one remains to be dealt with, and that is the close connection that style has with the history of specific culturally connected ethnic groups.

The recognition that those styles distinguished by Phillips come from equally distinctive areas leads directly to another important realization, that the language groups dominating these areas have something to do with the distinctive features of the art styles produced there. Thus, style geography leads to the recognition that regionalism governs the domination of a particular area by a specific language group (Brown 1989). The Craig style is at home at Spiro and the Red River drainage, where a sequence of three phases can be distinguished. This is an area dominated by Caddoan-speaking peoples in historic times. Other styles have distinct areas of distribution likewise in the areas dominated by one or more cultural formations. The Moundville area was dominated by the Hemphill style and the Southern Appalachian area was dominated by the Hightower style (Muller 1999).

The Classic Braden style can be placed at Cahokia very early in time (Brown and Kelly 2000). Braden style engravings on shell, pottery, and bone start as early as the Lohmann Phase and reach a peak in representation and stylistic development in the Moorehead Phase. This demonstration of Cahokia's early role in the development of the mother art style of the SECC points forcefully to this site's formative role in this complex. By antedating contexts at Etowah and probably Moundville and Spiro as well, the early expression of Braden forms of representation of the human figure and other motifs at Cahokia puts this expression outside of the traditional area of Muskogean speakers and into one dominated by Siouan speaking peoples. While Muskogean representatives are important in later expressions of the SECC, the early development of Braden at Cahokia reveals an obvious shift in geographical dominance and with it its dominating linguistic associations.

With the appearance of Late Braden in the fourteenth century the geographical linkages become less restricted regionally. To put it another way, the demonstrated linkages are to new areas. One such area lies in the vicinity of Memphis in the neighboring stretch of the Lower Mississippi Valley. Another appears to be the Nashville basin (Brown 1989). Although the Eastern Prairies was the source of the Braden style prior to 1300, the geographical spread of this style clearly includes a much more southern base afterward, perhaps signifying a shift from one area to another in political and ritual importance.

Summary and Conclusion

The burden of this chapter is to show that the seminal figurative style of the SECC develops over a period of one to two centuries from Classic Braden images of the thirteenth century to Late Braden ones of the succeeding century. Key to this historical presentation of SECC figurative material is a recognition of the importance of Phil Phillips's analysis of engraved shell cup imagery from the Spiro site (Phillips and Brown 1978, 1984). Phillips's stylistic criteria are robust enough to apply to a much larger set of images from a multitude of sites and well beyond the medium of engraved shell. As a consequence it has been possible to delineate Classic Braden human imagery from Late Braden forms. Late Braden, which has been relatively undeveloped conceptually beyond the "Braden B" phase of engraved shell cups, has been refined by the recognition that the snarling mouth, the Wulfing mouth, and the scalloped cheek marking are useful in tying together imagery on shell, pottery, and copper. During the Classic Braden stylistic phase of the thirteenth century, the Eastern Prairies was the primary locus of production. A stylistic development well into the fourteenth century proceeds logically from this phase in copperwork and in engraved shell, pottery, and stone found at many sites. The upshot of this demonstration of continuity is the necessity of considering the SECC as a widespread development over many centuries within the Mississippian Period.

Conclusions reached here are based on the application of a rule-based perspective to style that follows the principles developed in the Spiro site shell engraving study (Phillips and Brown 1978, 1984) but not followed in the Southeastern engraved shell gorget studies (Brain and Phillips 1996). This has allowed the stylistic assignment of images irrespective of thematic context and physical medium, and it has meant breaking away from the idiosyncrasies present in assemblages that happen to be recovered by archaeologists from specific sites. Phillips's criteria for analyzing human imagery have proved to be the necessary means for defining the Classic and Late Braden style phases respectively. This reanalysis was accomplished with only minor additions to the corpus available in the 1970s (Brain and Phillips 1996, Childs 1993, Schatte 1997). Finally, an up-to-date radiometrically informed knowledge of the age of the archaeological contexts completed the historical patterning.

Another conclusion to emerge from this review of the history of the Braden style sequence is the realization that many copper plates, particular but probably not exclusive to Wilbanks Phase Etowah, were deposited long after they were produced. Key to this argument was the application of the chronologically sensitive development of the heart-shaped apron into the ovoid pendant. Schatte's sequence of winged serpents from Moundville was helpful in anchoring the latest manifestations.

The development of Classic Braden at Cahokia from a regional base in the Eastern Prairies allows a linkage of high style with political, ritual, and economic development. With the loss of Cahokia's preeminence, Late Braden of the fourteenth century shifts locale to the south when other polities gain strength in the Southeast. With this shift comes a sub-regionalization of the Greater Braden style that probably mirrors the proliferation of peer polities in the Southeast.

Finally, this study supplies an answer to the oft-raised problem of why the Wilbanks Phases Etowah grave goods assemblage should be so rich in preciosities compared to Moundville, for instance, as if a cult existed there on a spiritual level different from other sites, and that level defining the "true cult." The answer lies in the widely varying types of grave goods concentrated in the elite graves of the Wilbanks phases. These goods have varying histories of use and sometimes come from distant locations. Long histories of use and far distant origins are epitomized by the Rogan plates, which, as expressive works of art, have arguably little to do with their final resting place at Etowah. Rather, they serve as indicators of networked connections and the rate of accumulation and disposal with the dead. On the other hand, expressive artwork on pottery has everything to do with local forms of representation. They form coherent series, unlike the heterogeneous imagery present among elite goods, and because of the prominence of locally received forms of representation are highly likely to be fundamentally different from most of the objects consigned to the graves of elite dead. With this readily understandable segmentation of the record along divisions consequential of the political economy, those regions that support a representation of iconography on locally made and consumed objects will exhibit a different pattern of SECC objects than those in which pottery is not the vehicle for iconographic expression.

Notes

This chapter is an expanded and revised version of the paper "The Braden Style and Southeastern Ceremonial Complex Regionalism," presented at the panel "Iconography and Mississippian Period Archaeology" held at the 56th SEAC, Pensacola, Florida, Saturday, November 13, 1999.

1. Muller's Eddyville incorporates anthropomorphic and spider themes from the Ohio-Mississippi confluence that Brain restricted to the human figure theme (Brain and Phillips 1996).

2. The place of Braden C shell cup engraving is more problematic, although its inclusion under the Greater Braden umbrella would almost certainly raise the likelihood that substyles other than that connected with Cahokia and the American Bottom existed.

3. The answer to the question of what followed Late Braden is not readily apparent. In the Prairie Plains during the fifteenth century, vaguely related imagery is found engraved on catlinite tablets (Bray 1963).

4. In addition to this two-dimensional art are the Cahokian red claystone statues of the twelfth century reviewed by Emerson et al. (2003) that must be included in the Braden style, if not specifically Classic Braden.

5. But see a more compatible view expressed (Phillips and Brown 1978:200).

6. Larson (1971) placed the pre-final mantle graves in an earlier time. The presence of Wilbanks sherds corrects this preliminary interpretation.

7. Note the connection with ceramic types from the Rudder site, located on the Tennessee River in Jackson County, Alabama. Mound B at that site produced grave goods that included gorget style types and distinctive bulbous pipes that were also found at Etowah Mound C (Brain and Phillips 1996:249–251, Webb and Wilder 1951). Note also the presence of the same distinctive bulbous pipes at the Hollywood site.

8. A total of four are known, two from the Hamilton-Chapman Stack cache at Spiro, one from Jackson County, Alabama, and one from Old Okahumpka in Florida (Hamilton, Hamilton, and Chapman 1974:Figs. 4, 24, 96, 97). Although the latter has lent its name to the group, it is the least complete and is missing the upper portion of the plate.

9. A sheet copper bi-lobed arrow hair ornament from the Citico site bears rows of arrows sticking out of the arrow shaft at right angles and roughly in the same position as the vertical band of horizontal arrows pointing out the back of the head (Brain and Phillips 1996:245). Note that the same row of arrowheads follows the back of the figures playing chunkey on a Classic Braden gorget from Spiro (Fig. 9.7).

10. This type of lower facial division differs from the scalloped line that runs over the nose on the face of the figure in Spiro cup 19, a major Classic Braden document. The orientation of the scallops is reversed.

11. This extension may have an analogue in the "extension" of Classic Braden into the Caddoan area that laid the foundation of an independent stylistic tradition with Craig A.

12. Now placed in the Hollywood Phase, dating around 1250 to 1350, and contemporary with the Wilbanks phases (Anderson 1994:189–193), notwithstanding the citation by Phillips and Brown (1978:194) of Joseph Caldwell's assignment to a Lamar horizon provided in 1952.

13. In the case of the "Piasa" pot the image of a winged serpent has significant features that enable us to place this important document within a stylistic sequence (Phillips and Brown 1978:Fig. 262). The serpent on this vessel of Walls Engraved, *var. Beck* (but *var. Walls* in Brain and Phillips [1996:394]) bears back-curved antlers, basal tine, and distinctively rendered wing tips that connect with an important series of winged serpents engraved on Moundville ceramics (Childs 1993:143).

14. To these can be added the frontally placed hawk with spread wings from Lubbub Creek.

15. The fragmentary hawk plates that Moorehead recovered from graves 6 and 51 do not appear to have coverts of any kind either.

10. Osage Texts and Cahokia Data

Alice Beck Kehoe

Cahokia has become an arena where proclaimed scientific evaluations of archaeological data meet more humanistic approaches, a contrast epitomized by George Milner's *The Cahokia Chiefdom* (1998) and Robert L. Hall's *An Archaeology of the Soul* (1997). Differences have been exacerbated in that most of the more recent, more detailed, and better-controlled data come from the highway mitigation project FAI-270, deliberately located in predicted less significant zones of the American Bottom. Having invested the major part of their professional lives in recovering and analyzing these data, FAI-270 archaeologists are understandably loath to minimize the contributions they might make to comprehending Cahokia; thus we see volumes such as Muller's *Mississippian Political Economy* (1997a) and Emerson's *Cahokia and the Archaeology of Power* (1997) leaping from rural or suburban sites into assertions about the Cahokia polity. Against these "from the ground" approaches (to which are often tacked grand theory), I shall adduce Dhegiha Siouan oral traditions that correspond to a number of features at Cahokia: the Keller figurine, Mound 72, Ramey knives, "Woodhenges," and the mounds and plazas of the built landscape. Francis La Flesche's Osage and Omaha texts, from which I draw these correspondences, offer several parallels to Mesoamerican legendary histories and rituals that suggest connections between Mexico, Dhegihans, and Cahokia —perhaps through the persons with Mexican-style filed teeth buried in the American Bottom during Cahokian times (Griffin 1966:129).

Backgrounding the controversies, sociology of knowledge points to nationalistic ideology (Kennedy 1994) and the legacy of Positivism (Kehoe 1998:82–95, 126–128, 133–144) obfuscating an appreciation of Cahokia's grandeur. The central place analogy must hold in archaeological interpretation (Kelley and Hanen 1988:378) directs us to examine ethnographies of the nations geographically closest to the American Bottom, of which Dhegiha Siouans were the most powerful at the time of seventeenth-century European contact. Recent discussion over use of "oral history" for American archaeological material (Echo-Hawk 2000, Mason 2000, Watkins 2000) requires me to explain why I consider linking Dhegihans and Cahokia a tenable hypothesis. Some preliminary remarks on science, particularly historical sciences, underpin that discussion.

Archaeology as a Historical Science
The doyen of twentieth-century paleontologists, George Gaylord Simpson, laid out the method for historical sciences:

> We . . . observe present configurations and from them infer configurations that preceded them. The principle of actualism is essential for such inferences. Historical inference depends less on projection into the past of the immanent, construed in a static sense, than on projection of processes, which of course do depend upon immanent characteristics. For the most part, these processes are recognized and characterized as they occur in the present. . . .
>
> In the total study of . . . any history, there are three phases:
> (1) obtaining and studying the historical data, . . .
> (2) determination of present processes, . . . and
> (3) confrontation of (1) and (2) with a view to ordering, filling in, and explaining the history. (Simpson 1970:81, 84–85)

Note that "configuration" is key to Simpson; processes occur within configurations. "Present processes" include ethnographically observed rituals and the myths they embody.

Karen Knorr-Cetina's ethnography of a chemistry laboratory led her to realize that

> Scientific enquiry [is] . . . *constructive* . . . in terms of the decision-laden character of knowledge production, [is marked by] *indeterminacy* and . . . *contextual contingency* — rather than non-local universality [and by] *analogical reasoning* which orients the opportunistic logic of research. (Knorr-Cetina 1981:152; her italics)

Heisenberg's 1927 statement of the indeterminacy principle established the contingency of all human observations (Kitcher 1989:449). The impact of physicists' indeterminacy upon historians, examined by Peter Novick (1988:138–140), reflects the breadth of its implications.

From a more historical sociology, Steven Shapin and Simon Schaffer discovered that "matters of fact" are constructed within "a disciplined space, where experimental, discursive, and social practices were collectively controlled by competent members" (Shapin and Schaffer 1985:39, 51–72, 78). Competency, they make clear, is declared by the members admitted to the discipline, a practice heightened by professionalization (Kehoe 1999:5). The barrier erected by extended formal academic credentialing may be challenged by members of marginalized classes (according to Patterson [1995:114–115], "the old buffer races from southern and eastern Europe . . . , gays and lesbians . . . , women . . . , and outside the profession . . . Native Americans"). Joe Watkins, a Choctaw and an archaeologist, remarks that for some Indians, "the scientific method might also be considered to be only a thinly disguised way of separating archaeologists from other grave desecrators" (Watkins 2000:x).

Archaeological inference proceeds from a drastically pauperized database, in regard to cultural knowledge, and within hypothesized paradigms that ideally should be struggling with the archaeologists' own natal and professional enculturation (Barnes and Shapin 1979). The direct historic approach was one logical but, as increasing data may demonstrate (e.g., Ritterbush and Logan 2000),[1] limited method. Knight, Brown, and Lankford (2001:1, 8) argue that the "principle of parsimony" justifies juxtaposing archaeological data with ethnographic material from the same geographical region, especially if "only a matter of a few centuries" interpose (Knight, Brown, and Lankford 2001:9). To put it more plainly, where at historic contact there was a block of nations closely related linguistically and similar culturally, it is reasonable to examine the degree of congruence between their societies and those in the region prehistorically, insofar as the archaeologically available residue permits.

Contention arises over the persistence of orally transmitted information (Mason 2000:256–259). Jan Vansina (1985) and Jack Goody (2000), each drawing upon several decades of fieldwork in Africa, find oral tradition to consist, basically, of what the cognitive psychologists call "schemas" (Rubin 1995:21–23; Lakoff 1987:68; Lakoff and Johnson 1980), images associated through a theme. Oral traditions are structured by formulaic utterances and standardized forms, such as meter and stanzas, but do not rely on exact verbatim rote repetition (Goody 2000:49–53; Vansina 1996:137). In his *The Theory of Oral Composition*, Foley felicitously sees "any given performance or text is but one perishable avatar" of the "work" (Foley 1988:111). David Rubin studied samples of such material from the standpoint of cognitive psychology, concluding,

> what is being transmitted is the theme of a song, its imagery, its poetics, and some specific details . . . an organized set of rules or constraints . . .

[i.e.,] schemas (Rubin 1995:7). These constraints include the organization of meaning, imagery, and patterns of sound, including the poetic devices of rhyme, alliteration, and assonance, as well as rhythm and music. . . . these constraints cue memory (Rubin 1995:10). . . . Recall of a piece in an oral tradition is serial. It starts at the first word and proceeds sequentially to the end. . . . Cues must distinguish the item to be recalled. . . . Each of the various forms of constraint acts in its own way. Having many different kinds of cues makes it much more likely that there will be a unique solution (Rubin 1995:12). . . . [O]ral traditions are stable, in large part, because of the combination of these constraints. There are few options that can simultaneously fit the constraints of a theme, an image, and the multiple forms of sound patterns. Combined constraints produce effects much larger than those of the individual factors by decreasing the memory load and increasing the number of cues to recall [Rubin 1995:90]. . . . The expertise developed is maintained through singing, often at spaced intervals. This overlearning, practice, and spacing ensure long-term retention. (Rubin 1995:307)

The aides-mémoires listed by Rubin dominate the texts transcribed by La Flesche from Osage priests. Especially given the priests' belief that the songs and recitations in their custody "kept them in constant touch with Wa-ko$^{n'}$-da," a mysterious vitalizing power (La Flesche 1921:47, 1932:193), it is possible they preserve concepts active centuries earlier among Osage ancestors (Bailey 1995:6).

Contact documentation begins with Marquette, 1673, who placed Osage with Missouri and Kansa upstream from the mouth of the Missouri at its confluence with the Mississippi in the American Bottom (Yelton 1998:280). Cahokia had collapsed in the thirteenth century, following which an attenuated Mississippian population and marginal Oneota resided in the region (Jackson 1998:111–112; Farnsworth and O'Gorman 1998:88). Algonkian-speaking Illini (including the eponymous Cahokia) had villages in the Illinois River Valley and adjacent Mississippi Valley during Marquette's traverse. From Cahokia's collapse until Euroamerican colonization, the region seems to have been a frontier discouraging intensive habitation. Bailey remarks (1995:29) that by locating away from the great rivers Missouri and Mississippi, historic Osage were in a stronger position to maintain their culture and prosperity, until at last they were forced to Oklahoma in 1872.[2]

The proposition that Osage priests' oral tradition preserved schemas over seven hundred years is a working hypothesis. Francis La Flesche's native fluency in Omaha, carrying over into the closely related Osage language, and full command of English provide texts—configurations—of a depth perhaps unparalleled in American ethnography. Cahokia archaeological data are the historical data, La Flesche's texts the present configuration confronting them. This chapter orders data and fills in the configurations, in accordance with Simpson's method for historical science.

Cahokia Female Figurines

I begin with the artifact that, like the Omahas' Venerable Man (Ridington and Hastings 1997:xxii), speaks even to the archaeologist. Keller is a red fire-clay figurine of a woman, half found in a shallow pit in a substantial building, Structure 87, in the BBB Motor Site (11-Ms-595) in the American Bottom, three-and-one-half kilometers northeast of Monks Mound, the center of Cahokia. The other half of the figurine lay in a garbage pit outside (south of) the building. Thomas Emerson, the excavator, dates the figurine to the earlier of the two major phases of the Mississippian, late Lohmann and Stirling phases at Cahokia, A.D. 1050–1200 (calibrated radiocarbon [Hall 1991]).

Interpreting the site as the center of a farming district, Emerson believes both Keller and the associated Birger figurine are symbols of fertility, water, and the Underworld (Emerson 1989:90–91), although Keller, unlike Birger, has no signs relating her to vegetation, serpents, or farming. Instead, she sits like a woman weaving on a small portable loom, singing or chanting as she works. She kneels on a thick pad, superficially resembling a mat but possibly a bearskin folded so that the paws form its edge. Her surviving hand grasps a horizontal rod-like object that may be a batten or weaving sword (cf. Hecht 1989:61). The batten rests on a foreshortened horizontal loom, its warps represented by vertical stripes. La Flesche (1930:Pl. 26) published a photograph of the parts of an Osage loom used in the Rite of the Wa-Xo'-Be; it consists of a pair of longer stakes, a pair of short stakes, and a pair of flat multiply perforated slats, with a polished, curved deer antler tine for a batten (La Flesche's term). It seems reasonable to dissociate Keller, and her object, from the figurines entwined with likely symbols of the earth and its regenerative powers.

Osage Texts and the Keller Figurine

"The Weaver," a passage in the Osage Rite of the Wa-Xo'-Be (La Flesche 1930:682–699), describes Keller remarkably closely. The Wa-Xo'-Be is a hawk, "symbol of the courage and valor of the warrior," and its ritual, Wa-xo'-be A-wa-thon, is "first in the order of the seven tribal war rituals as observed by the Tho'-xe (Buffalo Bull) gens of the Tsi'-zhu [Sky] moiety" (La Flesche 1930:529).

The hawkskin Wa-xo'-be is kept rolled up in a small rush mat woven for it by a woman who has purchased the right to perform this ritual act (La Flesche 1930:694). When a man was to be inducted into the Wa-xo'-be priesthood, priests representing the twenty-four clans of the nation assembled for the ritual. So assembled, they constituted the "House of Mysteriousness." The officiating priest directed the ceremonial caller (Sho'-ka) to go to the selected woman and place before her "the buffalo robe, the black bearskin, and other articles of value which the candidate [for initiation as a priest] has procured for her ceremonial use and for her fees." She was then formally asked "as a great favor to the $No^{n'}$-ho^{n}-zhi^{n}-ga [priests] to weave for them the emblematic matting." When she consented, the priest recited the Recitation of the Green Cattail (which would be used for the weft) and the Recitation of the "Linden" (pawpaw)—although nettle was actually preferred and used for the warp. The existing old rush shrine was put into a kettle and given to the weaver, who returned to her house. Water People clan owns the Green Rush Recitation.

Four days are allotted for the weaving of the shrine (i.e., mat). The weaver secluded herself behind a partition or in a separate small house, freed from all household and social duties. Ignorant persons are not to look upon the design of the mat on the loom. Each morning when the "Great Star" appeared, the woman went out, took a bit of earth, moistened it, and rubbed half on the left side of her forehead and half on the right: this represented the two great tribal moieties. The earth face-painting was a sign she was keeping vigil. She then "puts on her buffalo robe, spreads her bearskin before the loom, sits down and waits" for the candidate who had also put on the sign of vigil when the Great Star appeared. He had then walked to the weaver's house, and at her door, begun a wail, at which the woman sang her Lament for deceased relatives, then recited her Recitation of the Rush (Cattail), all the while the man continuing his wail. At the conclusion of the Recitation, the man went out on the prairie to keep vigil all day as the woman worked steadily all day. Neither took any food. At the end of each of the four days, the candidate returned to the village and joined the weaver for a supper prepared by a relative of the woman. Before they ate, the Weaver recited verses giving symbols of reaching old age.

The woman's Recitation of the Rush (Cattail) cannot be recited by any man. La Flesche obtained it by purchase, along with the loom, in 1917 from the elderly initiated Weaver Hon-be'-do-ka, who feared that when she died "harm should come to [her grandchildren] through inadvertence or misuse of the sacred articles" (La Flesche 1930:694). The Recitation names four phases of night, the sun, and the sky, each symbolized by one colored line in the mat: the yellowish line along the eastern horizon at the coming of the sun; the moon; the "pallid hue that succeeds the yellow" as dawn develops; the crimson line along the horizon as night departs; the sun full upon the horizon, deep red; the blue sky of day "whose border is like that of a flower"; the blue-black line along the western horizon as the sun goes down (La Flesche 1930:697–698). Overall, half the mat is light-colored, representing the day, and half is darker with a diamond design, representing the earth, night, galaxies, and clouds.

In 1910, Tse-zhi^n'-ga-wa-dai^n-ga told Francis La Flesche,

> There are some things that are not spoken of by the No^n'-ho^n-zhi^n-ga in the rituals they made, things that are not confided to the thoughtless and irreverent, but are discussed only by men who are serious minded and who treasure the thoughts that are sacred and mysterious. . . .
>
> The ancient No^n'-ho^n-zhi^n-ga have likened the arch of the sky to a great head in which are contained all of the things above; within this head life is conceived and put into bodily forms of all kinds. This thought is symbolized by the shrine ceremonially made of woven rush for the safe-keeping of the Wa-xo'-be, the symbol of the courage of the warrior. . . . The upper part of the shrine [rush mat] is made to symbolize the arch of the sky with all that it contains, the figure woven on the flap represents the single stars, the stars that move in groups, like the Three Deer [Orion's Belt], the Litter [Big Dipper], the Deer's Head [Pleiades], and the Path of the Ripening of all Fruits [Milky Way]. . . . The space between the upper and the under parts of the shrine [mat] which represents the space between the sky and the earth is called "cavity of the mouth." The under part, the pocket of the shrine [where the hawk is placed], symbolizes the earth where life takes upon itself bodily forms of all kinds. . . . comes through birth and departs therefrom by death. (La Flesche 1930:530–531, 681)

The woman's Recitation of the Rush concludes, "Verily, here lies a new shrine, they exclaimed, A new shrine wherein shall lie, unharmed, the sacred emblem, they exclaimed" (La Flesche 1930:699).

On the sixth day of the Rite of the Wa-Xo'-Be, following a day in which the priests cut and sewed new moccasins for the candidate, the new shrine was consecrated, beginning with a pipe ceremony, the priest blowing smoke upon the parts of the shrine:

- a buffalo-hide rope binding the bundle, by which it is hung, with an eagle leg and human scalp attached;

- the outer, buffalo-hair woven bag, the hair taken from the shoulder of a young bull;
- the inner, deerskin bag;
- the mat itself;
- the hawk;
- and a pipe and deerskin tobacco pouch to go into the pouch of the mat with the hawk.

The ends of the earth/sky/night lower portion of the mat had been ritually perforated with awls, seven on the Ho[n]-ga[3] end where the hawk's head will lie, six on the Tsi'-zhu (feet) end, these two ends representing the Osage moiety division. By drawing cord (made of nettle) through the two sets of end perforations, a pouch was made for the hawk, pipe, and tobacco pouch. The upper, day half of the mat is rolled around the pouch and the bundle tied. The shrine was used in war ceremonies and carried into battle (La Flesche 1930:726).

Comparing the Keller figurine with the Osage text, we note that Keller wears no face painting, ornaments, or apparent special costume; neither are any, other than the earth daubs, specified for the Osage Shrine weaver. If Keller had daubs of moistened earth on her temples, they would not be visible archaeologically. The vertically striped object in front of Keller shows no weft, and the priest told La Flesche that no ignorant persons should see the design on the mat. The edges of the pad she kneels on could be a fringed mat, or the clawed paws of a bearskin. Congruence between the figurine and the Osage text is close.

Osage Texts and Ramey Knives

Robert Hall called attention, twenty years ago, to Mixtec depictions of Nine Wind (Quetzalcoatl) born from an anthropomorphized Flint Knife, and to Aztec identification of the primal flint knife, *tecpatl*, as Mexica ancestor (Hall 1983b). At the beginning of the pre-conquest Mixtec codex known as the Vindobonensis (Vienna codex), an aged couple, perhaps One Deer and One Deer, or those later identified as Eight Alligator and Four Dog, create a series of stone objects, possibly representing places (Furst 1978:95). Flint Knife, shown with a face, then gives birth to Nine Wind, depicted as a small naked person tied by his umbilical cord to a cleft in the knife approximately where its vagina would be.

Nine Wind is given the attributes of the deity named Quetzalcoatl in Nahuatl: conch columella pendant (Nahuatl *ehécatlcoxcatl*, "wind jewel"), "duck bill" buccal mask, and hat or conical cap. There seems little doubt that Mixtec Nine Wind—his birthdate name, to which would have been added a personal name—is equivalent to Quetzalcoatl (Miller and Taube 1993:85; Byland and Pohl 1994:119; Dennis 1994:164), although the Aztecs did not describe him as born from a flint knife; instead, they sculpted feathered serpents with Flint Knife (with a face) for a tongue, sometimes with the wind jewel, and in some examples, with flint knives substituting for feathers (Nicholson 2000:147–156). This suggests that elongated oval flint knives were metaphorically feathers of the powerful Quetzal Serpent. Quetzalcoatl restored human life at the beginning of this world epoch, by bringing human bones from the Underworld, possibly the concept McKeever Furst notes in the association of skeletal-jawed deities with generation (Furst 1978:22–23). Some Mexica accounts of the creation of our world begin with a huge flint blade falling from the sky to Chicomoztoc ("place of the seven caves," wombs whence issued nations). The flint blade shattered into 1,600 chips that were gods; one of these was Quetzalcoatl, who followed instructions to descend to the underworld to obtain bones and ashes of humans from previous epochs (López Austin 1988:240).

Flint knives similar to Nine Wind's mother are shown in Mesoamerican paintings in the hands of sacrificing priests; perhaps Flint Knife as mother was conceptually associated with the idea that the gods are nourished with blood, self-offered and from sacrificed hearts (Miller and Taube 1993:46). The sacrificial flint knife is pictured as an elongated oval biface secured in a cylindrical handle (firmly grasped in priests' hands; the solid cylinder shape would facilitate a grasp delivering a power stroke). At Cahokia, finely flaked long oval bifaces are termed Ramey knives, from their discovery by Moorehead in the James Ramey mound east of Monks Mound. A beautiful Ramey knife (Moorehead 1929:45, Plate XXVI, 1) in that mound lay near a circle of postholes three to five inches in diameter, fourteen feet below the 1920s summit or twenty-nine feet below the postulated original summit, and nine feet above the base of the mound (Moorehead 1929:45). Conch shells and the small marine *Marginella* shell were abundant in the James Ramey mound, contrasted with absence (for *Marginella*) or rarity elsewhere. "Hundreds of specimens of the heavy axis [columella] occurred in the James Ramey Mound from top to bottom" (Baker 1929:150, Plate XXIV). Thus in this large mound in the principal plaza group east of Monks Mound were laid Nine Wind's mother and his ehécatlcozcatl.

Ramey knives appear rather suddenly in the American Bottom at the beginning of the initial full Mississippian Lohmann phase, approximately A.D. 1050. Lohmann phase shows a greater number of exotic cherts, with subsequent phases reducing these to two from southern Illinois quarries (south of Cahokia), Mill Creek and Kaolin (Pauketat 1994:93, 148–149; Cobb 2000:50, 71, 171). Marine shell (conch and *Marginella*) beads and pendants, and much debitage from their manufacture, were concentrated, so far as archaeological research goes, in the Kunnemann mound area north of Monks Mound, across Cahokia Creek (Pauketat 1994:154).

In the priestly texts of the Osage, the Wi'-gi-e To^n-ga (Great Wi'-gi-e) describes the Tsi'-zhu Wa-no^n gens origin legend. The

> people came down from the sky, as eagles, to the earth and alighted upon seven trees. . . . They came to the top of a rocky cliff, . . . White Rock. . . . From the White Rock the people went forth to wander over the earth. They thought to make for themselves a knife for ceremonial use. The Sho'-ka [Messenger] went again and again to find the right kind of stone of which to make the knife. He brought home the red flint, the blue flint, the flint streaked with yellow,[4] the black flint and the white flint . . . each of which was rejected as being unfit for use by the little ones [Osage priests] as a knife. Finally he brought home a round-handled knife which was accepted as suitable for the purpose [of making a club]. . . .

> Their round-handled-knife
> They quickly took from its resting place,
> And spake, saying: It is a fear-inspiring knife,
> Verily, it is a mysterious knife.
> Mysterious-knife [Mo^n'-hi^n Wa-ko^n'-da]
> The little ones shall take as their personal name.
> They lifted the round-handled knife
> and quickly stabbed with it the body of the willow tree.
> Then from its wound its life-blood streamed forth.
> (La Flesche 1928:84–85)

The willow is said to be "the-tree-that-never-dies" (La Flesche 1928:85), with "a mystical power—a power for resisting the forces inimical to life" (La Flesche 1921:272). The Osage ancestors killed a bison by merely brandishing the club four times in the air, and used the knife to cut a strong strap from its left hind leg, the prototype of the strap every warrior carried to tie up captives (La Flesche 1928:85). Strong parallels between the Osage origin legend and the Mixtec Vienna Codex, as interpreted by McKeever Furst, include: ancient heavenly pairs (identified as particular stars by the Osage); ancestral humans coming to earth via a tree (the codex pictured one, the Osage said seven); and war deities Red-star (Polaris) and Dog-star (Sirius) in addition to the set of eight deities (La Flesche 1928:75). "Round-handled" (cylindrical handle) knives with Ramey-like flint blades are pictured in several codices in the hands of priests performing human heart sacrifice, e.g., Nuttall page 69, and Vienna on the same page as the birth of Nine Wind, adjacent column. Preparing wide bands for wrapping around and tying medicine bundles (wa-xo'-be) was an Osage ritual celebrated in their origin legends (La Flesche 1921:262–268; 1925:92), and untying the band to open the bundle and take out the holy object within was spoken of with the verb used for passing out as in giving birth (La Flesche 1925:94).

Osage Texts and Mound 72
Concluding portions of the Rite of the Wa-Xo'-Be describe the Osage men successfully hunting animals and successfully going to war against enemy villages:

> They gave a forward stroke . . .
> It is a youth in his adolescence . . .
> They gave a second stroke . . .
> It is a maiden in her adolescence . . .
> They gave a third stroke . . .
> It is the man who is honored for his military achievements . . .
> They gave a fourth stroke . . .
> It is the woman who has given birth to her first child . . .
> On going against the enemy
> We shall always overcome them with ease, as we travel the path of life,
>   they said to one another.
> (La Flesche 1930:712–713)

Mound 72 at Cahokia was a small, oval mound oriented southeast-northwest, beyond the southern end of the Great Plaza and the massive upstanding mounds around it. Excavation revealed a series of mass burials strongly indicating human sacrifice (Fowler 1999:158). The set of burial pits is laid out to form a rough rectangle. At its southeast end is the principal person, a man placed on a blanket in the shape of a hawk with folded wings, entirely covered with shell beads. Underneath this, within an earthen platform, is another man, as if bearing the Hawk. The heads of both the principal person and the hawk figure beneath him lie to the southeast. When the Osage camped in ceremonial arrangement, the Hon-ga moiety occupied the southern half of the camp (La Flesche 1921:69); therefore the Hon-ga half of the Shrine mat, wherein is enclosed the hawk, would represent the south.

If the Hawk stood up, he would face the series of sacrifices: closest to him, what may be his four servants, and west of these, ten people with quantities of valuables (copper, mica, chunkey stones, and hundreds of fine arrows). Then, northward, there is a pit with two rows of young maidens, beside them four men decapitated and hands cut off, and west of these, a row of litters with corpses and bundle burials, and under the row, separated by matting, thirty-nine bodies. A row of eight bodies is next (proceeding northwestward along the long axis of the mound); then in the northern end, three pits with respectively nineteen, twenty-four, and twenty-two bodies, possibly all women (preservation conditions were so poor that not all skeletons could be sexed). Finally, at the north end, an apparently dismantled wooden structure with piles of human bones and four corpses associated. Totals: 28 men, 142 women, 5 children, 83 adults of indeterminable age and sex; altogether 255–266 individuals (Rose 1999). The order of classes of people—"youth in his adolescence," "maiden in her adolescence," "man who is honored for his military achievements," "woman who has given birth to her first child"—parallels the Osage war chant. "On going against the enemy/ We shall always overcome them with ease, as we travel the path of life, they said to one another."

Mound 72 may represent the cosmological Shrine of the Wa-xo'-be and the genocide the Cahokians intended for their enemies.

Osage and Omaha Texts, "Woodhenges," and Mounds

The Omaha venerate two beings, one of cedar and one of cottonwood, both associated with Thunder power. Each has a wooden "leg" (the Omaha word) bound to it so that it rests, at a forty-five-degree angle, on the leg. The Cedar Pole has a wooden club attached, the Venerable Man a bow wristguard. Knowledge of the tradition of the Cedar Pole in the Sacred War Tent apparently was lost by the 1880s (or not admitted to the ethnographers) (Fletcher and La Flesche 1911:229). Its Keeper was a priest of the We'zhi^{n}shte clan, responsible for war and Thunder (Fletcher and La Flesche 1911:142), who also was Keeper of the Sacred Shell, a complete mussel shell imbued with frightening power, kept in a leather bag (Fletcher and La Flesche 1911:454–457). Mound 72 at Cahokia contained mussel shells in a midden deposit, Feature 227, including one made into a hoe. A perforated mussel shell lay on the chest of Burial 69. Conch (*Busycon*) pendants were recovered from caches and on a shell bead choker worn by Burial 16, and some beads were made from conch columellae (Fowler 1999:132–137). Whether any of the thousands of shell beads not identified as to species in Fowler's 1999 monograph were made of mussel shell presumably could not be determined.

The Venerable Man in his tent was cared for by a clan of the Ho^n-ga moiety. He symbolizes the supernaturally granted authority of the Seven Chiefs of the nation, and he also "stands for the men of the tribe, the defenders and the providers of the home" (Fletcher and La Flesche 1911:243). His observances are divided into two parts, the first conducted by a man and the second centering on a woman who "shot the arrow along the bow [the Pole itself], simulating the shooting of the buffalo, to secure the gift of abundance" (in "shooting," she actually thrust the arrows by hand) (Fletcher and La Flesche 1911:242, 247). Thus, says La Flesche, the complete ceremony enacts the "union of the masculine and the feminine" (Fletcher and La Flesche 1911:243). Francis La Flesche and his father, Joseph (Iⁿshta'maza), persuaded the Keepers of the two Poles to entrust these venerable beings, with their accoutrements, to the custody of the Peabody Museum at Harvard. Later, by vowing to "cheerfully accept for himself any penalty that might follow the revealing of these sacred traditions," Joseph convinced Shu'denaçi to recite the Sacred Legend of Umon'hon'ti ("Real Omaha"), the cottonwood Venerable Man. "While the old chief talked he continually tapped the floor with a little stick he held in his hand, marking with it the rhythm peculiar to the drumming of a man who is invoking the unseen power during the performance of certain rites" (as students of oral tradition would expect). Two weeks later, Joseph La Flesche "lay dead in the very room in which had been revealed the Sacred Legend connected with the Pole" (Fletcher and La Flesche 1911:224).

La Flesche tells us, "The thunder birds were said to live 'in a forest of cedars'. . . . The phenomenon of lightning striking a tree was explained as, 'the thunder bird has lit on the tree.'. . . There is a tradition that in olden times, in the spring after the first thunder had sounded, in the ceremony which then took place this Cedar Pole was painted and anointed" (Fletcher and La Flesche 1911:457–458). The Omaha Sacred Legend states that the father of the young man who had discovered the Venerable Man told the assembled chiefs of the nation,

> My son has seen a wonderful tree. The Thunder birds come and go upon this tree, making a trail of fire that leaves four paths on the burnt grass that stretch toward the Four Winds. When the Thunder birds alight upon the tree it bursts into flame and the fire mounts to the top . . . yet [it] remains unconsumed. . . . [F]our animal paths led to it. These paths were well beaten . . . animals came to the tree and had rubbed against it and polished its bark by so doing. This was full of significance to the older man. (Fletcher and La Flesche 1911:217–218)

Warren Wittry (1969, 1980) and Melvin Fowler (1999) discovered plaza areas at Cahokia with arcs of large pits interpreted to have held wooden posts like that recovered from the Mitchell site (Young and Fowler 2000:92). Following Wittry, these have been interpreted as astronomical observation markers (Fowler 1996), although such a function fails to account for the number of posts and lengths of arcs. Whether at any one time there was a complete circle of posts in a plaza cannot be determined from existing data, since sections of investigated plazas have been destroyed, or only portions were studied. In the center of the plaza at Mitchell, and in the middle, slightly off center, in the Tract 15A plaza excavated by Wittry, stood single large posts. Regardless of whether circles or only arcs of posts once stood in the plazas, they would have resembled forests of cedars. The single great wooden being in the center could have been the Venerable Man of Cahokia, symbol of the nation's unity and the authority of its anointed leaders. Astronomical and directional alignments would have reinforced its power, as would have the likelihood that these poles, if higher than nearby structures, would have attracted lightning.

Osage and Omaha Texts and Cahokia Mounds

Cahokia, above all, is a stupendous theater of power (Rapoport 1993). Its huge mounds and plazas redundantly reiterate drama transcending mere mortal lives.[5] The mounds loom like mountains. We turn to the Osage "Songs of the High Hills," associated with "the great war rite." La Flesche informs us, "The title of this group of songs is metaphorical and refers to the clouds that appear along the horizon like lofty hills" (La Flesche 1925:349).

This set of four songs (La Flesche 1925:349–355) begins by invoking the hills of clouds to come to give aid, to march in and "move apart from each other as they come." The second song could not be translated. Song 3 is translated,

Behold the beauty of yonder moving black sky.
Behold the beauty of yonder moving gray sky.
Behold the beauty of yonder moving white sky.
Behold the beauty of yonder moving blue sky.

The word *Mo^n-xe*, "sky," "is used as a trope for clouds" in this song. The last song "is expressive of the awe that arises in the mind of the warrior as these colored clouds gather together and in angry turmoil approach, sweeping through the sky in a swift, undulating movement." La Flesche states, "Four of these standing clouds are spoken of as being the greatest in mystery. In these two songs the word for the standing position, 'Mo^n-gthe,' is used for the clouds rather than the ordinary name [for clouds], 'Mo^n-xpi.'"

Are the "high hill" mounds at Cahokia metaphors for lofty clouds?[6] Thunderclouds? (Monks and the other largest mounds around the Great Plaza would have been lightning attractors, higher than surrounding structures.) If this hypothesis is correct, it explains several features: the impression, as one stands on a plaza, of tall standing hills like thunderheads, the varied forms of the mounds, and the colored clay caps encountered in excavations—white, black, and blue-black (Young and Fowler 2000:284–286). Cahokia's location at the northern head of the Gulf Coastal Lowlands, where the Missouri Valley comes in and the Mississippi narrows, makes it prone to massive thunderstorms (a bane to its archaeologists' trenches, e.g., Fowler 1999:147). This is not to say that Cahokia was built at its prime hub location because the great thunderclouds came rolling in, only that the frequency of such display of almighty power added to the redundant signs of this traditional capital's status. "In this dramatic fashion the ancient Non'-hon-zhin-ga have given expression to their conception of the inseparable unity of the Sky and the Earth out of whose combined mystic power the great pageant of life goes forth on its endless journey" (La Flesche 1925:360).

Conclusion

The premise that Dhegihan Siouan priestly texts expound religious knowledge ritually maintained from Cahokia's florescence leads to a series of interpretations of the site's features, from its great mounds to the simply-dressed Keller figurine. Congruence of so many features with the holy texts enhances credibility. It seems to me that Osage parallels with Mesoamerican iconography further strengthen the hypothesis, for Cahokia's scale and urban grid plan are unique in Anglo America, although similar to those of contemporary cities in Mexico, such as Mixtecan-Pueblan Cholula.

Cahokia is unique, and so is La Flesche's compendium of Dhegihan texts; his status as native son, his education, and his training with Alice Fletcher, his strong commitment to saving the holy knowledge, and the crisis in Osage society arousing repudiation of traditional priestly leadership all converged to make possible these thousands of extraordinary dictated pages. As Cahokia is monumental, so is La Flesche's work: that they form a complementary set, icons and texts, is, I submit, a tribute to the dedication of generations of Osage priests.

Notes

1. I select this example because it comes from the Nebraska Central Plains where William Duncan Strong exemplified the method (Strong 1935).

2. Other standard sources on the Osage are G. Dorsey 1904b, J. Dorsey 1888, Mathews 1961, and Rollings 1992; see also Callahan 1990.

3. "Ho^n-ga" is usually given as "Earth moiety," but in fact "Ho^n-ga" means "sacred or holy, an object that is venerated," and is used to refer to the eagle (La Flesche 1932:65). In Fletcher and La Flesche 1911:153, he states of the Omaha Ho^n-ga gens, "Ho^n-ga means 'leader,' or 'first,' and implies the idea of ancient, or first, people; those who led."

4. In the Mixtec codices, stone is regularly shown as striped red, blue, yellow (G. McCafferty, personal communication, Calgary, September 13, 2002).

5. George Milner disagrees: "Much is made about very little. Nothing found at or around Cahokia is out of line with Mississippian developments elsewhere, except for the number of mounds and the size of some of them, particularly Monks Mound" (Milner 1998:12). His "except for" contradicts his opinion.

6. Mountains and rain, coming in the form of clouds, are closely related in Meso-america, to the extent that Sahagún was informed that "images of the mountains . . . are dedicated to those gods of rain" (quoted in Stone 1995:32).

References

Abler, T. S., and M. H. Logan. 1988. The Florescence and Demise of Iroquoian Cannibalism: Human Sacrifice and Malinowski's Hypothesis. *Man in the Northeast* 35:1–26.

Adair, J. 1775. *The History of the American Indian*. Dilly, London.

———. 1930. *Adair's History of the American Indians*, edited by S. Cole Williams. Watauga Press, Johnson City, TN.

Anderson, D. C. 1975. A Long-nosed God Mask from Northwest Iowa. *American Antiquity* 40:326–329.

Anderson, D. G. 1994. *The Savannah River Chiefdom: Political Change in the Late Prehistoric Southeast*. University of Alabama Press, Tuscaloosa.

Axtell, J., and W. C. Sturtevant. 1980. The Unkindest Cut, or Who Invented Scalping? *William and Mary Quarterly* 37(2):451–472.

Bailey, G. A. (editor). 1995. *The Osage and the Invisible World from the Works of Francis La Flesche*. University of Oklahoma Press, Norman.

Baker, F. 1929. The Use of Molluscan Shells by the Cahokia Mound Builders. Appendix A. In *The Cahokia Mounds*, edited by W. K. Moorehead, 147–154. University of Illinois Bulletin 26(4), Urbana.

Bareis, C. J. 1965. Excavation of Two Burials at the Material Service Quarry Site, LaSalle County, Illinois. *Wisconsin Archeologist* 46:140–143.

Bareis, C. J., and W. M. Gardner. 1968. Three Long-nosed God Masks from Western Illinois. *American Antiquity* 33:495–498.

Barnes, B., and S. Shapin (editors). 1979. *Natural Order*. Sage, Beverly Hills.

Barnouw, V. 1977. *Wisconsin Chippewa Myths and Tales*. University of Wisconsin Press, Madison.

Beauchamp, W. M. 1976 [1922]. *Iroquois Folk Lore*. AMS Press, New York.

Beckwith, M. W. 1930. *Myths and Hunting Stories of the Mandan and Hidatsa Sioux*. Vassar College, Poughkeepsie.

———. 1938. *Mandan-Hidatsa Myths and Ceremonies*. Memoirs of the American Folklore Society No. 32, New York.

Bell, R. E. 1972. *The Harlan Site, Ck-6, A Prehistoric Mound Center in Cherokee County, Eastern Oklahoma*. Oklahoma Anthropological Center, Memoir 2.

Bolton, H. 1987. *The Hasinais*. University of Oklahoma Press, Norman.

Bowers, A. 1950. *Mandan Social and Ceremonial Organization*. University of Chicago Press, Chicago.

———. 1963. *Hidatsa Social and Ceremonial Organization*. Bureau of American Ethnology Bulletin 194, Washington, DC.

Brain, J. P., and P. Phillips. 1996. *Shell Gorgets: Styles of the Late Prehistoric and Proto-historic Southeast*. Peabody Museum of Archaeology and Ethnology, Harvard University, Cambridge. Copyright © 1996 by the President and Fellows of Harvard College.

Bray, R. T. 1963. Southern Cult Motifs from the Utz Oneota Site, Saline County, Missouri. *Missouri Archaeologist* 25:1–40.

Bridges, P. S., K. P. Jacobi, and M. L. Powell. 2000. Warfare-Related Trauma in the Late Prehistory of Alabama. In *Bioarchaeological Studies of Life in the Age of Agriculture: A View from the Southeast*, edited by P. M. Lambert, 35–62. University of Alabama Press, Tuscaloosa.

Brinton, D. 1976 [1868]. *Myths of the New World: Symbolism and Mythology of the Indians of the Americas*. 1976 facsimile ed. Multimedia, Blauvelt, NY.

Brown, C. 1982. On the Gender of the Winged Being on Mississippian Period Copper Plates. *Tennessee Anthropologist* 7:1–8.

Brown, J. A. 1975. Spiro Art and Its Mortuary Context. In *Death and the Afterlife in Pre-Columbian America*, edited by E. P. Benson, 1–32. Dumbarton Oaks Research Library, Washington, DC.

———. 1976. The Southern Cult Reconsidered. *Midcontinental Journal of Archaeology* 1:115–135.

———. 1989. On Style Divisions of the Southeastern Ceremonial Complex—A Revisionist Perspective. In *Southern Ceremonial Complex, Artifacts and Analysis: The Cottonlandia Conference*, edited by P. Galloway, 183–204. University of Nebraska Press, Lincoln.

———. 1991. The Falcon and the Serpent: Life in the Southeastern United States at the Time of Columbus. In *Circa 1492: Art in the Age of Exploration*, edited by J. A. Levenson, 529–534. Yale University Press, New Haven.

———. 1996. *The Spiro Ceremonial Center: The Archaeology of Arkansas Valley Caddoan Culture in Eastern Oklahoma*. 2 vols. Memoirs of the Museum of Anthropology No. 29, University of Michigan, Ann Arbor.

———. 2001. Human Figures and the Southeastern Ancestor Shrine. In *Fleeting Identities: Perishable Material Culture in Archaeological Research*, edited by P. Drooker, 76–93. SIU Press, Carbondale.

———. 2003. The Cahokia Mound 72 Sub 1 Burials as Collective Representation. In "A Deep-Time Perspective: Studies in Symbols, Meaning, and the Archaeological Record," edited by J. D. Richards and M. L. Fowler, pp. 81–97. *Wisconsin Archeologist* 84(1–2).

———. n.d. Chronological Implications of the Bellows-shaped Apron. In *Chronology, Iconography, and Style: Current Perspectives on the Social and Temporal Con-*

texts of the Southeastern Ceremonial Complex, edited by A. King. University of Alabama Press, Tuscaloosa.

Brown, J. A., and D. H. Dye. 2007. Agnathic Decapitation: Middle Mississippi Ritual Regalia and Trophy Taking Practices. Paper Presented at the 69th Annual Meeting of the Society for American Archaeology, Montreal.

———. n.d. Severed Heads and Sacred Scalplocks: Mississippian Iconographic Trophies. In *The Taking and Displaying of Human Trophies by Amerindians*, edited by Richard J. Chacon and David H. Dye. Kluwer Academic/Plenum Publishers.

Brown, J. A., and J. E. Kelly. 1997. The Context of Davis Rectangle Motifs at Cahokia. Paper presented at the 56th SEAC, Baton Rouge, LA.

———. 2000. Cahokia and the Southeastern Ceremonial Complex. In *Mounds, Modoc, and Mesoamerica: Papers in Honor of Melvin L. Fowler*, edited by S. R. Ahler, 469–510. Illinois State Museum Scientific Papers 55, Springfield, IL.

Brown, J. A., and J. D. Rogers. 1989. Linking Spiro's Artistic Styles: The Copper Connection. *Southeastern Archaeology* 8:1–8.

———. 1999. AMS Dates on Artifacts of the Southeastern Ceremonial Complex at Spiro. *Southeastern Archaeology* 18:134–141.

Brown, J. E. (editor). 1953. *The Sacred Pipe*. Penguin Books, Baltimore.

Brumbaugh, L. 1995. Quest for Survival: The Native American Ghost-Pursuit Tradition ("Orpheus") and the Origins of the Ghost Dance. In *Folklore Interpreted: Essays in Honor of Alan Dundes*, edited by Regina Benedix and Rosemary Lévy Zumwalt, 182–198. Garland, New York.

Brumfiel, E. M. 1992. Breaking and Entering the Ecosystem—Gender, Class, and Faction Steal the Show. *American Anthropologist* 94:551–567.

Bushnell, D. I., Jr. 1920. *Native Cemeteries and Forms of Burial*. Bureau of American Ethnology Bulletin 71, Washington, DC.

Byers, D. S. 1962. The Restoration and Preservation of Some Objects from Etowah. *American Antiquity* 28:206–216.

Byington, C. 1915. *A Dictionary of the Choctaw Language*. Bureau of American Ethnology Bulletin 46, Washington, DC.

Byland, B. E., and J. M. D. Pohl. 1994. *In the Realm of 8 Deer: The Archaeology of the Mixtec Codices*. University of Oklahoma Press, Norman.

Callahan, A. A. 1990. *The Osage Ceremonial Dance I'n-Lon-Schka*. University of Oklahoma Press, Norman.

Catlin, G. 1967. *O-Kee-pa, a Religious Ceremony and other Customs of the Mandans*, edited by John C. Ewers. Yale University Press, New Haven.

Chamberlain, A. F. 1900. Notes and Queries. *Journal of American Folklore* 13:146–147.

Chamberlain, Von Del. 1982. *When Stars Came Down to Earth: Cosmology of the Skidi Pawnee Indians of North America*. Ballena, Los Altos, CA.

Chang, K. C. 1983. *Art, Myth, and Ritual: The Path to Political Authority in Ancient China*. Harvard University Press, Cambridge.

Childs, T. 1993. Variations of Walls Engraved and Rhodes Incised Pottery. *Arkansas Archeologist* 32:139–152.

Churchill, M. C. 1996. The Oppositional Paradigm of Purity versus Pollution in
    Charles Hudson's *The Southeastern Indians. American Indian Quarterly* 20:563–
    589.

Cobb, C. R. 2000. *From Quarry to Cornfield: The Political Economy of Mississippian
    Hoe Production.* University of Alabama Press, Tuscaloosa.

Coleman, Sr. B., O.S.B. 1947. *Decorative Designs of the Ojibwa of Northern Min-
    nesota.* Anthropological Series No. 12. Catholic University of America Press,
    Washington, DC.

Conkey, M., and C. Hastorf (editors). 1990. *The Uses of Style in Archaeology.* Cam-
    bridge University Press.

Davidson, T. 1965. Moths that Behave Like Hummingbirds. *National Geographic*
    127(6):770–775.

Davis, W. 1990. Style and History in Art History. In *The Uses of Style in Archaeology,*
    edited by Margaret Conkey and Christine Hastorf, 18–31. Cambridge University
    Press.

DeBoer, W. R. 1993. Like a Rolling Stone: The Chunkey Game and Political Organiza-
    tion in Eastern North America. *Southeastern Archaeology* 12:83–92.

De Marrais, E., L. J. Castillo, and T. Earle. 1996. Ideology, Materialization, and Power
    Strategies. *Current Anthropology* 37:15–31.

Dennis, B. J. 1994. Narrative Sequences in the Codex Borgia and the Codex Zouche-
    Nuttall. In *Mixteca-Puebla: Discoveries and Research in Mesoamerican Art and
    Archaeology,* edited by H. B. Nicholson and Eloise Quiñones Keber, 153–173.
    Labyrinthos, Culver City, CA.

Diaz-Granados, C., and J. R. Duncan. 2000. *The Petroglyphs and Pictographs of Mis-
    souri.* University of Alabama Press, Tuscaloosa.

Dietler, M. 1996. Feasts and Commensal Politics in the Political Economy: Food,
    Power, and Status in Prehistoric Europe. In *Food and the Status Quest: An Inter-
    disciplinary Perspective,* edited by P. Wiessner and W. Schiefenhövel, 87–126.
    Berghahn Books, Oxford.

Dobres, M., and C. R. Hoffman. 1994. Social Agency and the Dynamics of Prehistoric
    Technology. *Journal of Archeological Method and Theory* 1:211–258.

Dorsey, G. A. 1903. *The Arapaho Sun Dance: The Ceremony of the Offerings Lodge.*
    Field Museum Anthropological Series, vol. 5, Chicago.

———. 1904a. *Traditions of the Skidi Pawnee.* Memoirs of the American Folklore
    Society No. 8.

———. 1904b. *Traditions of the Osage.* Field Columbian Museum Publication No. 88,
    Anthropological Series 7(1):127–140. Field Columbian Museum, Chicago.

———. 1905. *The Ponca Sun Dance.* Field Columbian Museum Anthropological
    Papers 7:69–88, Chicago.

Dorsey, G. A., and J. R. Murie. 1940. *Notes on Skidi Pawnee Society.* Field Museum
    Anthropological Series 27, 67–119, Chicago.

Dorsey, J. O. 1885. Mourning and War Customs of the Kansas. *American Naturalist*
    19:670–680.

———. 1886. Migration of Siouan Tribes. *American Naturalist* 20:211–222.

———. 1888. *Osage Traditions*. Sixth Annual Report, Bureau of American Ethnology, Smithsonian Institution, 127–140. Government Printing Office, Washington, DC.

———. 1889. Teton Folk-lore Notes. *Journal of American Folklore* 2:133.

———. 1893. Modern Additions to Indian Myths, and Indian Thunder Superstitions. *Journal of American Folklore* 6:232–233.

———. 1895. Kwapa Folk-lore. *Journal of American Folklore* 8:130–131.

Dorsey, J. O., and J. R. Swanton. 1930. *A Dictionary of the Biloxi and Ofo Languages*. Bureau of American Ethnology Bulletin 47, Washington, DC.

Duffield, L. F. 1964. *Engraved Shells from the Craig Mound at Spiro, LeFlore County, Oklahoma*. Memoir 1, Oklahoma Anthropological Society, Norman.

Dye, D. H. 1995. Feasting with the Enemy: Mississippian Warfare and Prestige-Goods Circulation. In *Native American Interactions: Multiscalar Analysis and Interpretations in the Eastern Woodlands*, edited by M. S. Nassaney and K. E. Sassaman, 289–316. University of Tennessee Press, Knoxville.

———. 1997. Metaphors of War: Iconography, Ritual, and Warfare in the Central Mississippi Valley. Paper presented at the 62nd Annual Meeting of the Society for American Archaeology, Nashville.

———. 1998. An Overview of Walls Engraved Pottery in the Central Mississippi Valley. In *Changing Perspectives on the Archaeology of the Central Mississippi Valley*, edited by M. J. O'Brien and R. C. Dunnell, 80–98. University of Alabama Press, Tuscaloosa.

Earle, T. 1997. *How Chiefs Come to Power: The Political Economy in Prehistory*. Stanford University Press.

Echo-Hawk, R. C. 2000. Ancient History in the New World: Integrating Oral Traditions and the Archaeological Record in Deep Time. *American Antiquity* 65(1):267–290.

Eggan, F. R. 1952. The Ethnological Cultures and Their Archeological Backgrounds. In *Archeology of the Eastern United States*, edited by J. B. Griffin, 35–45. University of Chicago Press.

Eliade, M. 1974. *Shamanism: Archaic Techniques of Ecstasy*. Princeton University Press, New York.

Emerson, T. E. 1989. Water, Serpents, and the Underworld: An Exploration into Cahokian Symbolism. In *Southern Ceremonial Complex, Artifacts and Analysis: The Cottonlandia Conference*, edited by P. Galloway, 45–92. University of Nebraska Press, Lincoln.

———. 1997. *Cahokia and the Archaeology of Power*. University of Alabama Press, Tuscaloosa.

Emerson, T. E., R. E. Hughes, M. R. Hynes, and S. U. Wisseman. 2003. The Sourcing and Interpretation of Cahokia-Style Figurines in the Trans-Mississippi South and Southeast. *American Antiquity* 68:287–313.

English, T. 1922. The Piasa Petroglyph: The Devourer from the Bluffs. *Art and Archaeology* 14:151–156.

Eyman, F. 1962. An Unusual Winnebago War Club and an American Water Monster. *Expedition* 5(4):31–35.

Farnsworth, K. B., and J. A. O'Gorman. 1998. Oneota in the Lower Illinois River Valley. *Wisconsin Archeologist* 79(2):62–92.

Fenton, W. 1962. This Island, the World on the Turtle's Back. *Journal of American Folklore* 75:283ff.

Fisher-Carroll, R. L. 1997. Sociopolitical Organization at Upper Nodena (3MS4) from a Mortuary Perspective. M.A. thesis, University of Arkansas, Fayetteville.

Fletcher, Alice C. 1884. *The Religious Ceremony of the Four Winds or Quarters, as Observed by the Santee Sioux.* Annual Report of the Peabody Museum 3(3–4): 289–295, Harvard University, Cambridge.

———. 1903. Pawnee Star Lore. *Journal of American Folklore* 16:10–15.

Fletcher, A. C., and F. La Flesche. 1911. *The Omaha Tribe.* Bureau of American Ethnology Annual Report 27, Washington, DC.

Fletcher, R. V., T. L. Cameron, B. T. Lepper, D. A. Wymer, and W. Pickard. 1996. Serpent Mound: A Fort Ancient Icon? *Midcontinental Journal of Archaeology* 21(1):105–143.

Foley, J. M. 1988. *The Theory of Oral Composition.* Indiana University Press, Bloomington.

Fowke, G. 1910. *Antiquities of Central and Southeastern Missouri.* Bureau of American Ethnology, Bulletin 37. Washington, DC.

Fowler, M. L. (editor). 1996. The Ancient Skies and Sky Watchers of Cahokia: Woodhenges, Eclipses, and Cahokian Cosmology. *Wisconsin Archeologist* 77(3/4): 1–158.

Fowler, M. L. 1999. Chapter 10, Stone, Shell, Copper, and Other Artifacts, 129–139; Chapter 11, Mound 72 and Woodhenge 72, 141–155. In *The Mound 72 Area: Dedicated and Sacred Space in Early Cahokia,* by Melvin L. Fowler et al. Reports of Investigations, No. 54, Illinois State Museum, Springfield.

Fowler, M. L., J. Rose, B. V. Leest, and S. R. Ahler. 1999. *The Mound 72 Area: Dedicated and Sacred Space in Early Cahokia.* Illinois State Museum, Reports of Investigations, No. 54, Springfield.

Fundaburk, E. L., and M. D. Foreman. 1957. *Sun Circles and Human Hands: The Southeastern Indians Art and Industry.* Privately printed, Luverne, Alabama.

Furst, J. L. [McKeever]. 1978. *Codex Vindobonensis Mexicanus I: A Commentary.* Publication No. 4, Institute for Mesoamerican Studies, State University of New York.

Gatschet, A. S. 1899. Water-Monsters of American Aborigines. *Journal of American Folklore* 12:255–260.

Gayton, A. H. 1935. The Orpheus Myth in North America. *Journal of American Folklore* 48:263–293.

Gillies, J. L. 1998. A Preliminary Study of Moundville Hemphill Representational Engraved Ceramic Art Style. M.A. thesis, Department of Anthropology, University of Alabama, Tuscaloosa.

Goggin, J. A. 1949. A Southern Cult Specimen from Florida. *Florida Anthropologist* 2:36–38.

Goodman, R. 1992. On the Necessity of Sacrifice in Lakota Stellar Theology as Seen in "The Hand" Constellation, and the Story of "The Chief Who Lost His Arm."

In *Earth and Sky,* edited by R. Williamson and C. Farrer, 215–220. University of New Mexico Press, Albuquerque.

Goody, J. 2000. *The Power of the Written Tradition.* Smithsonian Institution Press, Washington, DC.

Graham, M. 1998. The Iconography of Rulership in Ancient West Mexico. In *Ancient West Mexico: Art and Archaeology of the Unknown Past,* edited by R. F. Townsend, 191–203. Thames and Hudson, New York.

Griffin, J. B. 1966. Mesoamerica and the Eastern United States in Prehistoric Times. In *Handbook of Middle American Indians,* vol. 4, edited by G. F. Ekholm and G. R. Willey, 111–131. University of Texas Press, Austin.

Grim, J. A. 1983. *The Shaman: Patterns of Religious Healing among the Ojibway Indians.* University of Oklahoma Press, Norman.

Grossman, M. L., and J. Hamlet. 1964. *Birds of Prey of the World.* Clarkson H. Potter, New York.

Hagar, S. 1896. Micmac Magic and Medicine. *Journal of American Folklore* 9:170ff.

———. 1906. Cherokee Star Lore. In *Boas Anniversary Volume: Anthropological Papers Written in Honor of Franz Boas,* 354–366. G. E. Stechert, New York.

Hall, R. L. 1976. Ghosts, Water Barriers, Corn and Sacred Enclosures in the Eastern Woodlands. *American Antiquity* 41(3):360–364.

———. 1977. An Anthropocentric Perspective for Eastern United States Prehistory. *American Antiquity* 42:499–518.

———. 1983a. Long Distance Connections of Some Long-Nosed Gods. Paper presented at the 82nd Annual Meeting of the American Anthropological Association, Chicago.

———. 1983b. A Pan-Continental Perspective on Red Ocher and Glacial Kame Ceremonialism. In *Lulu Linear Punctated: Essays in Honor of George Irving Quimby,* edited by R. C. Dunnell and D. P. Grayson, 74–107. University of Michigan Museum of Anthropology, Anthropological Papers 72, Ann Arbor.

———. 1989. The Cultural Background of Mississippian Symbolism. In *Southern Ceremonial Complex, Artifacts and Analysis: The Cottonlandia Conference,* edited by P. Galloway, 239–278. University of Nebraska Press, Lincoln.

———. 1991. Cahokia Identity and Interaction: Models of Cahokia Mississippian. In *Cahokia and the Hinterlands: Middle Mississippian Cultures of the Midwest,* edited by T. E. Emerson and R. B. Lewis, 3–34. University of Illinois Press, Urbana.

———. 1993. Red Banks, Oneota, and the Winnebago: Views from a Distant Rock. *Wisconsin Archeologist* 74:10–79.

———. 1995. Relating the Big Fish and the Big Stone: The Archaeological Identity and Habitat of the Winnebago in 1634. In *Oneota Archaeology: Past, Present, and Future,* edited by W. Green, 19–30. Office of the State Archaeologist, University of Iowa, Iowa City.

———. 1997. *An Archaeology of the Soul: North American Indian Belief and Ritual.* University of Illinois Press, Urbana.

Hamilton, H. W., J. T. Hamilton, and E. F. Chapman. 1974. *Spiro Mound Copper.* Missouri Archaeological Society, Memoir 11.

Harn, A. D. 1975. Another Long-nosed God Mask from Fulton County, Illinois. *Wisconsin Archeologist* 56:2–8.

Harrod, H. L. 1995. *Becoming and Remaining a People: Native American Religions on the Northern Plains.* University of Arizona Press, Tucson.

Hathcock, R. 1983. *The Quapaw and Their Pottery: A Pictorial Study of the Ceramic Arts of the Quapaw Indians, 1650–1750.* Hurley Press, Camden, AR.

———. 1988. *Ancient Indian Pottery of the Mississippi River Valley.* (2nd edition). Walsworth, Marceline, MO.

Hayden, B. 1996. Feasting in Prehistoric and Traditional Societies. In *Food and the Status Quest: An Interdisciplinary Perspective,* edited by P. Wiessner and W. Schiefenhövel, 127–147. Berghahn Books, Oxford.

Hecht, A. 1989. *The Art of the Loom.* British Museum Publications, London.

Helms, M. W. 1998. *Access to Origins.* University of Texas Press, Austin.

Hilgeman, S. L. 1985. Lower Ohio Valley Negative Painted Ceramics. *Midcontinental Journal of Archaeology* 10:195–213.

———. 2000. *Pottery and Chronology at Angel.* University of Alabama Press, Tuscaloosa.

Hoffman, W. J. 1896. *The Menomini Indians.* Bureau of American Ethnology Annual Report 14, Washington, DC.

Holland, W. J. 1968. *The Moth Book.* Dover, New York.

Holmes, W. H. 1903. *Aboriginal Pottery of the Eastern United States.* Twentieth Annual Report of the Bureau of American Ethnology, 1898–99. U.S. Government Printing Office, Washington, DC.

———. 1906. Certain Notched or Scalloped Stone Tablets of the Moundbuilders. *American Anthropologist* 8:101–108.

Horse Capture, G. P., et al. 1993. *Robes of Splendor: Native American Painted Buffalo Hides.* New Press, New York.

Howard, J. H. 1960. When They Worship the Underwater Panther: A Prairie Potawatomi Bundle Ceremony. *Southwestern Journal of Anthropology* 16:217–224.

———. 1965. *The Plains Ojibwa or Bungi.* Anthropological Paper No. 1, South Dakota Museum, University of South Dakota, Vermillion.

———. 1968. *The Southeastern Ceremonial Complex and Its Interpretation.* Missouri Archaeological Society Memoir No. 6.

Hudson, C. 1975. Vomiting for Purity: Ritual Emesis in the Aboriginal Southeastern United States. In *Symbols and Society: Essays on Belief Systems in Action,* edited by C. E. Hill, 93–102. University of Georgia Press, Athens.

———. 1976. *The Southeastern Indians.* University of Tennessee Press, Knoxville.

———. 1978. Uktena: A Cherokee Anomalous Monster. *Journal of Cherokee Studies* 3(2):62–75.

———. 1988. A Spanish-Coosa Alliance in Sixteenth Century North Georgia. *Georgia Historical Quarterly* 72(4):599–626.

Hultkrantz, A. 1953. *Conceptions of the Soul among North American Indians.* Ethnological Museum Monograph Series 1, Stockholm, Sweden.

————. 1957. *The North American Indian Orpheus Tradition.* Ethnological Museum Monograph Series 2, Stockholm, Sweden.

————. 1992. *Shamanic Healing and Ritual Drama.* Crossroad, New York.

Jackson, D. K. 1998. Settlement on the Southern Frontier: Oneota Occupations in the American Bottom. *Wisconsin Archeologist* 79(2):93–116.

Jacobson, J. 1991. The 1678 Piasa. *Illinois Antiquity* 16(4):7–8.

Johnsgard, P. A. 1990. *Hawks, Eagles, and Falcons of North America.* Smithsonian Institution Press, Washington.

Jones, B. C. 1982. Southern Cult Manifestations at the Lake Jackson Site, Leon County, Florida: Salvage Excavation of Mound 3. *Midcontinental Journal of Archaeology* 7:3–44.

Jones, W. 1911. Notes on the Fox Indians. *Journal of American Folklore* 24:209–237.

————. 1919. *Ojibwa Texts Part 2.* Publications of the American Ethnological Society No. 7, Washington, DC.

————. 1939. *Ethnography of the Fox Indians.* Bureau of American Ethnology Bulletin 125, Washington, DC.

Kehoe, A. B. 1998. *The Land of Prehistory: A Critical History of American Archaeology.* Routledge, New York.

————. 1999. Introduction. In *Assembling the Past: Studies in the Professionalization of Archaeology,* edited by A. B. Kehoe and Mary B. Emmerichs, 1–18. University of New Mexico Press, Albuquerque.

Kelley, J. H., and M. P. Hanen. 1988. *Archaeology and the Methodology of Science.* University of New Mexico Press, Albuquerque.

Kelly, J. E. 1991. Cahokia and Its Role as a Gateway Center in Interregional Exchange. In *Cahokia and the Hinterlands: Middle Mississippian Cultures of the Midwest,* edited by T. E. Emerson and R. B. Lewis, 61–80. University of Illinois Press, Urbana.

Kelly, J. E., J. A. Brown, J. M. Hamlin, L. S. Kelly, L. Kozuch, K. Parker, and J. Van Nest. n.d. Mound 34: The Context for the Early Evidence of the Southeastern Ceremonial Complex at Cahokia. In *Chronology, Iconography, and Style: Current Perspectives on the Social and Temporal Contexts of the Southeastern Ceremonial Complex,* edited by Adam King. University of Alabama Press, Tuscaloosa.

Kelly, L. S. S. 2000. Social Implications of Faunal Provisioning for the Cahokia Site: Initial Mississippian, Lohmann Phase. Ph.D. dissertation, Washington University.

Kennedy, J. G. 1971. Ritual and Intergroup Murder: Comments on War, Primitive and Modern. In *War and the Human Race,* edited by M. N. Walsh, 40–61. Elsevier, New York.

Kennedy, R. G. 1994. *Hidden Cities.* Free Press, New York.

Keyes, G. 1994. Myth and Social History in the Early Southeast. In *Perspectives on the Southeast,* edited by P. B. Kwachka, 106–115. University of Georgia Press, Athens.

King, A. 1996. Tracing Organizational Change in Mississippian Chiefdoms of the Etowah River Valley, Georgia. Ph.D. dissertation, Pennsylvania State University.

————. 2003. *Etowah: The Political History of a Chiefdom Capital.* University of Alabama Press, Tuscaloosa.

Kinietz, V. (editor). 1938. *Meearmeear Traditions; C. C. Trowbridge's Account*. Occasional Papers of the Museum of Anthropology No. 7. University of Michigan, Ann Arbor.

Kinietz, V., and E. W. Voegelin (editors). 1939. *Shawnese Traditions; C. C. Trowbridge's Account*. Occasional Papers of the Museum of Anthropology No. 9. University of Michigan, Ann Arbor.

Kitcher, P. 1989. Explanatory Unification and the Causal Structure of the World. In *Scientific Explanation*, edited by Philip Kitcher and Wesley C. Salmon, 410–505. Minnesota Studies in the Philosophy of Science, vol. 13. University of Minnesota Press, Minneapolis.

Klotz, A. 1951. *A Field Guide to the Butterflies of North America, East of the Great Plains*. Houghton Mifflin, New York.

Knight, V. J., Jr. 1986. The Institutional Organization of Mississippian Religion. *American Antiquity* 51:675–687.

———. 1995. An Assessment of Moundville Engraved "Cult" Designs from Pottery. Paper presented at the Annual Meeting of the Southeastern Archaeological Conference, Knoxville, TN.

Knight, V. J., Jr., J. A. Brown, and G. E. Lankford. 2001. On the Subject Matter of Southeastern Ceremonial Complex Art. *Southeastern Archaeology* 20:129–141.

Knight, V. J., Jr., and V. P. Steponaitis (editors). 1998. *Archaeology of the Moundville Chiefdom*. Smithsonian Institution Press, Washington, DC.

Knorr-Cetina, K. D. 1981. *The Manufacture of Knowledge*. Pergamon, Oxford.

Koehler, L. 1997. Earth Mothers, Warriors, Horticulturalists, Artists, and Chiefs: Women among the Mississippian and Mississippian-Oneota Peoples, A.D. 1000 to 1750. In *Women in Prehistory: North America and Mesoamerica*, edited by C. Claassen and R. A. Joyce, 211–220. University of Pennsylvania Press, Philadelphia.

Kraft, H. C. 1986. *The Lenape*. New Jersey Historical Society, Newark.

Kroeber, A. L. 1900. Cheyenne Tales. *Journal of American Folklore* 13:184ff.

Krupp, E. C. 1995. Negotiating the Highwire of Heaven: The Milky Way and the Itinerary of the Soul. *Vistas in Astronomy* 39:405–430.

Kubler, G. 1970. Period, Style, and Meaning in Ancient American Art. *New Literary History* 1:127–144.

———. 1973. Science and Humanism among Americanists. In *The Iconology of Middle American Sculpture*, edited by D. T. Easby, Jr., 163–167. Metropolitan Museum of Art, New York.

Lacefield, H. L. 1995. A Preliminary Study of Moundville Engraved Pottery. M.A. thesis, Department of Anthropology, University of Alabama, Tuscaloosa.

La Flesche, F. 1921. The Osage Tribe: Rite of the Chiefs; Sayings of the Ancient Men. *Thirty-sixth Annual Report of the Bureau of American Ethnology (1914-15)*, 35–604. Washington, DC.

———. 1925. The Osage Tribe, the Rite of Vigil. *Thirty-ninth Annual Report of the Bureau of American Ethnology (1917-18)*, 31–630. Washington, DC.

———. 1928. The Osage Tribe: Two Versions of the Child-naming Rite. *Forty-third*

Annual Report of the Bureau of American Ethnology (1925–26), 23–164. Washington, DC.

———. 1930. The Osage Tribe, Rite of the Wa-Xo'-Be. *Forty-fifth Annual Report of the Bureau of American Ethnology (1927–28)*, 523–833. Washington, DC.

———. 1932. *Dictionary of the Osage Language.* Bureau of American Ethnology Bulletin 109, Washington, DC.

———. 1939. *War Ceremony and Peace Ceremony of the Osage Indians.* Bureau of American Ethnology Bulletin 101, Washington, DC.

Lakoff, G. 1987. *Women, Fire, and Dangerous Things.* University of Chicago Press, Chicago.

Lakoff, G., and M. Johnson. 1980. *Metaphors We Live By.* University of Chicago Press, Chicago.

Landes, R. 1968. *Ojibwa Religion and the Midéwiwin.* University of Wisconsin Press, Madison.

Lankford, G. E. 1975. The Tree and the Frog. Ph.D. dissertation, Indiana University, Bloomington.

———. 1987. *Native American Legends.* August House, Little Rock.

———. 1993. Red and White: Some Reflections on Southeastern Symbolism. *Southern Folklore* 50(1):54–80.

Larson, L. H. 1971. Archaeological Implications of Social Stratification at the Etowah Site, Georgia. In *Approaches to the Social Dimensions of Mortuary Practices,* edited by J. A. Brown, 58–67. Memoir of the Society for American Archaeology No. 25.

———. 1989. The Etowah Site. In *Southern Ceremonial Complex, Artifacts and Analysis: The Cottonlandia Conference,* edited by P. Galloway, 133–141. University of Nebraska Press, Lincoln.

———. 1993. An Examination of the Significance of a Tortoise-shell Pin from the Etowah Site. In *Archaeology of Eastern North America, Papers in Honor of Stephen Williams,* edited by J. B. Stoltman, 169–185. Archaeological Report No. 25, Mississippi Department of Archives and History, Jackson, MS.

Levy, J. E. 1999. Gender, Power, and Heterarchy in Middle-level Societies. In *Manifesting Power: Gender and the Interpretation of Power in Archaeology,* edited by T. L. Sweely, 62–78. Routledge, London.

Liberty, M. 1980. The Sun Dance. In *Anthropology on the Great Plains,* edited by W. R. Wood and M. Liberty, 164–178. University of Nebraska Press, Lincoln.

Linton, R. 1923. *Annual Ceremony of the Pawnee Medicine Men.* Anthropology Leaflet No. 8. Field Museum of Natural History, Chicago.

López Austin, A. 1988. *The Human Body and Ideology: Concepts of the Ancient Nahuas.* Translated by T. Ortiz de Montellano and B. Ortiz de Montellano. Salt Lake City: University of Utah Press. [Original title: *Cuerpo humano e ideología: Las concepciones de los antiguos Nahuas,* 1980, Universidad Nacional Autónoma de México.]

Lowie, R. 1919. *The Hidatsa Sun Dance.* American Museum of Natural History, Anthropological Papers 16, 411–431.

Lutz, F. E. 1948. *Field Book of Insects*. 3rd edition. G. P. Putnam's Sons, New York.

MacCauley, C. 1887. *The Seminole Indians of Florida*. Bureau of American Ethnology Annual Report 5, 469–532, Washington, DC.

Malinowski, B. 1926. *Myth in Primitive Psychology*. W. W. Norton, New York.

———. 1936. *The Foundations of Faith and Morals*. Oxford University Press.

———. 1954. *Magic, Science and Religion and Other Essays*. Doubleday, Garden City.

Mallam, R. C. n.d. *Site of the Serpent: A Prehistoric Life-Metaphor in South Central Kansas*. Occasional Publications of the Coronado-Quivira Museum, No. 1.

Martin, J. 1991. *Sacred Revolt*. Beacon Press, Boston.

Martin, T. 1998. Feasting at Monks Mound: A Unique Example of Animal Exploitation by the Cahokia Illini. Paper presented at the 8th Congress of the International Council for Archaeozoology, Victoria, British Columbia, Canada.

Mason, R. J. 2000. Archaeology and Native American Oral Tradition. *American Antiquity* 65:239–266.

Mathews, J. J. 1961. *The Osage: Children of the Middle Waters*. University of Oklahoma Press, Norman.

McCleary, T. P. 1997. *The Stars We Know*. Waveland, Prospect Heights, IL.

Mensforth, R. P. 2001. Warfare and Trophy Taking in the Archaic Period. In *Archaic Transitions in Ohio and Kentucky Prehistory*, edited by Olaf H. Prufer, Sara E. Pedde, and Richard S. Meindl, 110–138. Kent State University Press, Kent, OH.

———. 2004. Human Trophy Taking in Eastern North America during the Archaic Period: Its Relationship to Demographic Change, Warfare, and the Evolution of Segmented Social Organizations. Paper presented at the 69th Annual Meeting of the Society for American Archaeology, Montreal.

Michelson, T. 1935. The Menomini Hairy Serpent and the Hairy Fish. *Journal of American Folklore* 48:197–199.

Miller, M., and K. Taube. 1993. *The Gods and Symbols of Ancient Mexico and the Maya*. Thames and Hudson, New York.

Milner, G. R. 1995. An Osteological Perspective on Prehistoric Warfare. In *Regional Approaches to Mortuary Analysis*, edited by Lane A. Beck, 221–244. Plenum, New York.

———. 1998. *The Cahokia Chiefdom: The Archaeology of a Mississippian Society*. Smithsonian Institution Press, Washington, DC.

Mitchell, R. T., and H. S. Zim. 1987. *Butterflies and Moths, a Golden Guide*. Golden Press, New York.

Mooney, J. 1891. *Sacred Formulas of the Cherokees*. Seventh Annual Report of the Bureau of Ethnology, 301–397. Washington, DC.

———. 1900. *Myths of the Cherokee*. Annual Report of the Bureau of American Ethnology 19(1):3–548.

Moore, C. B. 1895. Certain Sand Mounds of the Ocklawaha River, Florida, Part I. *Journal of the Academy of Natural Sciences of Philadelphia*, Second Series, vol. 10, part 1. Philadelphia, PA.

———. 1905. Certain Aboriginal Remains of the Black Warrior River. *Journal of the Academy of Natural Sciences of Philadelphia* 13:125–244.

————. 1907. Moundville Revisited. *Journal of the Academy of Natural Sciences of Philadelphia* 13:335–405.

Moorehead, W. K. 1929. *The Cahokia Mounds.* University of Illinois, Urbana.

————. 1932. Exploration of the Etowah site in Georgia. In *Etowah Papers.* Published for the Phillips Academy, Andover, by Yale University Press, New Haven, CT.

Morse, D. F., and P. A. Morse. 1983. *Archaeology of the Central Mississippi Valley.* Academic Press, New York.

Morse, D. F., and P. A. Morse (editors). 1998. *The Lower Mississippi Valley Expeditions of Clarence Bloomfield Moore.* University of Alabama Press, Tuscaloosa.

Muller, J. 1966. An Experimental Theory of Stylistic Analysis. Ph.D. dissertation, Department of Anthropology, Harvard University, Cambridge.

————. 1979. Structural Studies of Art Styles. In *The Visual Arts, Plastic and Graphic,* edited by J. Cordwell, 139–211. Mouton, The Hague.

————. 1989. The Southern Cult. In *Southern Ceremonial Complex, Artifacts and Analysis: The Cottonlandia Conference,* edited by P. Galloway, 11–26. University of Nebraska Press, Lincoln.

————. 1997a. *Mississippian Political Economy.* Plenum Press, New York.

————. 1997b. Review of Brain and Phillips: Shell Gorgets: Styles of the Late Prehistoric and Protohistoric Southeast. *Southeastern Archaeology* 16:176–178.

————. 1999. Southeastern Interaction and Integration. In *Great Towns and Regional Polities in the Prehistoric American Southwest and Southeast,* edited by Jill E. Neitzel, 143–158. University of New Mexico Press, Albuquerque.

Müller, W. 1968. North America. In *Pre-Columbian American Religions,* edited by W. Krickeberg, H. Trimborn, W. Müller, and O. Zeries. Holt, Rinehart, and Winston, New York.

Munro, P., and C. Willmond. 1994. *Chickasaw: An Analytical Dictionary.* University of Oklahoma Press, Norman.

Murie, J. R. 1914. *Pawnee Indian Societies.* American Museum of Natural History Anthropological Papers 11, 543–644.

————. 1981. *Ceremonies of the Pawnee.* Smithsonian Contributions to Anthropology No. 27, Washington, DC.

————. 1989. *Ceremonies of the Pawnee.* University of Nebraska Press, Lincoln.

Newcomb, W. W. Jr. 1961. *The Indians of Texas from Prehistoric to Modern Times.* University of Texas Press, Austin.

Nicholson, H. B. 2000. The Iconography of the Feathered Serpent in Late Postclassic Central Mexico. In *Mesoamerica's Classic Heritage: From Teotihuacán to the Aztecs,* edited by D. Carrasco, L. Jones, and S. Sessions, 145–164. University Press of Colorado, Boulder.

Novick, P. 1988. *That Noble Dream: The "Objectivity Question" and the American Historical Profession.* Cambridge University Press, Cambridge.

O'Brien, M. J. 1994. *Cat Monsters and Head Pots: The Archaeology of Missouri's Pemiscot Bayou.* University of Missouri Press, Columbia.

Overstreet, D. F. 1995. The Eastern Wisconsin Oneota Regional Continuity. In *Oneota*

Archaeology: Past, Present, and Future, edited by William Green, 33–64. Office of the State Archaeologist, University of Iowa, Iowa City.

Owsley, D. W., and H. E. Berryman. 1975. Ethnographic and Archaeological Evidence of Scalping in the Southeastern United States. *Tennessee Archaeologist* 31(1):41–58.

Panofsky, E. 1939. *Studies in Iconology: Humanistic Themes in the Art of the Renaissance* (1936), 3–31. Oxford University Press, New York.

Parsons, E. C. 1925. Micmac Folklore. *Journal of American Folklore* 38, 60ff.

Patterson, T. C. 1995. *Toward a Social History of Archaeology in the United States.* Harcourt Brace, Ft. Worth.

Pauketat, T. R. 1994. *The Ascent of Chiefs: Cahokia and Mississippian Politics in Native North America.* University of Alabama Press, Tuscaloosa.

———. 2003. Materiality and the Immaterial in Historical-Processual Archaeology. In *Essential Tensions in Archaeological Method and Theory*, edited by Todd L. VanPool and Christine S. VanPool, 41–54. University of Utah Press, Salt Lake City.

Pauketat, T. R., and T. E. Emerson. 1991. The Ideology of Authority and the Power of the Pot. *American Anthropologist* 93:919–941.

Perino, G. 1971. The Yokum Site, Pike County, Illinois. *Mississippian Site Archaeology in Illinois I*, 149–186. Illinois Archaeological Survey (Bulletin 8), Urbana, IL.

Phelps, D. S. 1970. *Mesoamerican Glyph Motifs on Southeastern Pottery.* Transactions of the International Congress of Americanists, 38th Session, Munich, 2:89–99.

Phillips, P. 1939. Introduction to the Archaeology of the Mississippi Valley. Ph.D. dissertation, Department of Anthropology, Harvard University, Cambridge.

Phillips, P., and J. A. Brown. 1975a. *Pre-Columbian Shell Engravings from Craig Mound at Spiro, Oklahoma.* Vol. 1. Copyright © 1975 by the President and Fellows of Harvard College. Cambridge, MA: Peabody Museum Press, Harvard University.

———. 1975b. *Pre-Columbian Shell Engravings from Craig Mound at Spiro, Oklahoma.* Vol. 2. Cambridge, MA: Peabody Museum Press, Harvard University. Copyright © 1975 by the President and Fellows of Harvard College.

———. 1975c. *Pre-Columbian Shell Engravings from Craig Mound at Spiro, Oklahoma.* Vol. 3. Cambridge, MA: Peabody Museum Press, Harvard University. Copyright © 1975 by the President and Fellows of Harvard College.

———. 1978. *Pre-Columbian Shell Engravings from the Craig Mound at Spiro, Oklahoma,* Part I (paperback edition). Peabody Museum of Archaeology and Ethnology, Harvard University, Cambridge. Copyright © 1978 by the President and Fellows of Harvard College.

———. 1979. *Pre-Columbian Shell Engravings from Craig Mound at Spiro, Oklahoma.* Vol. 4. Cambridge, MA: Peabody Museum Press, Harvard University. Copyright © 1979 by the President and Fellows of Harvard College.

———. 1980. *Pre-Columbian Shell Engravings from Craig Mound at Spiro, Oklahoma.* Vol. 5. Cambridge, MA: Peabody Museum Press, Harvard University. Copyright © 1980 by the President and Fellows of Harvard College.

———. 1982. *Pre-Columbian Shell Engravings from Craig Mound at Spiro, Okla-*

homa. Vol. 6. Cambridge, MA: Peabody Museum Press, Harvard University. Copyright © 1982 by the President and Fellows of Harvard College.

———. 1984. *Pre-Columbian Shell Engravings from the Craig Mound at Spiro, Oklahoma.* Part II (paperback edition). Peabody Museum of Archaeology and Ethnology, Harvard University, Cambridge. Copyright © 1984 by the President and Fellows of Harvard College.

Phillips, P., J. A. Ford, and J. B. Griffin. 1951. *Archaeological Survey in the Lower Mississippi Alluvial Valley, 1940–1947.* Papers of the Peabody Museum of Archaeology and Ethnology, vol. 25. Harvard University, Cambridge.

Powers, W. K. 1975. *Oglala Religion.* University of Nebraska Press, Lincoln.

Prentice, G. 1986. An Analysis of the Symbolism Expressed by the Birger Figurine. *American Antiquity* 51(2):239–266.

Radin, P. 1923. *The Winnebago Tribe.* Bureau of American Ethnology Annual Report 37, Washington, DC.

———. 1948. *Winnebago Hero Cycles: A Study in Aboriginal Literature.* Indiana University Publications in Anthropology and Linguistics, Bloomington.

———. 1950. *The Basic Myth of the North American Indians.* Eranos-Jahrbuch 1949 17:359–419.

———. 1954. *The Evolution of an American Indian Prose Epic: A Study in Comparative Literature Part I.* Special Publications of the Bollingen Foundation No. 3.

Rapoport, A. 1993. On the Nature of Capitals and Their Physical Expression. In *Capital Cities: International Perspectives/Les capitales: Perspectives internationales,* edited by J. Taylor et al., 31–67. Carleton University Press, Ottowa.

Rappaport, R. A. 1999. *Ritual and Religion in the Making of Humanity.* Cambridge University Press, Cambridge.

Reichard, G. A. 1921. Literary Types and Dissemination of Myths. *Journal of American Folklore* 27:269–307.

Reilly, F. K., III. 1995. Art, Ritual, and Rulership in the Olmec World. In *The Olmec World: Ritual and Rulership,* edited by G. Guthrie, 27–46. Harry Abrams, New York.

———. 1999. A Proposed Function for the Bi-Lobed Arrow Motif. Paper presented at the Annual Meeting of the Southeastern Archaeological Conference, Pensacola.

———. 2000. The Striped Pole Motif and the Ritual Construction of Cosmic Order in the Southeastern Ceremonial Complex. Paper presented at the 57th Annual Meeting of the Southeastern Archaeological Conference, Macon, GA.

Reyna, S. P. 1994. A Mode of Domination Approach to Organized Violence. In *Studying War: Anthropological Perspectives,* edited by S. P. Reyna and R. E. Downs, 29–65. Gordon and Breach, New York.

Ridington, R. 1993. A Sacred Object as Text. *American Indian Quarterly* 17.

Ridington, R., and D. Hastings (In'aska). 1997. *Blessing for a Long Time: The Sacred Pole of the Omaha Tribe.* University of Nebraska Press, Lincoln.

Ritterbush, L. W., and B. Logan. 2000. Late Prehistoric Oneota Population Migration into the Central Plains. *Plains Anthropologist* 45 (173):257–272.

Roberts, J. C. 1969. An Unusual Engraved Pottery Vessel. *Redskin* 4:60–66.

Rolingson, Martha A. 1994. Symbolic and Calendric Aspects of Community Design in Eastern North America. Paper presented at the Annual Meeting of the Midwest Archaeological Conference, Milwaukee.

Rollings, W. H. 1992. *The Osage: An Ethnohistorical Study of Hegemony on the Prairie-Plains*. University of Missouri Press, Columbia.

Rose, J. C. 1999. Chapter 6. Mortuary Data and Analysis. In *The Mound 72 Area: Dedicated and Sacred Space in Early Cahokia*, by Melvin L. Fowler et al. 63–82. Reports of Investigations, No. 54, Illinois State Museum, Springfield.

Rubin, D. C. 1995. *Memory in Oral Traditions: The Cognitive Psychology of Epic, Ballads, and Counting-out Rhymes*. Oxford University Press, New York.

Salzer, R. J. 1987. Preliminary Report on the Gottschall Site (47Ia80). *Wisconsin Archeologist* 68:419–472.

Salzer, R. J., and G. Rajnovich. 2000. *The Gottschall Rockshelter: An Archaeological Mystery*. Prairie Smoke Press, St. Paul, MN.

Sampson, K., and D. Esarey. 1993. A Survey of Elaborate Mississippian Copper Artifacts from Illinois. *Illinois Archaeology* 5:452–480.

Sasso, R. F. 1993. La Crosse Region Oneota Adaptation—Changing Late Prehistoric Subsistence and Settlement Patterns in the Upper Mississippi Valley. *Wisconsin Archeologist* 74:246–290.

Schatte, K. E. 1997. Moundville's Winged Serpents: An Analysis of Style. Paper presented at the 54th Annual Meeting of the Southeastern Archaeological Conference, Baton Rouge, LA, 1997.

Schele, L., and M. E. Miller. 1986. *The Blood of Kings: Dynasty and Ritual in Maya Art*. Kimbell Art Museum, Fort Worth.

Schlesier, K. H. 1994. Commentary: A History of Ethnic Groups in the Great Plains, A.D. 150–1550. In *Plains Indians, A.D. 500–1500*, edited by K. H. Schlesier, 308–381. University of Oklahoma Press, Norman.

Schutz, N. W. 1975. The Study of Shawnee Myth in an Ethnographic and Ethnohistorical Perspective. Ph.D. dissertation, Indiana University, Bloomington.

Sears, W. H. 1958. *The Wilbanks Site (9CK-5), Georgia*. Bureau of Ethnology, River Basin Papers, no. 12, Washington, DC.

———. 1964. The Southeastern United States. In *Prehistoric Man in the New World*, edited by J. D. Jennings and E. Norbeck, 259–287. University of Chicago Press, Chicago.

Shapin, S., and S. Schaffer. 1985. *Leviathan and the Air-Pump*. Princeton University Press, Princeton.

Sievert, A. K. 1992. The Craig Mound at Spiro, Oklahoma: Artifacts in the Collection of the Smithsonian Institution. Report submitted to the Office of Repatriation and the Department of Anthropology, National Museum of Natural History, Smithsonian Institution, Washington, DC.

Simpson, G. G. 1970. Uniformitarianism: An Inquiry into Principle, Theory, and Method in Geohistory and Biohistory. In *Essays in Evolution and Genetics in Honor of Theodosius Dobzhansky*, edited by M. K. Hecht and W. C. Steere, 43–96. Appleton-Century-Crofts, New York.

Skinner, A. 1923a. *Observations on the Ethnology of the Sauk Indians.* Public Museum of the City of Milwaukee Bulletin 5.

———. 1923b. *Prairie Potawatomi Indians.* Public Museum of the City of Milwaukee Bulletin 6.

Smith, M. O. 1997. Osteological Indications of Warfare in the Archaic Period of the Western Tennessee Valley. In *Troubled Times: Violence and Warfare in the Past,* edited by D. L. Martin and D. W. Frayer, 241–265. Gordon and Breach, New York.

Smith, T. S. 1995. *The Island of the Anishnaabeg.* University of Idaho Press, Moscow, ID.

Speck, F. G. 1909. *Ethnology of the Yuchi Indians.* Anthropology Publication No. 1, University of Pennsylvania Museum, Philadelphia.

———. 1931. *A Study of the Delaware Indian Big House Ceremony.* Pennsylvania Historical Commission, Harrisburg.

Spier, L. 1921. *The Sun Dance of the Plains Indians: Its Development and Diffusion.* American Museum of Natural History Anthropological Papers XVI, Part VII, 458–527.

Spinden, H. J. 1913. *A Study of Maya Art.* Memoirs of the Peabody Museum, vol. 6, Harvard University, Cambridge.

Springer, J. W., and S. R. Witkowski. 1982. Siouan Historical Linguistics and Oneota Archaeology. In *Oneota Studies,* edited by Guy E. Gibbon, 69–83. University of Minnesota Publications in Anthropology No. 1, Minneapolis.

Steponaitis, V. 1983. *Ceramics, Chronology, and Community Patterns: An Archaeological Study at Moundville.* Academic Press, New York.

Stone, A. J. 1995. *Images from the Underworld.* University of Texas Press, Austin.

Strong, J. A. 1989. The Mississippian Bird-Man Theme in Cross-Cultural Perspective. In *The Southeastern Ceremonial Complex: Artifacts and Analysis,* edited by P. K. Galloway, 211–238. University of Nebraska Press, Lincoln.

Strong, W. D. 1935. *An Introduction to Nebraska Archeology.* Smithsonian Miscellaneous Collections, vol. 93, no. 10. Government Printing Office, Washington, DC.

Stuiver, M., and R. S. Kra, eds. 1986. *Radiocarbon* 28(2B):805–1030.

Styles, B. W., and J. R. Purdue. 1991. Ritual and Secular Use of Fauna by Middle Woodland Peoples of Western Illinois. In *Beamers, Bobwhites and Blue-points: Tributes to the Career of Paul W. Parmalee,* edited by J. R. Purdue, W. E. Klippel, and B. W. Styles, 420–436. Illinois State Museum, Scientific Papers 23, Springfield.

Sullivan, W. 1996. *The Secret of the Incas.* Crown Publishing, New York.

Swanton, J. R. 1907. Mythology of the Indians of Louisiana and the Texas Coast. *Journal of American Folklore* 20:285ff.

———. 1911. *Indian Tribes of the Lower Mississippi Valley and Adjacent Coast of the Gulf of Mexico.* Bureau of American Ethnology Bulletin 43, Washington, DC.

———. 1928a. *Social Organization and Social Usages of the Indians of the Creek Confederacy.* Bureau of American Ethnology Annual Report 42, Washington, DC.

———. 1928b. Sun Worship in the Southeast. *American Anthropologist* 30:206–213.

———. 1928c. *Creek Religion and Medicine.* Bureau of American Ethnology Annual Report 42, Washington, DC.

————. 1928d. *Social and Religious Beliefs and Usages of the Chickasaw Indians.* Bureau of American Ethnology Annual Report 44, 169–273, Washington, DC.

————. 1929. *Myths and Tales of the Southeastern Indians.* Bureau of American Ethnology Bulletin 88, Washington, DC.

————. 1931. *Source Material for the Social and Ceremonial Life of the Choctaw Indians.* Bureau of American Ethnology Bulletin 103, Smithsonian Institution, Washington, DC.

————. 1946. *The Indians of the Southeastern United States.* Bureau of American Ethnology Bulletin 137, Washington, DC.

Taylor, L. A. 1940. *Plants Used as Curatives by Certain Southeastern Indians.* Botanical Museum of Harvard University, Cambridge.

ten Kate, H. 1889. Legends of the Cherokees. *Journal of American Folklore* 2:53ff.

Thomas, C. 1894. *Report of the Mound Explorations of the Bureau of American Ethnology.* Twelfth Annual Report of the Bureau of Ethnology. Washington, DC.

Thompson, S. 1956. *Tales of the North American Indians.* Indiana University Press, Bloomington.

Thwaites, R. G. (editor). 1896–1901. *The Jesuit Relations and Related Documents.* 73 vols. Burrows Brothers, Cleveland.

————. 1897. The Jesuit Relations and Allied Documents, vol. 10. Burrows Brothers, Cleveland.

Tooker, E. 1964. *An Ethnography of the Huron Indians 1615–1649.* Bureau of American Ethnology Bulletin 190, Washington, DC.

Townsend, R. F. 1979. *State and Cosmos in the Art of Tenochtitlan.* Studies in Pre-Columbian Art and Archaeology 20, Dumbarton Oaks, Washington, DC.

Tregle, J. G., Jr. (editor). 1975. *The History of Louisiana.* Louisiana State University Press, Baton Rouge.

Turney-High, H. H. 1949. *Primitive War: Its Practice and Concepts.* University of South Carolina Press, Columbia.

van der Dennen, J. M. G. 1998. The Politics of Peace in Primitive Societies: The Adaptive Rationale behind Corroboree and Calumet. In *Indoctrinability, Ideology, and Warfare: Evolutionary Perspectives,* edited by Irenäus Eibl-Eibesfeldt and F. K. Salter, 150–185. Berghahn Books, New York.

VanDerwarker, A. M. 1999. Feasting and Status at the Toqua Site. *Southeastern Archaeology* 18(1):24–34.

Vansina, J. 1985. *Oral Tradition as History.* University of Wisconsin Press, Madison.

————. 1996. Epilogue: Fieldwork in History. In *In Pursuit of History: Fieldwork in Africa,* edited by C. K. Adenaike and J. Vansina, 127–140. Heinemann, NH.

Vecsey, C. 1983. *Traditional Ojibwa Religion and Its Historical Changes.* American Philosophical Society, Philadelphia.

————. 1988. The Ojibwa Creation Myth (written with John F. Fisher). In *Imagine Ourselves Richly,* 64–93. Crossroad, New York.

Voegelin, C. F. 1936. *The Shawnee Female Deity.* Yale University Publications in Anthropology, No. 10. Yale University Press, New Haven.

———. 1972. North American Indian Folklore. In *Funk and Wagnalls Standard Dictionary of Folklore, Mythology, and Legend,* edited by M. Leach, 798–802. Harper and Row, New York.

von Gernet, A. 1993. The Construction of Prehistoric Ideation: Exploring the Universality-Idiosyncrasy Continuum. *Cambridge Archaeological Journal* 3:67–81.

Wallis, W. D., and R. S. Wallis. 1955. *The Micmac Indians of Eastern Canada.* University of Minnesota Press, Minneapolis.

Waring, A. J., Jr. 1968. The Southern Cult and Muskogean Ceremonial. In *The Waring Papers: The Collected Works of Antonio J. Waring, Jr.,* edited by S. Williams, 30–69. Papers of the Peabody Museum of Archaeology and Ethnology 58, Harvard University, Cambridge.

Waring, A. J., Jr., and P. Holder. 1945. A Prehistoric Ceremonial Complex in the Southeastern United States. *American Anthropologist* 47(1):1–34.

Watkins, J. 2000. *Indigenous Archaeology: American Indian Values and Scientific Practices.* Altamira, Walnut Creek, CA.

Watson, V. D. 1950. *The Wulfing Plates, Products of Prehistoric Americans.* Washington University Studies, New Series, Social and Philosophical Sciences, No. 8, St. Louis.

Webb, W. S., and C. G. Wilder. 1951. *An Archaeological Survey of Guntersville Basin on the Tennessee River in Northern Alabama.* University of Kentucky Press, Lexington.

Weltfish, G. 1977. *The Lost Universe.* University of Nebraska Press, Lincoln.

Westbrook, K. C. 1982. *Legacy in Clay: Prehistoric Ceramic Art of Arkansas.* Rose, Little Rock.

Willey, G. R. 1973. Mesoamerican Art and Iconography and the Integrity of the Mesoamerican Ideological System. In *The Iconology of Middle American Sculpture,* edited by D. T. Easby, Jr., 153–162. Metropolitan Museum of Art, New York.

———. 1990. *New World Archaeology and Culture History: Collected Essays and Articles, Gordon Randolph Willey,* 297–303. University of New Mexico Press, Albuquerque.

Williams, M., and G. Shapiro. 1990a. Paired Towns. In *Lamar Archaeology: Mississippian Chiefdoms in the Deep South,* edited by M. Williams and G. Shapiro, 163–174. University of Alabama Press, Tuscaloosa.

———. 1990b. *Lamar Archaeology: Mississippian Chiefdoms in the Deep South,* edited by M. Williams and G. Shapiro. University of Alabama Press, Tuscaloosa.

Williams, S., and J. M. Goggin. 1956. The Long Nosed God Mask in the Eastern United States. *Missouri Archaeologist* 18(3).

Williams, S. C. (editor). 1930 [1775]. *Adair's History of the American Indian.* Promontory Press, New York.

Williamson, R., and C. Farrer (editors). 1990. *Earth and Sky.* University of New Mexico Press, Albuquerque.

Willoughby, C. C. 1932. Notes on the History and Symbolism of the Muskhogeans and the People of Etowah. In *Etowah Papers: Exploration of the Etowah Site in Georgia,* edited by W. K. Moorehead, 7–105. Yale University Press, New Haven.

Wittry, W. 1969. An American Woodhenge. In *Explorations into Cahokia Archaeology*,
    edited by M. L. Fowler. Bulletin 7, Illinois Archaeological Survey, Urbana.

———. 1980. Cahokia Woodhenge Update. *Archaeoastronomy* 3:12–314.

Wolf, E. R. 1990. Distinguished Lecture: Facing Power—Old Insights, New Questions.
    American Anthropologist 92:586–596.

———. 1999. *Envisioning Power: Ideologies of Dominance and Crisis.* University of
    California Press, Berkeley.

Wycoco-Moore, R. S. 1951. The Types of the North American Indian Folktale. Ph.D.
    dissertation, Indiana University.

Wylie, A. 1985. The Reaction against Analogy. In *Advances in Archaeological Method
    and Theory,* vol. 8, edited by M. Schiffer, 63–111. Academic Press, New York.

Yelton, J. K. 1998. A Different View of Oneota Taxonomy and Origins in the Lower
    Missouri Valley. *Wisconsin Archeologist* 79(2):268–283.

Young, B. W., and M. L. Fowler. 2000. *Cahokia: The Great Native American Metropo-
    lis.* University of Illinois Press, Urbana.

Index

Italic page numbers refer to illustrations and tables.

CPSIA information can be obtained
at www.ICGtesting.com
Printed in the USA
LVHW110830291222
735964LV00003B/15